The Path of Constructive Life

THE PATH OF CONSTRUCTIVE LIFE

Embracing Heaven's Heart

by Hua-Ching Ni and Maoshing Ni, Ph.D.

SEVEN STAR
COMMUNICATIONS
www.sevenstarcom.com

The authors wish to express their appreciation to all students and friends who devoted their time and efforts to transcribing, editing, proofreading, typesetting and designing of this book. Publication of this work was made possible by an anonymous donor.

Calligraphy by Maoshing Ni, Ph.D.

Published by:
SevenStar Communications
13315 Washington Blvd., Suite 200
Los Angeles, CA 90066

Library of Congress Cataloging-In-Publication Data

Ni, Hua-Ching.
The path of constructive life : embracing Heaven's heart / Hua-Ching
Ni & Maoshing Ni.—1st ed.—Los Angeles : SevenStar
Communications, 2006, c2005.

   p. ; cm.

   ISBN-10: 1-887575-21-9
   ISBN-13: 978-1-887575-21-8

 1. Spiritual life. 2. Spirituality. 3. Conduct of life. 4. Religious
Ethics. 5. Character—Religious aspects. I. Ni, Maoshing. II. Title

BJ1012 .N54 2006   2005930332
205—dc22   0604

*This book is dedicated to a great humanity
that chooses to live a constructive life
with a bright and radiant heart.*

To All Readers,

According to the teaching of the Universal Integral Way, or Heavenly Heart, male and female are equally important in the natural sphere. This fact can be observed and confirmed in the diagram of the T'ai Chi. Therefore discrimination is not practiced in our tradition. All of our work is dedicated to both genders of the human race.

Wherever possible, sentence constructions using masculine pronouns to represent both sexes are avoided. Where they do occur, we ask your tolerance and spiritual understanding. We hope that you will take the essence of these teachings and overlook the limitations of a language in which gender discrimination is inherent. Ancient Chinese pronouns do not differentiate gender. We hope that all of you will achieve yourselves well above the level of language and gender. Thank you.

Warning—Disclaimer

This book is intended to present beneficial information and techniques that have been used throughout Asia for many centuries. This information and these practices utilize a natural system within the body; however, no claims are made regarding their effectiveness. The information offered is according to the authors' best knowledge and experience, and is to be used by the reader at his or her own discretion and liability.

People's lives have different conditions, and their growth has different stages. Because the development of all people cannot be unified, there is no single practice that can be universally applied to everyone. It must be through the discernment of the reader that practices are selected. The adoption and application of the material offered in this book must therefore be the reader's own responsibility.

The authors and publisher of this book are not responsible in any manner for any harm that may occur through following the instructions in this book.

ABOUT THE AUTHORS

Hua-Ching Ni, author, teacher and healer, addresses the essential nature of human life and works to further the personal growth and spiritual development of this and future generations. He was raised in a family tradition of healing and spirituality that is being continued by his two sons, Drs. Daoshing and Maoshing Ni, and by his many friends and supporters throughout the world.

Dr. Maoshing Ni, D.O.M., L.Ac., Ph.D., Dipl. C.H., Dipl. ABAAHP, has lectured and taught workshops throughout the country on such diverse subjects as longevity, preventive medicine, Chinese nutrition, herbal medicine, acupuncture, facial diagnosis, *fengshui*, stress management, *I Ching*, meditation, *t'ai chi, chi kung* and the history of medicine.

Dr. Mao has also authored many books, audio/video tapes and DVDs. These include *Chinese Herbology Made Easy, The Tao of Nutrition, The Eight Treasures Energy Enhancement Exercises, Self-Healing Chi Kung, 18-Step Harmony Style T'ai Chi, T'ai Chi Sword, Meditation for Stress Release, Pain Management, The Yellow Emperor's Classic of Medicine* and *Secrets of Longevity*. He was also an editorial member for the best-selling book, *Alternative Medicine: The Definitive Guide.*

TABLE OF CONTENTS

PRELUDE

朝　宗

Homage to the Heavenly Heart

吾以天地心为心

As humans our hearts can be Heavenly.

天地之心寄在吾.

The Heavenly Heart lodges in our human heart.

吾心乃是天地主.

Therefore, our human heart can be the Heart of Heaven.

焉敢放逸为不仁?

How then can we dare to scatter ourselves and indulge in unkindness?

致　敬　宇　宙　之　大　生　命

Homage to the Big Life of the Universe

天地宇宙大生命.

The universe is the big life.

人身亦是小宇宙.

Our body is a small universe.

弃小就大是逃避.

Giving up the small to reach for the big can be the search for refuge.

弃大就小是昧心.

Giving up the big to reach for the small darkens the light of our hearts.

人间做人何为则?

What is the correct principle for us to choose?

小生命中全大生.

Accomplish the big life through our small personal lives.

世界天为大.

In the world, Heaven is the biggest.

天大命为贵.

In the sky, life is the most precious.

宝惜小生命,

We should treasure our small lives,

完成大生命.

while accomplishing the big life of the universe.

致 敬 吾 人 之 小 生 命

Homage to the Universal Life
in Our Small Human Lives

小生命是我,

The small life is ours.

大生命是天.

The big life is Heaven's.

在小生命中,

Through our small lives,

完成大宇宙.

we can accomplish the great life of the universe.

INTRODUCTION

A New Constructive Spiritual Effort

Spiritual health and harmony is the root of a healthy life and a healthy world. The unhealthy social rivalry and limiting conceptions of some religions are an expression of the world's spiritual ill health. Today there is need for openhearted and cooperative spiritual guidance.

With this in mind, a new spiritual effort has been summoned to uplift all people's spiritual condition, and to encourage healthy research into the spiritual sphere of life. It is called the "Path of Constructive Life" (PCL). Its focus is on the enjoyment of health in all aspects of life. Its source is the Way or the Teachings of the Heavenly Heart. It includes five branches of strength: philosophy, psychology, religion, biology and physical science. As a philosophy, the PCL is a constructive philosophy. As a psychology, the PCL is a constructive psychology. As a religion, the PCL focuses on the universal spirit that existed before conceptualized religions. It meets the spiritual tendency and need of humanity's original benign nature. It is the constructive contribution of all existing religions, and is not trapped or limited by any specific custom.

To facilitate the new direction, people are encouraged to apply the universal religious spirit of their lives, and link their constructive strength together to work for the common benefit of all. The new service takes the form of self-sustaining cooperatives that offer all people the opportunity for healthy, whole living, and deep, individual spiritual growth. Volunteers who recognize that a constructive life is the way out of the world's negative spiritual condition support it. It aims at worldwide spiritual cooperation.

You may think it is impossible to integrate the different spiritual cultures together, yet all of them have the common foundation of the universal religious spirit. The effort to bring about world spiritual integration is not for the purpose of placing them all on one plate. Rather it is to encourage the different religious cultures to deepen their exploration of life's spiritual sphere, and expand into new spiritual territory.

Truthfully, individual spiritual progress should be more the focus than social spiritual progress. This is because broad social beliefs can harm the spiritual nature of individuals, as we each possess different spiritual qualities, temperaments and dispositions. The new effort, therefore, is open to individual adaptation, and encourages us to exercise our own spiritual strength to move our lives towards a new and broader direction. Nothing like this has occurred before. Individuals may join the voluntary spiritual cooperatives to help strengthen and maintain their spiritual health, as well as for spiritual community life.

The social religions such as Brahmanism, Judaism, Christianity and Islam are culturally purposed. They differ from humanity's real spiritual heritage of early shamanism and natural spiritualism. It was this early spirituality that provided the raw material for objective spiritual research. The newer religions, as replacements for these earlier spiritual practices, could have reformed and improved the valuable aspects of the old practices for greater spiritual progress. Instead, they blocked the opportunity for direct research into life's spiritual sphere by separating God from people, and by adopting the principle that everything has a good and bad side.

Conventionally, God is depicted as an authority over life, the Earth and the universe. Truthfully, the beingness of God, of people and of things, are all latecomers compared to the nonbeingness of Great Nature. The universal spiritual nature of people exists before their various creations. The true support for all the religious creations and activities comes from this spiritual nature and the universal religious heart of humans. Unfortunately, this natural reality has been externalized into different styles of worship with numerous spiritual titles. All external efforts to look for God are in vain and cause confusion.

The new focus of sages like Jain and Sakyamuni, the original teachers of Jainism and Buddhism respectively, was to find spiritual liberation from religious reliance. They turned to the invisible mind for solutions, but the mind cannot be independent from the truth. Yet, through their meaningful efforts, they discovered that spiritual dignity is produced by personal spiritual effort. There is no need to seek blessings from an external force, nor is there any need for a priesthood to act as the middle man between one's own mind and body, and the spiritual realm. The two sages also proved the truth that living with fewer material comforts can strengthen one's life spirit. However, they over relied on asceticism as a spiritual way of life.

Although physics has contributed to the breakdown of religious dominance, it is limited by its superficial view of the universe. Physics is only one aspect of the universe. The discovered physical laws merely scratch the surface of things, and are but a small part of the greater Universal Subtle Law. Yet, on some levels, both the subtle law and physical law intersect, and there is coherence between the two.

The most reliable spiritual truth of the world is naturally stored within our own bodies. By objectively exploring our naturally endowed spiritual nature, we can find God internally as the high life of our being. We may discover that within each of our bodies there are numerous spiritual entities. They are formless and do not possess a mind. They are the force and natural foundation of life. This fact is provable by each one of us.

To experience one's spirits for the first time is similar to the modern discovery of bacteria, in that bacteria were always there, though we were unaware of them. Spirits are also there—unaware to most, but there just the same. They are at a much higher level than bacteria. Bacteria are the invisible formation of the environment. Our bodies can produce them and chemicals can destroy them. Spirits, however, are the force of life, and although they can be scattered by electricity, they cannot be destroyed. They are the invisible partners of our lives, and they can communicate with our conscious minds.

Emotions and desires come from the spirits inside of us. When these spirits are strong, they can emit a bioelectric current similar to that experienced in sex, *chi kung* and acupuncture. Spirits are a fact of life. Their small lives are everywhere, both inside and outside of our lives. The Native Americans have much to teach about spirits, although some may confuse these natural spiritual phenomena with their mental creations, just as many religions have done.

When I (Hua-Ching Ni or OmNi) first achieved myself to reach the natural spiritual world, I addressed the spiritual beings as God, but they called me God. I noticed that in the spiritual world, each being is God. This fact differs vastly from conventional spiritual beliefs, which separate God from people. The difference is due to the human mind, which creates separation. A pure spiritual being does not possess a mind and does not separate. In the spiritual world: one is many and many are one. There is no spiritual reality to support all the religious disputes, arguments and wars, because there is no difference in the spiritual levels of life. Differences are products of the conceptual mind at play.

In the natural spiritual sphere, humans are the leaders of their internal world and natural surroundings. Spiritual leadership does not come from the pure spirits because they do not possess a mind. To bring about a harmonious response from the spiritual world, we need to develop ourselves to offer healthy spiritual leadership in our own lives and in nature. Through our constructive living and virtuous behavior, we can achieve high spiritual reward. Improper and unbalanced behavior only leads to spiritual disharmony.

For the vast majority, conventional religions are mere psychological applications. They do not touch the deep spiritual reality of human life, nor support deep research into the spiritual sphere. Modern medical science is also ignorant of the spiritual sphere, and that the body contains numerous spirits. While medicine may serve the bodily life, like religion, it doesn't present the knowledge of a complete life.

Human life consists of three natural and equal spheres of the physical, spiritual and mental sphere. No one aspect is inferior to the others. To live a complete life, the PCL encourages you to explore the independent science, which I call the science of life or "lifeology." Although other sciences such as biology already cover a big range, lifeology focuses on the spiritual phenomena and subtle spiritual reality of human life.

If spirits, soul and God are more than mere concepts, then there must be a way to research and develop yourself to know this spiritual reality, and enjoy its high life. Living a constructive life is the key. You need to study life and positively develop your own life, as there is no other avenue to study life's spiritual nature.

The ancient natural philosophy of the Way is the source of the PCL. In contrast to social religions, the Way used life's natural spiritual background as the foundation for its development. Followers of the Way, or "Wayfarers," appreciate that people can live a constructive life by avoiding disturbances from the following three elements: primitive spiritualist practices, pressure and manipulation from social religions, and extreme asceticism. Although asceticism is designed to lead one to a lucid mind, it suppresses all other aspects of life. This approach ignores the true foundation of life.

In the ageless Way, respect for life, which includes serving and nourishing the body, is a great virtue of the mind. No matter how difficult your life becomes, you need to value and protect it, for there are numerous small lives within it. Living decently is a great virtue of life. From nature you can learn to discipline the mind to help the body.

Maoshing and I hope that in modern life, a new tri-partnership can be formed among three aspects: people's new intellectual growth, their renewed moral strength, and their new respect for natural human spirituality. Together, the three partners will open the way for new research and improvement in life. Then, there can be hope for a better and complete human life.

We offer the vision for this new spiritual movement in a series of five books known collectively as the Constructive Life Series. This book is the third in the series. It is presented as a service from a spiritual family with 5000 years of devotion to the truth. It comes from the research of the deep, subtle sphere of life by diligent and focused individuals. These individuals attained real spiritual development based on standards that meet the modern style of scientific research.

We present this effort of genuine spiritual research and objective intellectual attitude to update and uplift the modern services of medicine, politics, religions and international relationships, as well as other aspects of human life. The PCL contains guidance for all lives, and carries the hope for worldwide spiritual cooperation.

We hope this work will challenge the intellects of the world's outstanding researchers and encourage their personal research. Their spiritual challenge will be their own growth, and we wish them every success. To those of you who need support for a positive way to live, you can accept and use the PCL as one hypothesis to prove within your own life. Although the established religious teachings are mere hypotheses, people were forced to accept their teachings as absolute truths. Religious conceptions were lazily passed down and accepted throughout generations without any real proof of their truth. This is not our way of teaching. Spiritual existence is beyond mere mental beliefs and is a provable fact.

We wish to nurture and build a healthier recognition of God and spiritual life for the betterment of all lives. The world needs a healthy and truthful spiritual faith. Our purpose is to assist the growth of a healthy human society by guiding the way for self-reliant living and objective spiritual growth. People have suffered from a morally inferior world. Personal happiness and success come from the natural, benign qualities of life. It is for the goodness of all people that we offer our spiritual work and friendship.

We openly acknowledge that although we have gathered a great spiritual harvest from the highest spiritual stature, there is still room for supplementation. The basic foundation however is complete. It is our spiritual responsibility to present this work to you for your review.

A Sincere and Grateful Heart Is What You Need

Beloved friends,

The practice of the Teaching of the Heavenly Heart does not involve any personal returns or personal rewards. The teaching is a way that all people can attain spiritual health and strength by living a constructive life. People are motivated to be involved simply by an appreciation for the life with which Mother Nature endowed them.

No matter if you are rich or poor, or have a high or low social status, you can appreciate your life endowed by Mother Universe by expressing the greatest gratitude for it. This is the way to practice the Teaching of the Heavenly Heart with a grateful spirit everyday.

The Teaching of the Heavenly Heart achieves acceptance through people's mutual spiritual recognition, which is based on their spiritual growth. Through growth and understanding, people begin to see things differently, and they come to respect and devote themselves to the practice of the natural teachings of the Heavenly Heart.

These teachings do not suppress the normal desire for life, but encourage every-one to pursue success, health, wealth, happiness, longevity and most essentially, spiritual balance, in order to nurture the possibility of an everlasting soul.

Religions have channeled your natural emotion of awe and respect towards the vast nature and unknowable mystery of life, into an emotional faith in God as the ruler of your life. In truth, God is the Heavenly Heart. God is the love and appreciation from your developed soul, rather than the fear and confusion of your weak soul, before it becomes fortified by your positive responses to life's challenges and experiences.

God is spiritual. God is the latent potency of nature. God is nonbeing, and human life with its formed body is the temple of God. Any strong souls in human form, who have contributed a great service to people, and who have expressed a spirit-ual faith without any religious bias, are expressions of God. At the very least, they are true saints who carry God's will to humanity. Likewise, people who live with the constructive nature of life are the unexpressed God.

As a religion based on community service, the PCL aims to help you fortify your soul. This is so that all of you may constructively serve your own lives and the lives of others, and avoid being manipulated or deceived by fictitious religious stories or undeveloped souls, who would pull the world back into an animal-like existence for the sake of personal ambition.

The human race has evolved more physically than it has spiritually. People are in the process of spiritual evolution, but widespread spiritual progress depends on the majority of people's spiritual development. The realistic spiritual efforts of many individuals can contribute towards this progress. Through the teachings of the PCL, we hope to facilitate a conjoint trend of spiritual evolution. The reward is that each time you return to the water, it is cleaner and warmer than before. It may not be that the world has changed, rather you have changed. Through your individual hard work and genuine efforts, your soul has been strengthened.

A self-indulgent life can cause your life to become loose and lost, but an earnest life of balanced hard work can make you strong and undefeatable. May you all face the truth, and may your souls be strengthened against any spiritual threats and regressive social forces. Your upright soul is a testament to the existence of the divine personality and divine realm.

From the standpoint of the teaching of the Heavenly Heart, Maoshing and I need to clarify some existing spiritual confusion.

"Tao," or the Way, means Universal Morality.

"Teh," or Virtue, means the spiritual gain of your life.

"God" is the spiritually fortified soul of your life.

"Heaven" means the healthy spiritual condition of your soul with its natural joy and happiness.

"Hell" means the unhealthy spiritual condition of your soul with all its pain and suffering.

From your spiritual friends,
OmNi and Maoshing

The Source of the Path of Constructive Life: The Teachings of the Heavenly Heart

Five thousand years ago in the region of China, near the dawn of the first civilization, a war broke out. This war nearly destroyed the beginnings of civilization that had been initiated by the natural leaders of Fu Shi, Shen Nung and others.

The war began when an alliance of nine aggressive tribes, led by Chi Yu, opposed human social order and launched their barbaric forces against the peace-loving tribes led by Yen Ti, the last leader of the early social order. Yen Ti was a descendant of Shen Nung, who initiated the age of farming and agriculture. Yen Ti's army was often defeated as it was lured into a jungle of poisonous fog, where the barefooted and semi-naked soldiers were attacked and killed by venomous insects and snakes, and besieged by the half-beasts, half-human troops of Chi Yu. Chi Yu had also gathered a group of fierce beasts as part of his fighting arsenal.

At this crucial stage, a brave son from one of the peace-loving tribes gathered an army of his young friends to respond to Yen Ti's defeat. By this time, most people had awakened to the disastrous threat of the dangerous dark force. The young army also attracted help from many wise elders. Among them, the Lady-in-Blue was one of the wisest. In defense of a civilized and humanistic social order, she and other elders taught the young men and their leader the following four guidelines.

Be the heart to help the cruel and rough human world.

Be a trustworthy individual to all.

Be a follower of the highest wisdom.

Be an initiator of a genuinely harmonious world.

The young army was victorious and brought human life to a new stage of civilization. The army's young leader later became the Yellow Emperor, Huang Di, and under his rule the spiritual direction of the Lady-in-Blue continued as the Teachings of the Yellow Emperor or "The Way." The Way differs vastly from the religious or folk Taoism that was created by later Chinese cultural leaders in response to the newly imported Buddhism.

The teachings of the Way are based on those four guidelines from the Lady-in-Blue, which encourage you to be a warrior of self-improvement and constructive living. The young warriors shaped the guidelines into a prayer to use for their righteous cause. You may also use this prayer.

I devote my life to be the heart of the rough world.

I devote my life to be trusted by all.

I devote my life to continue the great endeavors of all wise people

for humanistic progress.

I devote my life to begin a harmonious and peaceful world.

The four guidelines are still spiritually valid today. They may be used to restart the early natural spiritual faith of the Way with its new title of the Path of Constructive Life. Maoshing and I cordially invite all of you as our friends to devote yourselves to a new spiritual direction as warriors for self-improvement and constructive living.

The first big war fought between the Yellow Emperor and Chi Yu is worthy of our attention. It could be called the "First World War," since it was a war fought between the humanistic social order and the barbaric tendencies of human life; a war fought between the ordered society and the disordered society.

The barbaric tribes opposed all attempts of civilizing life. They had no respect for life, not even women or children. The war was fought to decide if people should remain naked or begin to wear clothes; if they should continue to eat raw meats, including human flesh, or give up cannibalism and eat cooked food.

Although the young Yellow Emperor won the war, the half-beast people still exist in today's modern society. They have developed modern cultures that prepare people to be eaten by the new half-beasts with their conceptual tools. To the sadness of all wise people, the fight continues and is the basic pattern of social conflicts.

Generally, physical wars are social competitions with no absolute righteousness. Triumph and defeat are only superficial views. Universal justice belongs to Nature, the real God of all people. Only after many years can the positive or negative fruits of war be assessed. No one wants to be the loser, but you may observe the deep reality that the losers can be the real winners. In the deep sphere of human society, often the slave-owners end up serving the slaves and the winners end up serving the losers.

You need to defend the natural right to live. Even if you are a winner, you still need to look deeply into how you live your life. There may be wars there too. For example, do you try to compete with your life partner? It is better that you both adjust your lives so you can live and work harmoniously together, as symbolized by the T'ai Chi with its harmony of *yin* and *yang*.

Internally, most people have a basic conflict between their conscious mind and subconscious mind. The conscious mind is composed of your thoughts, actions and reactions. The subconscious mind includes your spiritual system; the deep self of your life. What this means is that you may follow your emotions and do one thing, while your heart or deep self has a different tendency or attitude. Herein lies the danger of splitting your personality in daily life. As a warrior for self-improvement, you need to unify your mind and heart. And, most importantly, you need to unite your shallow sensory self with your deep spiritual self. To help you in this endeavor you may use my version of the *I Ching: The Book of Changes and the Unchanging Truth* (*I Ching* or *Book of Changes*).

You may also observe in your life's conduct whether you are too serious, which causes strain, or whether you take things too lightly or are negligent, which causes mistakes and failures in your life. In most situations, you don't know when to be serious and when to take things lightly, when to go fast and when to slow down. As a result, you invite trouble. Could your life do with some self-improvement?

Who can say they have finished the battle of life? The work of self-improvement continues throughout life. You have been fighting external wars, but you may have neglected the big war within your own life. We offer you this message.

Be the heart of the universe.

Be the life of the universe.

Be the wisdom of the universe.

Be the strength of peace and health of the universe.

As a warrior of self-improvement, you plow your life for personal spiritual farming as well as for world spiritual farming. From both, you may derive the meaning of spiritual self-cultivation. As you boldly seek peace, internally and externally, with the realization of the four guidelines from the Lady-in-Blue, the Heavenly Truth is realized in your life. The Heavenly Heart is reached by your achievement. You are a true Heaven in the world and among people.

PART I

Enhance Your Understanding of God

Chapter 1

Faith, Value and Confidence

Faith, value and confidence are concepts that still influence people's vision of life, even at a time when a materialistic view tends to dominate, and people have turned to building an external life rather than staying with the deep substance of life.

Faith

Faith is the trust you place in someone, something or some creed. It can be public or private. Public faith is defined by the trust you place in some establishment, such as a social, religious or political faith.

Faith can influence a society. At a deeper level, it can invite serious consequences because you cannot always trust what people say. When people do not deeply understand what their faith is about, it makes it easy for egotistic people to manipulate the trend of the majority. Big and small social tragedies may result, and still people do not know how they came to be victimized.

People of independent judgment know that though you can personally select and project a faith, you can also be wrong. It takes time to build up a useful faith that can correctly serve your life. As faith is not absolute, you may need to personally scrutinize it and put it through different tests. Faith should, therefore, involve your personal growth. This is the reason why our teachings promote free spiritual learning, spiritual self-cultivation[1] and spiritual development as support for those individuals who attempt to live a self-responsible life.

---

1. You may look into our many other publications that we have written for fulfilling your inner potential through self-cultivation. You can start with *Stepping Stones for Spiritual Success* and *The Golden Message*, and see pgs. 99–100 (of this volume) for more book referrals.

Value

Value is different from faith. Value can be objective or subjective, and differences of value can exist between groups of people. What is valuable to one person or one group of people may be of little or no worth to another person or group of people.

For instance, among plants, some are valued for food, some for their nature, and some for water conservation, housing construction, medicinal purposes, artistic value and land- covering value. There are also fields of troublesome vegetation like poison ivy and poison oak, which most people don't like, but which can have an ecological value. Therefore, what is valuable to one person may be of little worth to another.

When people are hungry and starving, the value of food is higher to them than to those who have a full stomach. Food is often wasted and thrown away at festivals in certain areas of the world. The amount of food thrown away is much more than what is needed to feed people in the poorer areas. A baby in a well-to-do area generally weighs around 20 pounds, which is around the same weight of a three-year-old child in a destitute region.

Where food is cheap, the value of life is higher. Where food is hard to obtain, the value of human life is cheaper. You can figure out who cares more about living between the two groups in the two different places.

When wealthy nations wish to protect the security of their society, merely building up military strength cannot do a good job. Saving the food that would otherwise be wasted to help supply and feed world neighbors can do a better job. People will not gamble their lives on a political or religious leader's words, when they have enough to eat and enjoy times of plenty. As Lao Tzu[2] taught 2500 years

---

2. Active around 571 BCE.

ago, such times are times when the natural value of life among people has been restored.

Many city dwellers do not concern themselves with the natural world. They care more about things such as real estate, finance, industry and commerce, politics, social values and the value of their skills. That is to say, they care more about things related to monetary value. The personal, innate value of life seems to be ignored. Your birth certificate cannot describe this value. Changes in the means of living have changed the value of life to that of a modern social robot. People often risk their invaluable gift of life for a very small amount of money. Life is cheap to those people who blindly pursue monetary worth.

So the idea of value is still relative. It is your own spiritual learning and growth that sets the true value of your life.

Confidence

Just as an untested faith can victimize your life, the wrong valuation of your life can also cost you dearly by directing your life in unhealthy ways. What remains as the invaluable support of your life is your natural confidence in life, which includes your moral health. Confidence in life is the most fundamental support of life, and it involves two considerations: what is life and what is the value of moral health in life?

I (Hua-Ching Ni or OmNi) would like to share with you what I have learned. I was born into a traditional family that encouraged spiritual self-reliance. My family, the descendants of China's Yellow Emperor (reign 2698–2598 BCE[3]), collected and passed down the knowledge and experiences of humanity's early ancestors. Called the Way, or Teaching of the Heavenly Heart, these teachings

---

3. Please note that BCE stands for "Before the Common Era" and CE stands for "Common Era." The distinction is the same as between BC and AD.

gave me a measure of the possible confusion that can come from following cultural trends, and chasing after the myriad options in general life.

After many years of writing books and answering questions from seekers, I feel it is time to offer a conclusion from my learning and attainment in this package called the Path of Constructive Life (PCL), with its related public service. For future seekers, this can be a capsule of the long history of human development. It carries the clear direction to restore confidence in a natural life, just as our early human ancestors practiced and achieved. I hope it will help cure the modern confusion regarding the concepts of faith and value.

The following poem describes the faith, value and confidence my ancestors held and practiced. These differ from other cultures, which mostly have the effect of dwarfing people and their potential.

My head supports the Heavens,
My feet stabilize the Earth,
I hold the Humanistic Heart in the center of my being,
embracing all lives and all things.
I am the Divine Being above all.

Chapter 2

A New Spiritual Faith for a New Human Destiny

As we have mentioned, spiritual faith can affect the destiny of people individually and socially. It can also affect people globally. Today's spiritual crisis offers us the opportunity to discuss a new spiritual direction that could provide hope for the future.

Conventional Religious Views and the Value of a True Spiritual Teaching

Conventional religious faith often gives you an image of God as a single ruling entity who dictates all things. Yet people's belief of God has not always been like this. When the Catholic faith was declining in popularity, Saint Thomas Aquinas elucidated God as a nonbeing. Doing so helped establish God above human limitations and it helped people overcome the issue of God's gender. For the first time, God became a nonbeing above creation—a departure from the old Roman idea of God, which was represented by Mars, the god of war.

The ancient Chinese have a similar philosophy of nonbeing. They describe that all beings and creations are from what is called the post-heaven stage of the universe, and that there is also a pre-heaven stage of the universe that consists of nonbeing or that which is not created. Based on this philosophy, God, as the creator of all things, must come before the creation, so God cannot be a part of the creation or the stage of beingness. God must be a nonbeing from the pre-heaven stage. If God is described as a being, then it follows God has to be one of the created beings. As a created being, God would be equal in rank to all other beings. How then could God establish unique and sole authority as a single ruler over all other beings?

Aquinas saw that beingness created a sense of God's limitations and raised the issue of gender. Nonbeingness, however, escapes the dispute over whether God is male or female. Further, if you think deeply about it, nonbeingness implies another perspective on God: even if God is the source of all beings and creations, as nonbeingness God cannot be a ruler of all things. Therefore, the idea of God as a ruler is nullified and your paying homage to God as such is an irrelevant matter.

Historically, the Roman Emperor Constantine had used the image of God as a creator and single ruler to increase his power. His empire was declining and he decided to adopt Christianity to bolster his authority. The falling Roman Empire installed Christianity as the new state religion to gather the interest of people and expand its political glory.

In formulating such a vague image of God that was neither plural nor singular, it expressed weakness as a faith and raised a dilemma. If God was a singular being, then God had to be isolated from all other things. And, if God was pluralistic in being then that would raise the question whether everything was holy, which would deny a singular ruling God. In establishing a common social faith, spiritual unity is the goal to seek. Based on the above image, however, God remains a singular and unsupported bachelor.

Catholicism made the Bible too holy for the lay person. Most people at that time were illiterate, and so the thick book was set aside. People's religious interests were stimulated instead by ceremonial activities. So the Church, for social purposes, performed rituals and ceremonies that were gathered and updated from the different local customs.

Among its adopted rituals, the main one was Watching Mass where the priest would raise a cup high and cross it over his head. This was an imitation of the Egyptian religious officiates, who performed rituals in worship of the sun some thousand years ago. In early Christianity, the Cross symbolized the sun.

After the Protestant Reformation, the Bible became the driving force of Christianity. However, the Bible is full of contradictions—the fundamental one being the concept of a single man ruling the world like a dictatorship.

In the second century CE, after Jesus had passed, there were two schools of his legacy: the Gnostic teaching and the Latin school of Jesus study. The Latin school became more popular because it allied with the Roman Empire as part of a political conspiracy. When a pure spiritual teaching becomes a social movement, it diminishes in quality due to the changes made to bolster power. The Gnostic teaching, which is still available, can help Christians gain a more objective view and understanding of the true spiritual heritage of Jesus as a teacher.

For a while, Christianity held the dream of a worldly kingdom or empire that can last forever, even though most people knew that was impossible. When the Roman Empire fell, the religion survived by promoting Jesus as the spiritual king. In truth, Jesus was an innocent teacher who did not enjoy much popularity in his time. He was simply pulled into a social drama by the Catholics.

A Chinese proverb says, "When the water flows in the mountain, it is clean and clear. When it rushes downward to the land, it becomes murkier and murkier." As an observer of spirituality, I respect the initiatives of all spiritual teachings before they become religions. As teachings, they can be pure when the intention of the teacher is still present; as religions they become mixed with the different political and social agendas of the later leaders. In other words, I heed the original teachings more seriously than their later versions, which are contaminated by social struggles and political schemes.

Furthermore, the original teachings were created in response to the spiritual situation of the social environment. The original teachers had reflected spiritually and produced their teachings for the pure benefit of the people of their time. In contrast, later followers used the teachings to socially manipulate people, emphasizing certain aspects of them to achieve their own purposes.

In China, some 2500 years ago, the wise sage Lao Tzu once said that spiritual teaching should be beyond considerations of social success. The genuine value of a teaching is as a public offering that provides a true reflection, beneficial for the time. That reflection needs to be spiritual and above social struggle, offering real spiritual help to the world while asking for nothing in return. The main message here is that a spiritual teaching renews human faith.

The teaching of the ageless Way is not concerned with external authority and power. It offers the plain wisdom of nature with its deep spirituality. Lao Tzu embodies the Way. The foundation of the Way is nature, and its spiritual teaching includes the manifested and the unmanifested spheres of universal nature. The unmanifested sphere is the pre-heaven stage of universal nature. The manifested sphere is the post-heaven stage of nature. This was an interpretation of the Way's earlier ancestor Fu Shi,[1] and his vision of *yin* as the hidden aspect and *yang* as the apparent aspect.

Not everything is visible to the naked eye though, even in the manifested sphere. For example, you can only see into a small portion of the whole procession of universal movement and the ongoing development of nature.

Energy is a Natural Part of Life

What is nature? Whether you depend on your naked eye or on visual instruments, nature is seen as differing degrees of thickness of basic matter. This early physical vision of nature has produced a dead image of the universe. However nature is not a dead thing.

In the visible range of nature, basic materials give shape to the universe, but in the invisible range, it is energy that animates the life of nature. The two basic

---

1. Fu Shi is said by some to have lived between 6000 and 30000 years ago and by others to have lived between 3852–2738 BCE.

categories of matter and energy have been recognized by the human mind. From Fu Shi, the early people of China termed these as *yin* and *yang*, deeply perceiving them as two different sides of the one reality. The two are not separate. They are two interdependent and mutually supplementary forces, whose interplay is recognized to produce all of nature's variety.

The confusion over whether energy leads to matter, or vice versa, has led people's minds down the narrow alley of a materialistic world. This is the modern mental trap. It dominates people's vision, causing trouble to many. No one is prepared to admit their ignorance. Stubbornness is a great spiritual trouble, even among big social authorities and religions. As a result, the human world lives on in disputes and wars.

When the visual sense is used as the dominant sense for gathering knowledge, it easily reaches public agreement, even though it is a partial view. There are, however, three grades of basic materials: heavy, light and in-between, or the material, spiritual and living beings. Humankind has actively researched the material sphere of nature, but the spiritual sphere of the universe remains little known to its minds, even though it is a billion times vaster than the material sphere.

You are confused by your creations, and your knowledge is limited by your visual sense. The only way to grow is to develop your mind spiritually through spiritual research. However, unlike the visible reality, the invisible reality is unlikely to get the same agreement from the majority. This is because researchers are not interested in exploring its unclear sphere, as it brings little to no financial or emotional reward. This is a great pity, yet even talking about energy takes you one step closer to spiritual energy.

The modern conceptions of energy are still at a coarse level. In the lower sphere, the different materials of the myriad things provide various sources of energy, which you require and use in life to produce different energies. Humankind has learned to split an atom and use its resulting energy to kill. This same energy in different densities can be protective. On one level, the protective energy is the natural, benign conscious energy within you, before any hatred is brewed in your mind. Your mind can produce and contain both energies. It is your choice to apply the conscious energy in a creative or destructive direction.

Today, many religious countries compete with each other to build up a nuclear armory. The real solution is not to fear one another. Rather, you can study, improve and explore your personal religious faith to go beyond its expressible level, to the deeper inexpressible level. This level is beyond the source of human conflict. Between the expressible and inexpressible levels, anyone can easily see what is the real, just God and what is a product of human emotions.

The various world religions show how people shape their spiritual visions differently. You need to turn back to see the importance of the health and benignity of life's spiritual nature, which is close to the natural, benign conscious energy. All human minds can attain the reality of the natural conscious energy, which by nature is not a killing power unless it is associated with negative human emotions.

The natural, benign conscious energy, whether shallow or deep, is the God of human life, and your life is the vehicle that carries this conscious energy. Many of you have misappropriated its universal force for ill-use. Has anyone deeply studied how to apply this natural conscious energy that makes you think, plan and design your life? Many religions have applied it to form a concept of God that kills. The concept of God should not be used for killing; it should be used for universal protection. The root of evil and good is the same conscious energy. When misapplied, it is evil; when correctly applied, it is God. By recognizing the power of your mind, which has the potential to kill, you can move forward to appreciate that the depth of living things relates to the strength of their conscious energy.

Universal spiritual energy also contains a strong moral sense. Although you are clever, you cannot truly separate your life from this living universal environment, just as no single atom can exist apart from the rest of the world. You are all part of the universal order of great nature. The significance of life varies between living things, depending on how strongly a life distinguishes between harm and support. The definition of life also varies with the living conditions, whether to live like an animal or a human, there is a difference.

The Importance of Spiritual Cooperation and the Tri-Partnership of the Sky, Earth and People

The Way is the development of nature. The Way describes how nature takes steps to develop itself. The unformed oneness of the spiritual energy comes first. From this nondistinguishable oneness of spiritual energy, two random yet distinguishable spheres of *yin* and *yang* appear as the second step. The third step is when these two elements combine to form life. Then the myriad things come into being as the fourth step. These things are the supports and accessories to the main tripod, or cauldron of universal beingness.

The sky symbolizes the spiritual sphere of nature. The Earth symbolizes the material sphere of nature. Human life, as the offspring of the sky and Earth, contains both in one sphere. Human life, with its own impulses and emotions, has become the third category of nature. Each type of life, including the invisible beings and forces of the universe, has a different unique nature or quality. However humans, more than any other life, have developed a higher conscious energy.

Lao Tzu used the Way to elucidate his message of the triple partnership of the sky (or Heaven), Earth and people.

This tri-partner model replaces the one-creator concept of the world because the three partners of the sky, Earth and life need to cooperate and harmonize together for universal survival. It is not a matter of who should take credit for having created the world. This focus on credit is merely the sentimental attitude of some individuals.

The focus of a spiritual faith should be on continuous self-renewal of the individual and of the world. And the goal for establishing a common faith that serves this purpose is spiritual unity. The worship of dictatorship simply does not help, but the concept of cooperation between the spiritual and material spheres of life is a unique vision of reality that can support the goal of spiritual unity.

You do not need to be a 10,000-year-old soul to understand that true democracy is not a product of dictator worship. Your vision of democracy needs to extend beyond the victory celebrations of election campaigns to include the collective balance and mutual cooperation among people. Now is the time to prepare for such a universal society. That would be true success.

The concept of one God may not be the real trouble that misleads people, as this concept can also be interpreted to be a necessary spiritual unity among all people. Rather, the trouble is that this concept suggests a great conqueror.

Now after emerging from an era of dictatorship, the human world is ready to grow in the direction of cooperation between people. Humanity needs a new understanding of God that includes the triple reality of everlasting life. This reality includes the high life of humanity with its internal spiritual harmony, as well as the other material aspects of human life, such as impulses, desires and emotions. Whatever nature has given human life should be respected as part of the normalcy of life, as long as it does not extend to any extreme. Balance develops the wholeness of a high life, and can even be considered to be life's spiritual goal.

Some religions try to elevate the concept of spirituality by denying material and emotional needs. Yet partiality can create trouble for your everyday health. Without balance as a spiritual necessity how can people or society evolve? Balance is the important duty of spirituality in individual life and in society.

Although humans possess the highest conscious energy in life, many social religions fail to help people develop it. Some leaders and their followers fuel the tension among people, based on their fears that people of different beliefs will attack them. Such a response pulls people down to the level of animals, like barking dogs viciously defending their territories.

You need to trust the partnerships within life, nature and society, and that trust is a spiritual quality that cannot be demanded, commanded or built through fear. The hope for making spiritual progress is to change your concept from that of a single performance to one of a great cooperative partnership involving all humanity.

The Path of Constructive Life, a New Morality and a New Spiritual Worship

Constructive living requires respect for balance, which means no partial exaltation in life. While God represents the spiritual focus, it is a balanced life, not God, which leads to special favors. God is simply impartial spiritual reality.

The new spiritual path we offer does not suggest that you make sacrifices to God, or that you attain balance for God's sake. These conventional concepts of God only give a sense of self-aggrandizement. Being balanced in life is to realize the God that is the triple partnership of spiritual peace, physical health and emotional happiness.

The new generation has the same important need as the previous generations, which is to harmonize the inner and outer aspects of life. This is the Way of life as outlined in the *I Ching*. The *I Ching* is a system that presents the various outcomes of an event, whether it is good or bad, fortunate or troublesome, faulty or virtuous. When you are in a bad situation, you need to know how to move into a good situation. The aim of the *I Ching* is to present the constructive nature of life and the universe.

Life requires orderly connections on the outside, as well as an orderly and healthy conscious life on the inside. Inner and outer order is necessary for the health and normalcy of your life's functioning. The spiritual qualities of unity and neatness support external social normalcy, as well as internal health. The new service of the PCL focuses on both external improvement in society, and internal improvement and harmony within the individual.

The PCL, as a social service, adopts the form of social congregations, but it avoids any social or racial prejudice. It seeks to find a new and refreshed spiritual respect in life.

The PCL shares the spiritual root of the prehistorical faith of early people in recognizing that the sky is the father of life, the Earth is the mother of life, and all lives, especially human lives, are brothers and sisters. This is the foundation of the Way. It is a particularly significant view, as it gives a great deal of healthy confidence in humans by placing them equally in the context of the tri-partnership of the universe, along with the sky and the Earth.

You may think that this view came from the self-importance of humans, but in our view it relates more to spiritual strength. Humans hold an invisible spiritual potential in their lives that cannot be belittled, unless they are neurotic or insane and place themselves too high or too low.

The PCL presents the sky, which is the spiritual sphere of life; the Earth, which is the material sphere of life; and people, which are the realm of the mind and its healthy desires and emotions. In deciding whether your desires and emotions are healthy, you need to consider whether any one of them has been overly extended. The three partners need to accept one another by embracing one another. Partial dominance does not present the good, normal life of humanity. Therefore, the harmony of all three partners has become the spiritual learning and practice of the PCL.

The idea of the three partners is a more enlightened view compared to the general religious one that exalts the spiritual sphere over the other two. Spiritual dominance neglects that spiritual harmony is the foundation of a healthy human life. The PCL forsakes the old exaltation of a partial life, which has lost its vision of completeness. The conventional religions were shy to admit the physical and emotional spheres as equal partners in life. Yet everyone, especially the new generation, can benefit by correcting this mistake. Generally, religious teachings lack spiritual harmony and the necessary cooperation among people and their environment.

People need a spiritual life to completely fulfill their potential. The already harmonized relationship between the sky and the Earth has no need of specific attention, but we all need to attend to the cultivation and discipline of human development.

The PCL embraces spiritual wholeness. It is the Way of Heavenly Love. It is for spiritual enrichment, wealth and abundance in life, And, among all aspects of life, health is central. Life should have spiritual support, material support and emotional support. Life cannot be complete if it loses the support of any one of these. Harmony requires the cooperation of all three. A good life is defined by the balance, orderliness and unity among the three spheres.

Appropriate spiritual learning and worshipping in organized gatherings can help to attune and order the inner and outer aspects of your life. It can also help you live with pure spiritual piety. Personal spiritual practices protect the deep conscious self from the outer aggressive culture, to which the bare mind is vulnerable. Worldly culture contains an unhealthy and negative emotional network that constantly stimulates your physical, financial and social desires. This can burden the natural benignity and decency of your life.

You need to practice being constructive in your own life, and reflect this out to all other lives. Being constructive is the universal nature. It is in your nature, and it can be encouraged and awakened in anyone. Being constructive should be the nature of friendships and intimate relationships. People should be able to see that as a trend, the world wants to be more constructively minded. It is natural that people are motivated by it. By realizing the constructive and moral nature of the universe, you are able to secure the safety of your own life and the lives of others.

Finally, who or what will serve as the brighter God or spiritual leader for people's spiritual support and worship? As humankind is not beyond the human stage of spiritual growth, I propose borrowing the image of the Lady-in-Blue from the early people of ancient China to remind you of the boundless love from the deep, blue sky. The early people appreciated the Lady-in-Blue as the spiritual expression of the Mother Universe. She appeared in human form to teach the young Yellow Emperor the Way of Heaven, and helped him guide his people to civilization. Hence the sky, as her image, can be used to help the growth of your wisdom. The Lady-in-Blue's messenger is the Lady of the Subtle Light. This Light is invisible to your general vision, and has been called *Kwan Yin*.

Kwan Yin is the personification of all feminine-natured spiritual energy. *Kwan Yin* represents protection not killing, which is why this energy has been appropriately translated as the Goddess of Mercy. In a constructive life, the image of the Goddess of Mercy represents the spiritual capability of hearing the voice, seeing the colors, smelling the tastes, tasting the smells and touching the unformed. She is the universal conscious energy in all humans, presented in this way in order to reach the public.

The Lady of the Subtle Light is the Universal Spiritual Light. The Light means not to become confused by your senses, or by over extending one sense in the way the visual sense has probably dominated your life. Ask yourself whether you are over stimulating your life by watching television, listening to the news, needlessly chatting on the phone and so forth, in order to know you are alive? Don't these things limit how much you truly know about your life? To know the complete and real art of life means that sometimes you have to withdraw from the senses to witness the wholeness of life.

Chapter 3

Let Us Move Forward Into the Light

Today the world is like a drunken giant walking in a dark, dead-end alley. Society suffers from a conflict among natural values, social values and conventional values of life. It has been confused by the old religions, which are in need of updating. There should be true Light and constructive spiritual guidance to show the world the way to safety.

The natural value of life is the real value of your life. There is no way to escape life except to find an honest and healthy way to support it. When I first came to the United States in the 1970s, I was invited by a generation of young Americans who needed my spiritual help in light of the suffering from the Vietnam War. They had been to the East and had studied its religions, which encouraged them to give up mainstream life as a way of dealing with its pressures. Those religions, like many others, taught them to hide away.

There were also other students who settled on some skills that I taught, like *t'ai chi,* and sought to make a living from them. Some of them even proclaimed themselves to be masters. Other people of limited vision made a big deal out of them. Such matters have become part of the new age of confusion.

This is not my or my family's teaching purpose. What my spiritual family does is completely different from the general religious and new age approaches. Our teaching is not a business for making a personal living; it is a renewed social service based on the Way of subtle nature to assist the rejuvenation of the world.

Life itself is a process for building true Divinity. Often those who do not look deeply for the truth would rather worship an external divinity to make them happy. And then they try hard to please the divine. Yet Divinity is not something you can force or insist upon: it is what you achieve through life's many tests with its real anger, pain and even agony.

No one should try to escape from life's difficulties, even if many religions try to tell you that the world is a rough ocean with sea monsters that could swallow you. In times of peace, life is a preparation of the strength you will need to fight the monsters when you encounter them. Sometimes these monsters are within you. My family's spiritual tradition provides the correct and healthy life path to support peace among people, and to help everyone live constructively and happily in the world.

As we have mentioned, the truth of a good life is about balance, both internally and externally. Such balance is maintained and cared for by your own honest strength and self-reliant efforts. We ask you to face the challenges of today, and correct your own and the world's mistakes, which are causing so much sickness. You need to be able to show people the constructive way in order to reach a personal bright future and better world.

The social value of life is the accommodations you make each day. These include the adornments and disruptions to a naturally healthy style of living. On a personal scale, no one can ignore the presence of society whether big or small, even if society usually brings more pressure than pleasure. Many spiritual seekers tend to shun societies, but truthfully, by learning to cope with them well you can become enlightened, and you can use what you know to help others with emotional difficulties like your own.

The conventional religious values of life, most of which are fictitious, need some correction and improvement to help balance the conflict between the natural and social values of life. You also need an improved presentation of spiritual matters, so you can live effectively and honestly in mainstream life.

The PCL is offered as a spiritual solution to the world crisis. While conventional religions presented themselves as the boss and wrongly demanded that people serve them, the PCL recognizes that human life is the substance that religious and spiritual teachings need to support if humankind is to progress.

The PCL seeks to ease conflicts among individuals and societies, to balance life's natural and social values, and to provide a sound connection between the two, through open learning and constructive activity.

What follows are five principles of the PCL that I have put together.

Return to Sun Worship

To help clean up the spiritual confusion among people we need to understand that the real God or Creator is in the sky, not in books containing the twisted conceptions of people. Books reflect people's understanding at different times, when they possessed different capabilities in communication, accuracy and clarity. Progress can be expected when people make sufficient growth. The early written teachings can still be used for your life's support and understanding, but be aware that they can confuse. If you do not wish to be confused or fooled by the existing answers to who has created human life, you need only look up at the sky. The only Heavenly Father in the sky is the sun with its numerous children as the different human races. All humanity comes from the sun. The sun is the one father and one life source of all.

Sun worship is natural and universal, although the styles of worship differed throughout different communities. Without the sun's support, people could not grow crops or hunt. Through millions of years and generations of development, the sun has been the only God as a guide to all.

It was through the sky's influence that human civilizations began, and early societies were shaped. Later people became idealistic. Their growing minds developed religions with notions and intentions from the developing social background. They invented many rituals and decorations to reinvent the creator of life, replacing the real God in the sky. Human life began to deviate from the broad and natural universal life.

In the deep truth, religions can trace back to find unity in the worship of the subtle Light as the soul and deep spirit in life. By washing away religious decorations, the single truth can be revealed, the practical effect of which is to direct people towards the subtle Divine Light. This has been proven by such spiritual teachers as Lao Tzu, Jesus, Mani, and through teachings such as the Pure Land of Buddhism and Tibetan Buddhism. However, the most direct and scientific approach to the discovery of the subtle Light is through the ancient Chinese teachings of immortality.

The foundation of the different spiritual promotions, if they are truthful, is the same subtle, inner Light in life. No matter what the name or style of the promotion, the secret is that nurturing one's inner Light supports spiritual health and longevity. One of the most advanced training systems is the spiritual system of the Pure Light from my mother's teaching. As well as nourishing health and longevity, it includes the enlightenment of the mind. Master Maoshing Ni, as the current master of the Integral Way, may offer to teach it to some spiritual coaches. The PCL is one level of practice. The depth of its teaching is the Path of Subtle Light. At this level the teaching will be individually based. The broad and correct direction is to guide you to live a constructive life, as this is the foundation for your subtle spiritual growth. Both a constructive life and the subtle Light are completely connected.

Jesus, in his time, was the only one of his people who understood the truth of life and the universe. Although born a Jew, Jesus was a spiritual child of the Way. He was influenced by the Way's teachings of the subtle Light and immortality that grew out of the ancient regions of China and elsewhere. His teaching refers to the Heavenly Father and the trinity of the light, the life and the truth. He hints that there is a close connection between the light of the sun, the life of people and the truth of life. Of the three, the sun is the most fundamental. To Jesus, the sun is the Heavenly Father. Jesus learned that the *yang* energy of the sun is the origin of life, and that one's life and soul are gifts from the sun. If you lose your soul, you lose your light in life.

Jesus intended to bring people back to sun worship, but Catholicism did not support his wish. Instead, the Catholic establishment promoted Jesus as a type of hero to facilitate their politico-religious control of the masses.

The sun, as the provider of light and warmth, never taxed people or drove them to build pyramids. The price of turning away from the natural reality to the fictional creations of the mind was a high one to pay.

The natural environment, most significantly the sun, vitally influences a human life—particularly at birth. The sun gives you physical life. It affects your looks as well as your mental and spiritual tendencies. Through self-cultivation, you can learn to develop your positive tendencies and control the extreme ones. But first, if you wish to improve your spiritual condition, you need to clean away the artificial concepts and creations of others. Then you will see that the real God is in the sky, and is always bright and ready to support and guide you. God means the direction where life is headed.

No life can give up the sun. You may wonder how I continue to do my voluntary spiritual teaching and writing. Let me pass the secret onto you. In my daily life, I always recognize the sun like this.

Dearest Heavenly Father,
I know that the early earthlings once knew you as the Mother.
We owe you love and respect forever, as you are the true source of our lives.
With your light you created life in this part of the universe.
Your beams of light are your limbs.
You touch and fulfill things as you wish.
As your children, we can do the same as you, but not more.

Your light shapes the initial form of all fleshed lives.
Your light helps to produce the ancestors of each different species on earth.
The continual development and evolution of life, which makes all lives different,
is also your work.

You have been the strongest supporter of us earthlings.

Your work can be traced spiritually.

Although you have completed the first stage of creation in its primitive style,

the work of completion needs to continue.

And I always pray like this.

Dear Heavenly Father,

Please help me, your child, with your light.

With your help, I am able to see the darkness inside my life,

and I am able to offer your light to my fellow people.

Please cleanse my soul with your divine golden light,

and absorb it into you.

Help me live the example of your life on Earth.

Amour!

Mostly I say this prayer during the cold winter mornings. During the hot summer, I joyfully greet the Heavenly Father by saying, "Papa," and in the evening of any season, I happily greet the Heavenly Father as "Mama." This was how my parents trained me. As a beginner, it is important to receive training and have some formality, but the core of spiritual connection is through your heart.

When I left my parents I was very young. I was not able to contact them, so I used the sky and sun for my emotional support. The sky shaped my young life. This was how my parents taught me about life and how they learned from their parents. The sky has given me the strength and interest to keep doing my work.

Many religions began out of social competition. Humankind needs harmony and cooperation if everyone is to enjoy a better life on Earth. Maoshing and I need your help for our work. Please understand that the sun is the light provider, the warmth giver, the spiritually inspiring image and the real life-giving example.

Keep the Week as a Spiritual Reminder

The seven-day cycle has been the pattern of time management for many people. This system is appropriate for physical and emotional refreshment, because people have two free days in a week. This pattern was a Babylonian custom of some 4000 to 5000 years ago.

The Babylonians discovered that the sun was the center of life and the five main planets, Jupiter, Mercury, Mars, Venus and Saturn, formed a closely related family in the sky. They therefore decided to name a seven-day cycle corresponding to the sun, moon and the first five planets.

Although there is no astronomical connection between the movements of the sun, moon and planets and the order of the days of the week, it is still a good custom to have at least one or two days break in a period of seven days, so you don't become a slave to your life. That is why we support it.

I would like to share with you some spiritual background that establishes the human preference for the number seven. In the *I Ching*, the sixty-four hexagrams describe 64 different situations of development in nature or in life events. Each change, or hexagram, has six stages represented by six lines. The top line expresses the last stage of the developing situation. Usually, the few top lines express the top condition or the accomplishment to come, but the top-most line indicates the final or even the worst development in the situation.

To express the continuity of changes, there is a possible new phase in which a completely new pattern can develop. In between two hexagrams, there is an implied stage, a transitory or neutral stage not expressed by a line, but it is still part of the development of an event. This in-between stage heralds the beginning of a new cycle for the purpose of renewal.

This unexpressed stage can also be in the middle of two trigrams, since a hexagram is composed of two trigrams. The three lines of a trigram trace the basic division of three stages of development, which can be formed as a curved line with one peak. A hexagram is two curves, and each developing stage expresses a curvature.

In describing an event in human history, an individual life, a family, a clan, a society or anything, a combination of small and big curved lines are used rather than a straight line to express each stage of development. The 64 hexagrams are a big cycle, and the six lines within one hexagram is one small cycle. Seven, therefore, means renewal, the time of finishing and restarting. It also means the neutral transitional stage.

The week was based on sun-centered worship so that every seven days there is Sunday, Monday, etc. If you understand that background, you can say it is a good custom. In truth, everyday is Sunday, and due to the rotation of the Earth around the sun, you have one hemisphere in the light and the other in the dark.

It is a good idea to use one day of the week as a spiritual day to do something for your body, mind and spirit. You can refresh your life with the sun. Therefore, continue the good custom of using one day out of seven for self-cultivation and/ or spiritual service for others. Actually, any day is a good day for constructive spiritual activities.

The Ageless Way

The Way is the recognized orderly and cyclical path of the heavenly bodies. It can also be expressed in the normal and regular style by which people relate to and treat each other. It has been developed since humankind was born on Earth, and has existed over a long period of time among the people in China and elsewhere. This is why the Way is the cultural root of humanity.

The ancients observed a natural order and relatively stable routine among the sun, moon and stars that was not created by anyone. They also observed that a natural order existed in human society among its families, clans and races, which was connected to the natural order of the sky. Humankind stills live a lifestyle that closely follows the orderliness of the sky, with the sun as the nearest center.

The sun offers its service free of charge, as long as people do not overuse its gifts. However, when people invented religions, they claimed to be the sky's regents on Earth and they charged others. Yet God, in the deep sense, is the harmony and orderliness of nature that has always been of great support to human life. You should appreciate what nature has done for you. You should not confuse these natural functions with the psychological applications of cunning leaders.

The center of life is life itself, not the government, even if the government does provide some services for a heavy price. In contrast, the natural orderliness charges no one. For example, you have a yearly cycle, monthly cycle and many other big and small cycles. Cycles form the routine of your lives, and they have existed long before humankind was born.

The orderliness of the universe is recognizable. It has been recognized as the Way. Though some small chaos can be experienced in nature, the overriding grand order has offered human life a relatively stable existence on Earth. The universe is not as chaotic as some people think, so no one can use this viewpoint to support irresponsible social behavior.

The Way, unlike the unnatural concepts of most religions, teaches harmony with nature and orderliness in life. Nature has a center. You can see the solar system with all its planets spinning around the North Star. The North Star, in turn, spins around the Spinning Damsel as its center. This star is also known in the West as the star Vega in the constellation of Lyra, and in the East as the Weaving Maiden. All these systems, from small to big, extend to the galaxies and beyond.

Those are the three spheres of universal spirituality. The space surrounding the solar system and beneath the North Star is the range of *T'ai Ching*, the Great

Purity. Peace is the required quality to reside there. The space above the North Star system but beneath the Weaving Maiden or Spinning Damsel is the range of *San Ching*, the Supreme Purity. Freedom is the required quality to reside there. The space above the Weaving Maiden is the range of *Yu Ching*, the Precious Purity, and wisdom is the required quality to be there. These three spheres are the deep universal valleys in the womb of Mother Universe. They are also the sacred places that are found in the spacious hearts of highly wise people. The three levels correspond to the three levels of soul in your life. The head of an achieved individual corresponds to the range of *Yu Ching* where wisdom resides, the center of the chest of such an individual is *San Ching* where there is a humanistic heart, and the center of the lower abdomen is *T'ai Ching* where harmony resides.

There is no other Way, but the recognizable orderliness of the universe. And although it is all right to conceive the entire universe as being under a unified ruling system, or what may be conceptualized as God, you should not erect a separate ruling system to compete with the natural orderliness of the sky. At the same time, you can adopt the orderliness of nature into your personal lives, your family lives, your work places and your societies. The Way is a natural inspiration to people. No teaching established by the mind can be greater than what nature teaches.

Maoshing and I confess that we would like all lives to directly appreciate nature as the real background of life, rather than the fictitious one of conceptual religious rule. However, we promote the PCL as a bridge to work with the thought patterns and social habits of the last two to three thousand years.

What follows are the primary principles of the PCL.

> God is a spiritual quality, not a position or a person.

> God is the virtue that loves and supports life, not the force or power ruling over life.

God is the spiritual respect you hold within and express in life, not a ritual or performance.

God is the spiritual dignity in life, not emotional pride or arrogance.

Nonduality is the identity of your spirituality. God is the faith in life's spiritual potential, not an external element added to life.

Impartiality to all religions and their leaders is encouraged, and respect is given to their humanistic efforts. Religious teachings are viewed with objectivity and nonattachment.

God is the end of self-discovery from the realization in life.

God is the substance of life, not the decorations such as your degree, position, house, job, car or clothes.

God is the work you do, not the enjoyment you take.

Being naïve and having no disappointment in life is how to protect the divine nature, while a suitable amount of sophistication is the lubrication among people.

Holding an indiscriminate attitude and image towards people, and expecting nothing in return will ensure that you never tire of helping them. If you attempt to help people out of the desire for something in return, you will tire easily.

How Do You Offer Service?

This point needs to be carefully explained. We have mentioned the importance of imitating the sky to improve order among people, as well as accepting support from Mother Nature rather than following the established styles of religions, as many have become the fuel for social rivalry.

Originally, I didn't agree with having a socially organized teaching because of their historical use as tools to manipulate people, as in the Dark Ages of the West. Even today, some dark corners of society still experience religious biases. However, organized teachings also have positive aspects. For example, today you enjoy the privileges and freedom promoted by the democratic style of politics, which was started by the parliamentary system of the Church, the foundation of Western society. Although the Church has performed many misdeeds, it also served well as a caretaker for humanity during its infancy. After many years, the church-style of organized religion has made many improvements, becoming an effective format to offer organized social services to society. Therefore, its form should be kept for this purpose, while its contents should be scrutinized openly and objectively.

A healthy social spiritual service contributes to the world. We, therefore, encourage you to use the weekend to offer social service for your own spiritual development, as well as for the development of society. It can be from an individual based spiritual pursuit to the social sharing of your own attainment.

Learn and teach from the ancient sages who elucidated the Way of wisdom, yet reduce any extreme teaching to be in line with the divine principles of balance, impartiality and non-duality. Be open to the good work and teachings of outstanding individuals regardless of their background. You can learn from the two outstanding individuals of Jesus and Mohammed. Both of them were spiritual children of the Way: they used its teachings to help the people of their time.

As you know, their teachings became popularized as the religions of Christianity and Islam, which are in rivalry today. This is the fault of the religious leaders and their followers, who do not see behind the teachings.

Jesus was born a Jew, but spiritually he was a child of the Way, drawing on it for his teachings. The substance of his teachings, as given in his Sermon on the Mount, corresponds to Hexagram 15 in the *I Ching*, which is titled *Chien* or Being Humble. It means moderation. This is the main guidance given by Lao Tzu in the

Tao Teh Ching and the *Heavenly Way*,[1] and it is the social goal and fulfillment of the PCL. Most of Jesus's other teachings are literary dramatizations created by others.

Jesus also conveyed the message of the sky's kindness and love towards people. He taught peaceful living as derived from the *Tao Teh Ching*. His main message was that people should cease all fighting, battling and warfare. Personally this means you should yield to one another. Jesus demonstrated this in his own life by living unselfishly and selflessly. Being tolerant and yielding is the core of his teaching, and he explained it figuratively by saying that if someone asks you to walk one mile with them, you could walk two miles with them. Or, if someone struck you on the left cheek, you would turn the other cheek and allow them to strike you again. This demonstrates the spiritual depth of an individual life.

To yield and cease fighting does not mean you become a coward. Rather, it means you exhibit deep humanistic love by offering harmony in human relationships. In the teaching of the Way, all life is one big life, and all human races are one family. All people should care for the total survival of humanity, not just for one individual, one clan or one race.

The salvation of Jesus is the harmony of the world. He taught and embodied the virtue of forgiveness by returning evil with good. He embodied the philosophy of the *Tao Teh Ching* by living its universal morality. Without Jesus's example, the *Tao Teh Ching* is a mere philosophical teaching, and without the *Tao Teh Ching*, Jesus' teachings may not have revealed the depth of life. Jesus, by giving his life and light to the world, was the only example in his time of the Heavenly Father sun, which is the highest example of universal morality. You can learn from Jesus's example.

Mohammed was also a child of the Way. When trading with the East, he searched for the truth, absorbing the wisdom from the learned and wise. He learnt and confirmed that the high truth is formless, unspeakable, unthinkable and inde-

---

1. Refer to Hua-Ching Ni's work of *The Complete Works of Lao Tzu*, and his booklet entitled *Heavenly Way*.

scribable, and that all objects and temples are mere symbols of the spiritual truth. These are all essential teachings of the Way. Upon returning to his homeland, he taught the same thing to his people, encouraging them to do away with idolatry, and worship the sky, the void, the emptiness and the subtle truth of no obstructions.

The worship of the vast, open sky is a wise improvement on idol worship. Mohammed may have over extended his insistence on those spiritual principles, but he was truthful in understanding that statues and idols can obstruct one's direct experience of the deep, subtle truth. As a message to the general people, he wisely chose the word, Allah. Deeply, it implies the one spiritual self of life and the universe.

Mohammed and Islam are two different things. Mohammed was an individual who developed himself to know the real substance that supports life, which contrasts with the Islamic religion which has become overly structured and unnatural. Mohammed demonstrated that the spiritual truth is formless, and above any symbols and titles. He was serious about practicing piety, an emotion which many modern people lack. Through practicing piety towards nature, and through healthy, balanced ritual, you can gather and strengthen spiritual energy and communicate with the subtle depths and substance of life.

As future teachers of the Way, you can utilize the positive examples of Jesus and Mohammed. You may adopt Jesus as the one who exemplifies the Way, and use Mohammed's organized style of gathering and devotion (or piety) to the truth. Although your confidence is in the oneness of the natural truth, your teaching styles can be flexible and varied. In this way, you will be able to moderate the confusing approaches of religions. The PCL intends to continue the spiritual achievement of the non-dualistic spirituality of the one universal life. At the same time, it also respects the different spiritual expressions of nature and in life's different circumstances.

Find the simplest and most effective way of helping people at their different levels and with their different mental tendencies. It is appropriate to construct a shrine, as long as you place its objects and images in perspective, as simple symbols and reminders of the spiritual essence and energy in people's lives. The shrine can also help to channel people's piety towards deep nature. The high spirit in life does not rely on symbols. The more symbols and rituals used, the lower and less truthful, even unhealthy, the expression of spirituality. Conventionally, the different religions rely and insist on symbols to express how spiritual they are. Consequently, they have become shallow and disconnected to the truth. Things should be made simpler and easier now. A suitable amount of symbolism may be required to communicate, but relying on more expresses regress rather than progress. The old forms of social spiritual service can be continued, but they need to be refined and improved to promote a healthy community spirit and spiritual service.

The PCL provides a healthy standard of spiritual life, as demonstrated by its ancient human spiritual leaders such as Fu Shi, Shen Nung (3218–3078 BCE, 140 years of reign) and the Yellow Emperor. They lived a normal life, while personally serving and benefiting all people. They did not lead by force. People were attracted to follow and listen to them, because of the qualities those natural leaders expressed in their lives.

The fulfillment of a constructive community comes from the level of its followers. Where do we find good students who fulfill the beauty in life? The truth is that the constructive spirit of life serves the life of all people, and that spirit should be expressed 100 percent in life. There is nothing more holy or sacred in life than this.

All good activities of the different aspects of life should be constructively performed with a healthy attitude. If the desire to do is overly extended, it will only lead to detriment rather than benefit. Some of the old religious disciplines, such as deep bowing, appropriate fasting or food reduction, healthy sexual activity and meditation have beneficial value if constructively and correctly applied. But they should not be promoted as holier than other activities. They can all be useful as the art of life. Among them, one of the most effective practices is the soft and gentle physical movement of *t'ai chi*. Conventionally, *t'ai chi* is used as a martial art, but it has little value for that, as no campaign can live for long. Regular practice of *t'ai chi* can save you from frequenting the doctor and can help slow down the aging process.

There is another aspect about social service from the perspective of the PCL. As followers of constructive living you still encourage people to be spiritually self-reliant, but you also agree to support the spiritual growth of the public. There is another important difference from the religious style of service: your intention is not to make a living from the PCL service. You do not intend to be like some religious leaders who used spiritual service as their sole means of income, with the result that they create things to make the service financially viable and continuous. In contrast, your service is a vehicle to connect to people and share what you have achieved. Among you all there are also different levels of attainment, and you each teach from your own level. Spiritual service is your virtuous fulfillment to society.

We therefore encourage you to give public service and support, but still have your own personal life support. You may learn from the positive examples of ministers in the improved Protestant churches, as well as from Lao Tzu's *Heavenly Way*. Lao Tzu teaches that once you have enough to take care of yourself, then you can give away what you do not need. However, if you don't have enough for yourself, how can you have anything to give away? How you decide on enough depends on your own spiritual growth and maturity.

There may also be situations where spiritually you have more than others, and they are better than you at making a living. In that case, a fair exchange would be appropriate, with them offering you something back in the sense of mutual support.

Unlike conventional religions that created hero worship, the PCL worships the spiritual quality that brings success, prosperity and great accomplishment in life. Rather than believing God is the highest position and highest authority in life that people can rely on, the PCL understands that God represents the highest spiritual qualities of the life-giving light. It is these spiritual qualities that people pursue to actualize, rather than rely on in their lives. The PCL does not define God as the authority of life and death who can be bribed, but as the quality of being that gives one's life and light to illuminate one's surroundings.

The Feminine Principle as Both the Old and New Spiritual Leadership

For the past 3000 to 4000 years, the world has suffered from an exaggerated application of the masculine principle with its emphasis on physical aggression and intense social competition. To balance the current extreme, you need to appreciate and uphold the feminine principle that values cooperation, tolerance, gentleness and harmony.

The valuable spiritual vision and virtue of the feminine approach is superior at raising families and managing human affairs. Both Lao Tzu and Jesus's teachings are based on the feminine principle.

We therefore encourage all women to exercise their feminine virtue, and accept the role of spiritual leadership in order to help spread the teachings of the *Heavenly Way* for social cooperation and world peace. The second book in the Constructive Life Series, *The Power of the Feminine* can help you in this endeavor. Know, too, that the Lady-in-Blue, as the hint for the boundless blue sky, is always ready to support those of pure heartedness and clear mindedness. The PCL adopts the Lady-in-Blue as the spiritual leader of all people. The Lady-in-Blue can also imply the Mother Universe. For a greater understanding of the Lady-in-Blue, refer to Chapter 29.

Chapter 4

Health Is Spiritual Faith
(Have Faith in the Spiritual Light)

Spiritual faith is a strong projection of the mind. The most trustworthy of spiritual faiths needs to be supported by strong objective grounds, even if having faith can be a subjective matter that helps strengthen your life.

The truth of a spiritual faith or teaching is not about how it is taught, or how the initiated leaders received their inspirations. It must be more than just a thought or a promotional slogan, and it must be related with the deep truth of life.

Though people freely shape their mental attitudes from their backgrounds, religious teachings are more than just a personal faith; they help influence the conjoint destiny of humanity. This is especially so in today's world, where improved communications have brought people closer together. Therefore, the world cannot afford to be manipulated by an individual's personal faith or private ideology. All religious groups can help solve the world's conflicts, and save humanity by relinquishing their narrow beliefs and embracing the universal spiritual faith.

The universal spiritual truth contains three premises: The first is that the Spirit is a subtle energy in the universe. The second is that human life is composed of spiritual entities. The third is that spiritual phenomena exist among people.

The Spirit as a Subtle Energy

The Spirit in human life is like the sun in the sky on a fine day. When there are no clouds, everything is bright and warm, and the great natural reality is clearly visible to the mind, along with the creations of humankind. Although it may be hard to see the actual light, you can see or contact everything revealed by it in describable ways.

Conventionally, people have mistaken some natural objects or human creations, or whatever they could see in the light, to be the Light. However, the things that are made visible by the light are not the Light itself. To say that they are misplaces the spiritual reality of life, as spiritual Light is not like a lamp or a lantern, though such objects do help light up the dark. The power of the Spirit is like an internal light source that helps your mind perceive things, the same way a lamp helps your eyes see things in the world.

The above example is a two-fold metaphor. First, we are saying that Spirit and light are similar in quality. Second, that Spirit can transform to become Light for your mind, and an invisible Light for your life, which is perceivable by the conscious mind during critical times of life and death. The Light is a sign for the life to revive and continue living.

The Spiritual Entities in Human Life

The spirits in your life are not a new experience or a new power that you suddenly possess. They have been with human life ever since the first human received life. Interestingly, human beings have the capacity to know great volumes of information and make things happen accordingly, however, they do not know what enables them to know and act. The soul is the power and support that drives humans to know and act. The Spirit or soul can also rescue you from your mind's mistakes that misuse your being.

The Need for Balance Among the Three Spheres of Human Life

All humans are born with three spheres of life. The physical sphere is the body, the part that you can see, feel and know; the mental sphere is the mind, the part that can feel and know; and the spiritual sphere is the part that knows what to support in order to maintain your life's functions.

Living things thrive under the sun on a fine day or a cloudy day, but behind this resilience the soul of life plays a serious role. When the soul is absent, life cannot function. At most, some physical function may last another hour or few days. Hence, the spiritual sphere of life, though hidden behind the mind and physical form, is one of three indispensable levels of reality. It is the subtle substance of your life.

By being aware of the three spheres of life, you may perceive that a human being is a tripled-natured reality: the physical body is the form and the force; the mind is the operator; and the spirit is the generator. In other words, force in life is produced from your physical being. At the same time, your mind operates your body with what it knows, and with the health of your life's moral condition. All healthy functions come from the spiritual sphere of your life—spiritual energy is the potency of your life.

The Conscious Unit or the Soul of Life

Living and dying may be apparent expressions of life, but what you don't see is the subtle substance that enhances or withdraws from the functions of life to express the reality of living. That subtle substance may be described as the conscious unit or the soul of the life.

The soul is a separate reality that can freely come and go at the moment when a fatal accident destroys the form or the vital internal transportation system or the communicative system. However, a mature individual with self-achievement can safely withdraw the soul from his or her body as one possible spiritual attainment.

Human life ranks on top of the wonders of the world. Scientists ambitiously try to duplicate life in the laboratory, and though they may succeed on some level of shape or form, the spiritual reality is beyond anyone's creation. That possibility is only endowed to life by nature.

The Research of the Soul

Although a few of humankind's small achievements have significantly contributed to improving life, most people remain ignorant of the subtle sphere of spiritual truth. The spiritual reality of life can be known as clearly as any scientific subject or object, even if to the academic world it is still a blank page.

Conventional religions harbor many misconceptions of the spiritual world. They tend to meet any mystical feelings from the subtle evidence of the spiritual sphere with misgivings. Spiritual fiction, like science fiction, is a product of the mind. No scholar or researcher has broken down the conceptual walls to reach the depth of the mind where both science and religion were created.

The Monkey King

The monkey king is the dominating human mind that shifts back and forth between the spiritual and physical realms to create religions and science, but it often misses the reality in between, which is the middle point. First, this restless monkey created religions and misguided the masses, and then it developed destructive weapons and brought harm to life. Both came out of its respect for the safety of life, but morality, as the domain of the spirit, was neglected.

Physical research and mental beliefs constantly rival reach other. Each devalues the other, yet both are simply different expressions from the same source. You may be awakened by seeing that created religions, by dominating people's thoughts and beliefs, add more fuel to world problems rather than solving them. Likewise, science offers no solution to the problems of the world, as it functions much like putting a steel hammer to a starving stomach—the needy world cannot digest it. In facing the world's crises, people have neglected the real spiritual truth in life.

The Plain Spiritual Reality

The confusion in life comes from a lack of correct understanding of the three facts of life that: One, the Spirit is the subtle potency of life. Two, spirits exist as numerous tiny entities in your life. And three, spiritual phenomena can be experienced.

These three facts of life need to be made distinct. They have not been established because people have been too busy competing with each other, and so not many people know what their life is. Some people die because of physical ailments, others for religious conflicts, and both die with spiritual confusion. This loss of life reflects how the spiritual Light is not seen as the internal or external reality. Without understanding these facts, people do not know the value of life and death.

A Human Life Rests on a Three-Footed Caldron

The number one spiritual reality is the Spirit, also called the spiritual nature or the Way. You can also call it God. Simply put, the Spirit is a common fact in the high life of humans. It differs from the psychological tendency of the mind. It is the naturally endowed will for safety in one's life. That internal demand produces the Spiritual Light. God can thus be a decorative concept, as well as the headlamp that lights up the way for miners.

The number two spiritual reality is the clusters of spirits. Traditionally, people have mistaken life to be a single spiritual unit. Actually, an individual consists of many spiritual units that can produce various spiritual phenomena. These phenomena can cause confusion, and some people have used the confusion as a foundation to structure spiritual beliefs.

In healthy conditions, spiritual entities work together with your life to produce internal activities such as dreaming, daydreaming, a sudden memory, an inspiration, or a sudden enlightenment. These are all common in daily life. You may also get a strange feeling about someone or something, which does not come from reading books, but is perceived through your silent spiritual functions. This is the internal reality, and it can happen to anyone. Often the internal spiritual functions are confused with the mind.

Today, scholars treat these phenomena as part of the conscious or subconscious mind. They do not know that such phenomena do not come from the brain, as the mind in the life, but from the body through the different spiritual units. The different groups of bodily spirits, which are not the mind or the brain, form the separate conscious systems in the body. Sometimes the spirits can appear as formed life too.

With spiritual training you are able to witness and experience the spiritual entities that are the foundation of your life. The traditional term for them is *chi*. *Chi* can be seen as particles forming a dense-like vapor. This truthful reality is not to be confused with ghost-like spirits (better known as *chi* beings), which are the disappearing lives of the past; the scattered life spirits of a person who has passed. Your body spirits are the hope and seeds of life for the future. If ghosts are true, they are the formation of the good or bad energy of the surroundings, appearing to a viewer incidentally, or as a result of their conscious condition or connection. Such phenomena have nothing to do with the tiny body spirits that are a fact and foundation of your living internal life.

The Spiritual Phenomena Among People

The number three spiritual reality is the spiritual experiences and prophecies of specific individuals. These are not common to most people, but can be particular to some spiritual leaders. These experiences may be reproduced in literature. Some may have been created fictionally to gather public faith, or draw attention to certain tensions.

Support for this category of spiritual experiences does exist, but it is mixed. The meaning and the degree of its trustworthiness must be carefully sorted. Often spiritual prophecies come from an unintended individual from an uneducated class, or from someone with an innocent mind, regardless of age or gender. They carry a message for some individual, some family, or some group of people. These spiritual phenomena do exist.

The Refined Essence is on Top

The spiritual reality of human life is expressed three-fold, as if it rests on a three-footed caldron. The caldron is used to refine the medicine, and the crystallized essence is on the top, not the bottom. The number one reality is the fruit of spiritual development and achievement. It is the Spiritual Light in an individual life and in society, an absolute necessity rather than an emotional luxury. Without the Spiritual Light, people would live in the darkness like low beasts, all too ready to kill each other, as well as themselves. Or, they would slowly poison or kill themselves and others with their productions.

The second reality of the spirits is the internal spiritual knowledge of life, which intersects with branches of modern intellectual knowledge such as biology, anatomy, physiology and biochemistry. The latter studies, however, fail to see or recognize the internal spirits as the connection.

The Spiritual Light is the important spiritual reality in life, but its foundation is the reality of the numerous spirits in life. That is to say, the healthy foundation of your inner spirits produces Spiritual Light.

The second reality of the cluster of spirits is related to the healthiness of life. For an individual life, self-knowledge is most valuable. By living a healthy life, you can quietly recognize your inner spirits and learn more about them, including how to strengthen them. The offering of service is a way to train professional healers and spiritual teachers about spirits. However, even with training, these people may remain as mere speakers of the mind without reaching the truth of the spirits.

As a spiritual individual you are responsible for your internal spirits. Your healthy mental and emotional being, your well-guided desires, and your spiritual formation are all connected to the health of your life spirits. Though the tiny spirits can each be a spiritual entity, they are more effective as a group. They respond to your mind as a group and are subject to conditioning. As you are responsible for their management, you need to select healthy influences with which to shape your conscious being, and avoid any negative ones. Living decently produces good spirits for your own health and the health of the world.

The third reality of spiritual phenomena can be truthful if it is produced by innocent people, and not used for social manipulation. The true understanding of these spiritual phenomena, both in reality and as fiction, is related to the development of the individual and the society.

Spiritual phenomena challenge your personal spiritual development. It requires you to know how much can be trusted, whether it happens to you or to someone else. Though you don't have to correct these matters, for your own and the public's safety you should at least know what to support or keep away from. This is because just as healthy people can produce Spiritual Light, so sick people can produce sick auras and misguided information. Fortunately, the first reality of Spiritual Light can be trusted as the open truth for everyone. It is the only hope for humanity.

The World Needs Spiritual Light

The big religions, as social experiments, have attained certain proven successes, but each has reached the end of the road. In facing today's problems, solutions can be found by combining the physical structures of those social religions with the Spiritual Light. The positive aspects of social religions can remain as specific social customs or local structures to help carry out the real hope of pursuing the Spiritual Light. We feel this is the way to avoid mutual destruction and sustain humanity's survival.

The Spiritual Light is the product of a healthy life. If people could lessen the time they spend watching television or listening to the radio, in exchange for developing the Spiritual Light, they would improve their mind's intelligence. Special vision like the Heavenly Eye and special audio power like the Heavenly Ear are innate human abilities. Both are spiritually connected. They are the benefits of spiritual self-cultivation through correct spiritual disciplines.

True and complete understanding of life's spiritual nature is important for society's health. The deep truth of life should also be a personal pursuit. What you attain can save you from the confusion resulting from people's erroneous or incomplete descriptions, and from their inventions that would otherwise influence you. Even if there was no specific design or plan intended, these creations can still confuse your mind and your spirit.

The Limitations of the Mind

Throughout generations many achieved individuals have reached the understanding of life's spiritual nature. Yet this truth cannot be communicated through the relative habit of the mind, as the truth is the direct knowledge of life. The truth of spiritual reality should not be limited by the mind, which has a hard time perceiving things beyond the pattern of its own constraints.

The mind knows things by discernable differences. For example, "long" is seen by a sense of "short," "front" is seen by a sense of "rear," "right" is known by a sense of "wrong" (even if people often confuse which is which) and happiness is known by a sense of painful suffering. These endless preferences, set by the pattern of mind, are taken as the reality of the world.

By using the mind to establish religions, people reinforce the mind's patterns. These patterns have caused much confusion about spiritual truth. Religions are supposed to guide people with spiritual truth to live a healthy and whole life, but a great divergence results when the basic mental frames are themselves taken to be the spiritual truth.

When the relative patterns of the mind dominate, dualism becomes the rule, such as heaven and hell, God and Satan, angels and devils, good and bad, sin and salvation, love and hate, justice and injustice and so on. This has intensified dualism in human culture. With this conventional religious fault, how can people expect to recognize and respect others in sharing universal harmony and cooperation?

The mind has the duty of fulfilling a real and practical life. To make better use of the mind and its products, God can be perceived as the collective wisdom that people respect and use to see their way out of trouble. God can also be the leadership that takes people from the dark to the light. Likewise, a devil can be a capable individual, whose partial vision and narrow-mindedness have brought disasters to people and their surroundings.

Nurturing Spiritual Awareness
Is the Support for a Healthy and
Truthful Spiritual Faith

Spiritual awareness is the main conscious function of your life. It is the ability to be aware of your life, and includes the knowledge and activity that are going on in your life. However, spiritual nature cannot be known as an object. It manifests as the direct function of spiritual awareness that subtly guides your life, especially if you do not confuse it with external knowledge.

All wise people should know that the spiritual nature of the universe is everywhere, and in the high life of all people. It is not a problem of who possesses more or less. All people equally possess spiritual nature. Everything is one thing, and one thing is everything. This is the spiritual truth. There is freedom for everyone. The obstruction to seeing this reality is caused by the mind. Conventional religions have not reached the Truth and do not teach the Truth, though they have expressed a kind heart in their attempts to pacify society.

In truth, the Spirit is the Light in life. Living a spiritual life is to live in the Spiritual Light. Both are not conspicuously seen or known. Wise people know that spiritual awareness comes from a healthy life, not from anywhere else. The strong spiritual awareness of sages comes from the Spiritual Light of their lives. They can be considered as God. Your life has the same potential. You can express it as the universal moral strength and clear vision in your practical life.

The spiritual nature in life treats all as the truth, and makes the truth available to all. It does not discriminate. With natural spiritual self-knowledge, one treats all others the same as oneself, for all life carries the same life nature. One who lives with the spiritual nature is with the spiritual truth, where there is no bondage, only boundless freedom. It is a wholeness and completeness that you do not need to seek out, but that is freely with you.

The darkness of the mind brings about vexation. Once the darkness of the dualistic mind is removed, there is sunlight from natural wisdom. What comes from the mind can also be changed by the mind, and what people call pain and trouble is the mind behaving like a bandit to pawn your life for its slavery. People need to understand the mind completely to further its development. A healthy mind has spiritual support available to it. Spiritual freedom, in a limited sense, is a mind that has reached maturity.

One should pursue the best orderliness that the mind can reach at each level, individual, familial and social. Spiritual benignity requires a spiritually open mind. This means living free from all mental conditions, for the spiritual reality is the natural, indefinable potential in your life.

Spiritual Cooperation

The Way is not a socially shaped force like established religions. The Way is the pure life spirit of universal nature. The religions and the Way need to cooperate together to save each other, like in the old story where the lame worked with the blind to help each other escape the fire.

We hope you see by now that the spiritual reality in human life is not a matter of language, but of real life. Such an indescribable spiritual reality was called the Way in old China. In the West, it is called God. To us, as humble seekers of truth from the many healthy achievements of all human ancestors, we courageously define the Way as the Spiritual Light produced by the healthy nature of life. And we define God as the executive of peace, harmony and cooperation among all people. There should be no more misunderstanding and contortion.

The Way is a path for the minds of people to unite with universal beingness. When the mind's negative projections are mingled with a high projection such as God, God can be used as an excuse for the mind's mistakes, resulting from its undeveloped condition. The best leadership for human life should be from the undisturbed Spirit of life, which supports the health of the mind.

A developed humanity comes from the development of its people. In this matter, the conventional religions do not help, but show how sick the mind can be from its own confusion. If the barbarism in the world is worse without rather than with religions, then with religions it becomes concentrated as the common obstacle to spiritual realization and world peace. When people reach enough development, they will relegate these old problems and misunderstandings to the religious halls. Such days are something to look forward to.

People are the children of Mother Nature. You are a child of the universe who proudly possesses the three complete spheres in life. You are no less than those born before you, during your time or after you. Externally, you rely on light from all sources to help you conduct your precious life. Internally, you have to nurture and develop your own Spiritual Light to enable you to see your life, your mistakes and the mistakes of others.

As a child of the universe you do not need a go-between, though you may occasionally have teachers. Whoever can live in the Spiritual Light, and conduct their life in the Spiritual Light is with the Spiritual Light. If you prefer to use conventional terms, it means that you are with God, you are a part of God and your life is to complete God. God is with you, and you are with God. This is the union of humanity and Divinity. This is the truth that will eventually unfold in your life.

Chapter 5

God Is the Optimal Rational Function in an Harmonious, Balanced Life

Every person in the world has the same natural foundation, only it has been overlaid and confused by the artifice of social religions. Religions were originally developed to correct and guide people's behavior, but their corrections became too extreme. By spreading their stylized activities across the world, they added an artificial flavoring to people's lives. Therefore, what is normal to a natural life, such as sexual union, has been viewed as subnormal. And what is subnormal has been viewed as normal, such as the self-punishing style of some spiritual practices and rituals.

Once people adopt the artificial habits of a religion, they find it difficult to accept a simple and normal life, considering it dull and boring. They may even find it painful after the pain-killing type of religious practices, which may remove them from life. The true value of life exists in a plain and painless way of living.

People's deep identification with the different religious expressions has also become a new way for people to compete socially. The plain truth of life is not respected as much as the artificial new additions. This plain and honest presentation may challenge some people who have been conditioned by conventional ideas since childhood.

The natural foundation of each individual consists of several elements or levels. These are the sensory, conscious, emotional, intelligent, rational, moral and spiritual levels. In the natural order, the sensory level produces the conscious level, and the conscious level produces the emotional level. These three are the most basic and general levels of life.

Rationality is a higher level attained through growth. It includes the condition of your intelligence, upbringing and education. It has taken humankind many years to grow the rational level.

Above the four basic levels, or subtle functions of life, human nature contains the precious moral and spiritual senses. With mental growth you can come close to your spiritual potential. This spiritual attainment is not free. You need to pay with your real life experiences, frequent personal inspection and spiritual self-reflection.

Although the moral and spiritual senses are the highest levels, even higher than the rational level, they are often not in charge. Generally, one's emotions tend to be the boss, and one's likes and dislikes dictate how one lives. In a more developed individual, rationality is the boss.

Morality is your strengthened conscience or strengthened rationality. As your life grows, morality starts to freely offer itself to others as considerateness, sympathy and compassion. Yet even at this level, there is still an awareness of the self.

Divinity, or the spiritual sense, is the highest level in life, even higher than the moral sense. An individual who reaches this level has transcended self-centered thoughts of benefit, goodness, gain and so forth. He or she does nothing to serve their self, but rather works for the benefit and gain of all. He or she has gone beyond the sense of a small or narrow self, and expanded to be close to the universal self. This is when Godly individuals are produced.

The PCL advocates the safe growth of all lives by pointing out the importance of maintaining balance among all the internal elements. Each level, whether it is the sensory, conscious, emotional, rational (conscience), moral or spiritual, needs to be in balance with all the other levels. This will give your life the health it needs to support itself. And by keeping the foundation of your truthful and natural life balanced and well protected, the solution to many problems will become apparent.

Once you have achieved balance, your life may seem uninteresting. You may not attract the attention of others because you no longer have any pain to yell about. In this case, no news is good news. If you are wise, you will value the absence of bad experiences as the best performance of life. Not all people see this, however.

On the other hand, if one level of your life dominates over the other levels without supervision from the rational function, you could end up sacrificing your own life, as well as the lives of others. Living an unbalanced life can be immoral. This is the spiritual law.

Some religious and social systems cause serious deviations from the normalcy and natural health of life. For instance, though conventional religions often exalt the moral sense above all other elements of life, the practical reality, as presented by some clergy, is a subnormal example that is very different from life's true natural morality. This fact escapes those who do not develop their spiritual vision.

The PCL recommends elevating rationality with conscience to be the boss and executive manager of your life. At the same time, you are encouraged to exercise your moral sense, and uplift the spiritual dignity of your soul. These elements are the important, high levels of life.

In your daily life, you should value poise and balance over artificial require-ments. Harmonize all the levels in your life to be balanced and poised in the middle or center. The equality among them is the measure to attain evenness in life. The PCL guides you to attune your emotions to be melodious, and in good rhythm to match your life's healthy, smooth actions.

Life has no ideal evenness, like the surface of a peaceful lake without any storms or winds. Therefore, a sudden attack or stimulation can cause you to react sub-normally. Naturally, when you are young your emotions tend to dominate. This can cause danger to others and yourself. With growth and maturity, you can become more rational, calm and peaceful. But no definite number of years can guarantee when you will outgrow the beast of emotion.

Emotions are the bosses of conventional religionists. Social religionists display the unhealthiest condition when they turn social sentiments into God. Religious morality is then used as an excuse to persecute others, and the divine nature, which should be the highest growth of human nature, becomes the force to debase and mistreat others. This is the source of humanity's darkness.

God should never be the title for human emotion as that can be destructive to all. Never ask God to do this or that for you. Such behavior comes from your emotional level and will end at the emotional level.

God should be the title of the optimal rational function in life. It is safe to exalt rationality as God in life; it is the constructive order in an individual life and in society. In prayer, you may say:

God, help me attain the balance and benignity of my life.
I follow your leadership above all.
You are connected to the rationality of my high life
rather than the sentiments of my low life.
You are the center of my greatly ordered life.
No low elements will rise above the throne of my life's rationality.
You are the true ruler and sovereign of my life.

If ever a low element attempts to usurp your rationality, rather than suppressing it, the PCL guides you look for harmony, balance and cooperation among all the inner levels of your life, and between the inner and outer fabric of your life. This will fortify the throne of your rationality, which is real spiritual attainment.

Your life is one of completeness and wholeness. Do not let yourself become segmented by worldly cultures or religious customs. Blindly following the world will only push you to run after more possessions, emotional excitement and social gains for momentary pride. All these things have unseen negative side effects on your life and soul. When you only see the gains but not the losses, you have made emotion the lord of your life. And you already know how this will end.

Most of humanity exalts religion. This is not so unreasonable, but real confusion is caused when spiritual matters are separated from moral matters. People find it difficult to wholly understand moral matters. Simply put, when your soul is healthy, your life is in good condition. Spiritual confusion is caused when you don't realize that your moral condition is the healthy spiritual foundation of your life, and vice versa. There has never been a case where individuals of high spiritual quality mess up their lives or the lives of others. Therefore, it's easy to see that those who deny things of moral value usually ignore the spiritual reality in life.

Your life should have only one integral direction, and that is to be balanced and strong. This enables you to attain success, happiness, health, longevity and spiritual dignity, evenly and wholesomely. Do not live for only one thing and neglect the other aspects of your life. Such an unwise practice will invite trouble to the whole.

We have just revealed to you the confusion among people. This knowledge does not come from living a blessed life, but from having experienced many human ordeals. After so much suffering, humans need to grow their spiritual vision to see how their own ignorance creates their problems. This awakening comes from the mercy of the Mother Universe or Tao. Poise, balance, harmony and the ability to yield and cooperate, are highly valued spiritual qualities. They should be the ministers of God or divinities in your life. The real being of God is your own achieved rationality.

God is the hidden spiritual nature behind the form of life. Although God has no gender, it is not improper to address God as "She." She becomes enthroned by gentleness, not by force. She is kind to all lives both inside and outside of your life.

In life, you also need spiritual enthusiasm, which is the Heavenly Heart. The Mother Universe produces the Heavenly Heart. Life comes from the Heavenly Heart. The multiple divinities in the universe form the heavenly, spiritual functions of the giant universal life. From these multiple spiritual functions in life and in nature, people have misconceived too many deities. Yet, the value of spirituality is unity for all. Only one divinity oversees life and that is the Heavenly Heart. Only one God, one Lord, one Sovereign, one Superior and one Senior Authority is on duty, and that is the Heavenly Heart of Mother Universe.

Because of your contorted conceptions, you may not know Mother Universe, but she knows you. She is deeply related to you as your life's spiritually constructive nature. All godly or divine spiritual leaders come from her universal constructive nature. They are the corresponding response, and reflect the different spiritual functions of the kind Mother Universe to the needs of people in different regions and times. Once each god or divine leader accomplishes their mission, they merge back to the Mother again. The Mother contains all gods. Those who hold the belief in one god appearing in the different times and regions, hold a partial image of the spirituality of the Mother Universe. Whereas those who cherish the faith in the complete image of the everlasting life of Mother Universe, respect and value all the different expressions of her spiritual functioning as part of spiritual completeness.

The Mother Universe is known as the Heart of the Universe because of her concern for wholeness, and for the high divine virtues of balance, impartiality and evenness. The spiritual heart of the universe generates and operates the entire cosmos with the highest function of spirituality. The physical universe can be viewed as her body.

The heart contains the potency of life, and the head is the function of life. Mother Universe is not the head; she is the heart that supports the entire being of life. She is the generator and operator of universal life, which is great nature to people. Her natural potency is the freedom to form and reform herself, as well as all other things and beings. Though the early people knew her as the Lady-in-Blue, she can wear any healthy color. The sun gives birth to all lives in the solar system, whereas Mother Universe or Tao gives birth to the cosmos and all divinities. The Mother Universe is the source of the ultimate Three Pure Realms. She is the Subtle Origin, the Spiritual Sphere of the universe and the pivot of Subtle Light or Mother of Wisdom.

The sun forms your life and endows you with the potential to develop your soul. The soul is the core of your life. Though human beings are the highest form of life on Earth, they still allow their biological influence to dominate. They remain in the same big level as other forms of life. Your soul can be damaged by dark behaviors, or by bending to external, dark forces. The sun makes it possible for a damaged soul to regenerate, revitalize and reincarnate. However, it is the Subtle Light of Mother Universe that nourishes your soul with wisdom. The sun maintains your soul in its natural cycles, while the Mother Universe can uplift your soul above these cycles to the high sphere of supreme beingness.

You have been confused by too many teachings. The only genuine teaching of life is the Path of Constructive Life, and there is only one Divinity with many names and that is the Heavenly Heart of the Mother Universe. The Divine Heart is the origin of your soul. The Divine Heart is the destination of your soul. Live with the Divine Heart. Nothing is higher than the Divine Heart shared by all high lives.

Be constructive and spiritually enthusiastic in your life. You do not need to search around. The Way to a good life is right under your feet. Where there is normalcy, there is God. Where there is the unspoiled condition of your life nature, there is an angel. Everything is right here. Just watch the balance among the levels of your life, and you will find the highly achieved life.

The Heavenly Heart is the very spirituality of the universe. People express the Heavenly Heart by living a virtuous life. Let go of artificial moral standards, both right and wrong. Live constructively and harmoniously. This is how all people can better survive.

Chapter 6

The Internal Spiritual World

I would like to further discuss the subtle spirits, which are the invisible subtle substance and foundation of life. My investigations came from generations of research done by Chinese healers in my family. Developed 5000 years ago, and still effective today, the findings of the classical Chinese healing system are based on the early discoveries of life, not on the partial and mechanical view of today's medical science. Chinese healers performed their experiments primarily on themselves, not on mice, frogs or rabbits. The laboratory animals cannot tell you how they feel. Furthermore, the data gathered from today's medical tests cannot truly discern what is wrong with you. Western medicine is taking the wrong route, for often the patient's symptoms emerge from his or her subjective feeling and internal knowledge of life. Physicians see the form of cells and organs without seeing the unformed subtle substance. They think they can fix the physical form, yet they are unable to fix the trouble that comes from the unformed spiritual sphere of life.

I use my tradition's research in the hope of correcting the one-track medicine that views life as absolutely physical and measurable. As well as the one-track social religions that falsely evaluate life based on absolute assertions of externalized and unearthly ideals in place of the real value of human life. You can be poorly conditioned by these conventional scientific and religious views. I hope you can slow down your modern mind to look deeply into what has been produced through humanistic efforts from a different side of the ocean. All people of the world should know that the tiny internal spirits are the foundation of their lives.

The Internal World

A fundamental view of life in classical Chinese medicine is that life and nature both develop from the subtle substance. The internal world can be explored based on this provable knowledge of life. The spiritual world of an individual human life consists of spirits, the spirit and the soul, as well as other related aspects. Here is a simplified outline.

The spiritual groups inside your life make your life tick. Spirits are the tiny spreading particles that join together and attach to activate the functions of the different organs and systems in your body. These are the *Po* group of spirits.

Spirit in the single sense of the life spirit is the *Hun*, whose interest and direction in life inclines towards morality. The presence and health of the moral condition decides the levels in life and between lives. Some animals have *Hun*, but it is lower than that of humans. The *Hun* can also be at different levels in humans. Personal spiritual effort can improve the health of the *Hun*.

Your soul is a combination of the two big elemental spiritual realities of the *Hun,* the spiritual soul, and *Po,* the physical soul. The differently proportioned strength of the *Hun* and *Po* affect individual character and personality. A person of strong *Po* and weak *Hun* tends to be more forward and less considerate. Conversely, when the *Hun* is stronger than the *Po*, a person tends to be more considerate and less aggressive. This is the spiritual condition of life.

Life is a living thing. It gives birth to new aspects in the face of external conditions. Therefore, besides the *Hun* and *Po* there is the mind. Your mind influences your life. It absorbs the influences from your experiences and emotions. Personal tendencies are thus expressed, and personal destiny is shaped with the handling of each internal and external condition.

In order to find attunement and improvement, you can use spiritual development to monitor the internal condition of the *Hun* and *Po*, as well as the content of your mind. Spiritual development is an opportunity for people of sensitive spiritual awareness.

Your dreams can be related to your spirits. When you have dreams in shallow sleep, it is the brain interpreting and reporting the activity of the body spirits. Some dreams can be a reflection of your daily activities. These can be pure internal matters, and as such, the created copies can be erased immediately. When you have dreams in deep sleep, such as those at midnight, it can be the *Hun* communicating to your conscious mind via your brain. It may be trying to alert you about an external situation. Additionally, your subconscious spirits, at your suggestion, can help you wake at a certain hour. You may not get the required sleep though, if the spirits become overly active due to your over suggestion.

The lower conscious mind functions for general circumstances. It is the low self. The high conscious mind operates the importance of life, but it is not equal to the High Self. The High Self is the achieved clarity of the mind. It has the support of the *Hun* and *Po,* as well as the spiritual agreement or universal approval from the high sphere of spiritual life. This is the brightened soul in life.

In bodily life, the spiritual functions of the spiritual units are different, but they all serve your life. If your life is improperly managed, internal spiritual competition and conflict will arise. These are signs that you are ruining your life.

Knowledge of the *Hun* and *Po* has been clearly elucidated in the *Esoteric Tao Teh Ching.* You may refer to my book of that title, which was originally written by the Senior on the River. The source of knowledge of the *Esoteric Tao Teh Ching* is the *Yellow Emperor's Internal Classic* or *Neijing* (please refer to Dr. Maoshing Ni's translation). Many generations of knowledge about the *Hun* and *Po* were compiled and edited in the *Neijing.* There are also materials and experiences from that time period that have not been included, but they were spread among the early people. This internal knowledge affected the early Chinese people and shaped their cultural faith. We found the source from the grandson of the Yellow Emperor, the great Emperor Chuan Hsu (2514–2436 BCE).

The concepts of *Hun* and *Po* come from the moon. Sometimes people cannot see the full moon. The moon reflects the light of the sun, and the Earth shades the moon due to its position between the sun and the moon. The visible portion of the moon is called *Po*; the invisible portion is called *Hun*. Being invisible does not mean that it does not exist. The ancient ones were quite wise to associate light and shade to the internal human spirit. The lighted portion is called the white *Po* and the shaded portion is called the *Hun*. The soul is simply the light of the internal life.

The normal proportion of *Hun* and *Po* in the high life of humans, whether the formula or recipe of the Creator or Mother Nature, or both, should be identical. In a normal individual, the proportion of *Hun* and *Po* is like the seventh or eighth night of the moon. The seven portions of *Po* stand for the physical attributes, and the three portions of *Hun* stand for the spiritual attributes in life. This is the normal standard of good balance.

The *Hun* likes to move and be active, while the *Po* likes to stay and be inactive. The out-of-body game, like that performed by a child with a pure soul, is the *Hun* going out to play while one is asleep. Generally, one does not remember the places one visited in the dreams, until a real physical experience occurs and one has a *déjà vu* experience.

If the *Hun* is overly strong, the *Po* cannot maintain it, and subnormal disintegration can occur unexpectedly. Achieving total integration is a spiritual discipline. The *Hun* and *Po* are husband and wife and ideally they should always stay together. To learn more about this topic, refer to my book *The Story of Two Kingdoms*.

The Development of Morality and God

All useful knowledge begins from the normal, upright sense of life. Humans are born with the innate knowledge of right and wrong, good and bad. This innate knowledge is the basis of our normal, upright sense of life. What is right and good supports our life, and what is wrong or bad harms our life.

During the Ming Dynasty (around 600 years ago) a great scholar, Mr. Wong, Yang-Ming, promoted respect of this internal knowledge in conducting one's life. As he saw it, worldly trouble came from a lack of coherence between this innate knowledge of life and one's personal behavior. He produced simple guidance for human life; such as the coherence between knowing and doing, and that there can be no external moral standard to rely upon. He cleared the spiritual clouds of his time.

The innate knowledge of life is valuable as a high principle of behavior. Practically though, there are moral and emotional conflicts among people, and people tend to flock to social competitions. Sometimes, therefore, as a moral choice, one has to keep away from the convenience of living among the masses. High moral realization can lead to social isolation.

Because humans have an animal foundation, morality can be considered progress; it can hardly be deemed a natural gift. From an upright sense of life, you produce a sympathetic feeling to another's suffering or misfortune. Considerateness is then chosen and practiced in life. When you extend sympathy to others and begin practicing it habitually, your conscience develops, and the distinction between morality and immorality is clearly established.

Natural spiritual value is derived from five steps.

(1) A sympathetic feeling.

(2) The considerateness that comes with mental growth.

(3) Broad empathy.

(4) The conscience of life.

(5) The high moral sense of life.

This is how things develop provided there are no external interferences in the process. Most of the time, the growth of the high moral sense is interrupted and blocked by external situations. Your life presents itself as one experience at a time, and is therefore segmented and fractured. This causes difficulty, as your life seeks to grow and become whole. It is also the reason for the slow or lack of moral growth among people in general.

From the two spiritual groups, the *Po* group activates the function of the body, and the *Hun* animates the mind. There is no absolute God or authority among them, though the two may compete for the throne of life, as expressed by the varying external concepts of God. In reality, both the *Hun* and the *Po* are partners of your bodily life.

The inner harmony and the required unity in the normal and natural sense of life, is itself God. This same effort of unifying and harmonizing life should be made in human society and in the inner life of individuals. Personal success or failure can be seen by how long, how healthy and how happy an individual lives. Various religions promote these goals as social activities, but they don't fulfill them. Success in this social sense really means spiritual failure, while social failure doesn't necessarily mean spiritual success. Social undertakings and spiritual success are just different pursuits. Within such religious social programs, some individuals do benefit, but overall there is little spiritual progress made.

When you meticulously search for God in your natural existence, you inevitably fail. This is because God can be anything and everything that has been safely and healthfully established, since God is the safety and health of normal life. The external search for God is really the search for a ruler, and the farther the search, the bigger and heavier is the waste. This is because there is no giant, ethereal or phantomlike pre-existence in the universe, other than the giant life of the universe itself, with all lives and things within it.

The new direction we encourage you to pursue is the God of high spiritual qualities. The old concept of God as a physical sense or political sense, such as the power to conquer all, the power to suppress all and the power to make all obey, has caused a lot of trouble for a very long time. Our term for it is "power mania." There have been repeated shows of powers rising and falling, trapping human destiny in a permanently helpless situation, all as a result of the wrong projection of faith. Old conventional religions can be made into weapons of psychological warfare, but the truth is: all power has an enemy, and any power that has a rival is not the absolute power.

God is nonbeing. If there has to be God, then God is the evolving sense of life. To establish and support the sense of life in human life, there needs to be constructive spiritual qualities. God produces the spiritual attributes and the high spiritual qualities. Constructively speaking, God is the unity, the harmony, the safety and the cooperation of all humans. At least these qualities express the need of God in life.

If you want to summarize all those necessary spiritual qualities, they would all belong to human progress. Being spiritually constructive in your individual life and in your society can lead to spiritual progress. That means to meet God in a real and better place. You can begin by recognizing that God is your constructive nature, otherwise there is no God.

The Five Types of Personalities

According to the early classification of people, there are Five Personality Types.

The "Water" personality is easy-going, communicative and gets along well with others. Its spiritual symbol is Mercury.

The "Vegetation" or "Wood" type is kind and fair, asking for little in return. Its spiritual symbol is Jupiter.

The "Fire" type is quick-tempered and swift in movement and action. This type easily runs into trouble and conflict with others. Its spiritual symbol is Mars.

The "Metal" type is crafty, mechanically talented and apt to organize. Its spiritual symbol is Venus.

The "Earth" type is slow to respond and somewhat sluggish, but trustworthy. This type is stubborn, does not cheat and does not care about fashions. Its spiritual symbol is Saturn.

Each type has a positive and negative side.

People are not formed of a single energy, but are a combination of all five. Proportionally, everyone has more of some and less of some. The balance and completeness of all five energies within an individual personality is the desired aim. These observations are still valid today, and they invalidate the concept of an omnipotent creator that creates different fortunes by his special design.

The Esoteric Teaching

Careful readers can see that human life energy is affected by the close relationship of the first five planets. The question is, where is the sun and moon in relation to a human life? The sun is the *Hun* and the moon is the *Po* in human life. The sun is the real support of your life, the moon is the expression of that support, and the first five planets affect your personality. These things compose the subtle spiritual structure of human life.

It is interesting to know that the Egyptians also knew that the human soul is related to the sun. Why were they able to produce the same spiritual awareness as the early Chinese? This, to me, suggests a universal coincidence. All people are born with the same source; they share many natural similarities among their deep instinct. The Egyptians did not patent sun worship; all early people worshipped the sun. The sun symbolizes the leadership of kings, clans and family leaders, and it expresses itself through shining upon others. That was the political principle of earlier times. The symbol of the sun was not used to establish special privilege, but to be of service. The conception of Heaven was also derived from the light of the sun.

What is the difference between the early religionists and the forerunners of the Way? The early religionists engaged in sol or sun worship universally. Although the forerunners may also have practiced sun worship, their deep understanding of the spiritual meaning of life from the solar system became their life's philosophy.

How can the Way of Life guide people? Relative to the Earth, the sun appears to make a yearly rotation around the Earth with 24 periods of climatic variation. In reality, the sun has no variation except the increasing and decreasing of black spots, which has a subtle effect on the climate and the Earth's steadiness. The sun's constancy indicates that the *Hun* of life expresses no change.

Unlike the sun, the moon expresses variations: the eyebrow new moon; the crescent moon, the up-chord moon in the increasing procession; the full moon; then the down-chord moon, in the declining procession and then no moon. The moon's variations can affect the ocean tides as well as women's menstruation. The changing moon describes people's common emotional cycles. It affects blood pressure and can cause people to behave madly. It can also bring on a stroke, causing death. Furthermore, the moon has a natural correspondence with the brightness of the human mind. Children who are born during a moonlit night are brighter than those born during a dark night.

The moon can be a regular inspiration for people to recognize the law of life that: when anything reaches its fullness, a decline has to be experienced. This law applies to both natural matters and people's lives.

In the early stages of humanity, people divided the day into two big sections of day and night or light and dark. They later became aware that the length of the human life cycle, lived fully, is 120 years. They also noticed that people were more active during the day and less active at night. People of modern times do not have this conception of a natural cycle. Most live a day-to-day cycle, and the natural cycle of their lives have shrunk to adapt to the new fashion.

Through their observations of the daily solar energy cycle, the early people created a model depicting a human's life stages. Morning time represents youth—from babyhood to preadulthood; prenoon represents early adulthood; the time of midday, when the solar energy is at its highest point on Earth, represents the highest peak of people's life energy—the period of full adulthood; the afternoon resembles middle-age bringing with it a sense of maturity and harvest; and the evening and completion of the day represents old-age and the last stage of life. Similarly, the solar energy shapes and accomplishes the full cycle of a year with spring, summer, autumn (or fall) and winter.

If you use a curve graph to express this relationship between the daily solar cycle and the human life cycle, you would start with the lowest point of the curve on the left side of the graph as the early morning. Gradually, the curve would move upwards until it reached its highest point at noon. This expresses the upslope of the curve. When the highest point is reached, this is the peak of the day and beginning of the afternoon. The process then reverses, and is expressed by the downward slope of the curve, which represents the period of life when you experience a lowering of energy. If you haven't exhausted yourself by this time, you can still enjoy a wonderful "evening" or period of old age.

All wise people accept this natural cycle of life as the standard way, and throughout its process they follow the principle of balance. This means that no matter what stage of life you're in, whether you are experiencing the high or low part of the curve, it is best not to over extend yourself with all types of excessive activities.

Generally it is accepted that most people have "wet mornings." That is they live a poor, bad or even unwise life in the early stages. It is preferable to experience "fine weather" in the morning, as that leads to stability and contentment in life's later stages. Naturally one's life becomes wiser in the later stages, when one grows from immaturity to maturity.

No one can reverse this process. If you have overly enjoyed yourself in the morning, or early stage of life, it means you have already reached the high point of life. Inevitably you will then experience the downturn of the curve. And, as a result, you may shorten your whole life process.

In the morning, the sun rises in the east and slowly moves westward until it sets in the west. This natural daily routine has taught people how to live their lives. It was from this single daily cycle that the early, natural people derived the philosophy of the Way.

The teaching of the Way encourages you not to pursue extremes or high fullness in life or use your life's full strength. This behavior can invite early exhaustion, disabling you from continued regular performance. Followers of the Way, or wayfarers, value the regular, steady performance and normal expressions of life. In their knowledge of life, they understand that the climax of anything implies a corresponding falling. Any curved line has high and highest points, and low and lowest points. Whenever someone experiences the super high point in their life's performance, the opposite, lowest points have been created.

Both the *I Ching* and Lao Tzu's *Tao Teh Ching* express this law. The *I Ching* demonstrates this by lines. Lao Tzu noticed that so-called fortune and misfortune give birth to one another. The Way suggests staying low to experience a moderate rising in life rather than creating excitement, which inevitably invites depression when falling to extreme lowness. This means that you know the low valley and the high peak as you move steadily and regularly towards the high level, like the sun. The nine to 11 o'clock sun is the most preferable. Use this as the spiritual guideline in your life in order to experience the everspring or the ever-youthfulness in life. Having confidence in the gentle rising of life was the real essence of Jesus's natural message to people.

The natural cycle of human life is 120 years. When people are around 60-years old, it is like the period of the full moon, after which a decline naturally occurs. In order to slow down the decline, wayfarers should maintain the mentality of around 30-years old, which corresponds to the seventh and eighth of a moon. As humans living in the natural world, 120 years is one cycle, but nothing needs to stop our living one or more additional cycles.

In the big cycle, there are smaller cycles. There are twelve moons (lunar months) in a year. Similarly, people experience 12 smaller cycles of ten years each. During each decade, they can experience climbing to a fully stretched life, as well as a decline. The same is true even in a moon cycle, as well as a daily cycle. By proceeding gently and slowly, you can live beyond the influence of the cycles. If you do not push hard, you can gradually move towards certain set goals. Your personality may have been affected by the formation of the five planets, and the position of the sun and moon may also have affected your fortune. Living with the Way, however, is not about accommodating the fortune of life. It is about nurturing the spirit of life to go beyond the framed set of the sky with its planets, so as to live with the Milky Way. This is the big goal of life for people of the Way.

A classic work titled *Tsan Ton Chi* suggests spiritually refining yourself with the natural cycles. The simple truth is to live with an eighth of the moon, and not overly extend your life so that you may enjoy the happiness of health and longevity. This insight came from the early people who lived close to nature for a very long period of time.

Wayfarers worship the infinite life, while worldly religions hurry people on by alluring them to spiritual paradise. The Way keeps people moving along the far-reaching universal journey to the infinite by an inexhaustible, gradual pace of living. The key practice is moderation in all things you do. Moderation should be valued above any new or old faith in order to receive positive support, and to not extend into negative side effects.

As the prodigal child of my long family lineage, I will make a bargain with the world religionists. If you stop hurrying people to go to paradise, I will stop encouraging people to live with immortal life. Our true bargain is to let all people restore the genuine sense of being human, and live a normal human life. Do not make people take sides in meaningless struggles, and burn down our home, the Earth. This is my only hope.

Chapter 7

Faith in the Light

People react differently to spiritual matters. Those who react warmly may confuse spirituality with their emotional interest. They can be colored by the differing religious interpretations. Those who react coldly fail to see that the support for their lives comes from the invisible, subtle spiritual substance in their lives, and that this should be their focus. Instead, they apply their spiritual strength to a materially focused life. Hence, at death, their spiritual nature separates from their physical essence.

The nature of your living life is spiritual. To people of an open and balanced mind, I present the spiritual truth that the universal spiritual reality is the Light. The real God is the Light, or more accurately speaking, the Spiritual Light. Buddha, God and Allah, in the broad sense, are the Spiritual Light of humanity, and as such, are good inspirations for pursuing the health of the soul and of life. Those who have faith in the Light accept any good interpretation of the true spiritual nature of life.

Any names used to interpret spiritual life are all acceptable as different ways to address the Subtle Spiritual Light of the Eternal Life, provided these circumstantial interpretations are not insisted upon, or used to create a shadow on another's life or on the world. All interpretative efforts should be respectfully recognized as a response to people's needs in different stages, and in specific communities of the one human race. It does not matter that a shadow is created in the temporary process of responding to needs, but what is truly evil is the insistence on these spiritual interpretations.

All creations have a possible shadow. Even useful things are relative and cannot be treated as the absolute truth. In the tradition of the Integral Way, we define something as good or bad by whether the creation of a shadow is insisted upon or is an intentional act. All other creations are considered to be constructive.

In the life of an individual, a nation and humanity, the true spiritual matter is the Great Spiritual Unity. No god is above this God for anyone. The segmented spiritual efforts of small communities at various times are much less significant than the effort to appreciate the Universal Spiritual Unity.

The Way is the way of the Tao. The Tao covers the sphere of being and nonbeing, existence and nonexistence and coexistence. As human beings, the Light is our guide, and we follow the Subtle Light of Tao.

What Is the Difference Between Human Immortality and Spiritual Divinity?

During my childhood, I would occasionally serve warm tea to the elders of my family's community when they met together in the beautiful garden. On those occasions, whatever questions I had in my mind would usually be answered by listening to them chatting and picking up a line or two. I was very curious to know how people, such as the Eight Immortals, became immortal. The popular folk stories on this subject may be far from the reality. The elders never directly answered my interest, although I did receive their smiles.

Many times I practiced my calligraphy with short poems like this.

The prince went to the mountains searching for immortality.
Immortality can be achieved through the refinement
of the Immortal Medicine inside one's life.
Though it took only seven days in the cave,
a thousand years had passed in the world.

Although I had been a bookworm for a long time, even new discoveries in books did not greatly surprise me. But the content of the elders' conversation that day was memorable. It went like this.

All things are formed and shaped by human hands and minds. They are subject to human control. There are also things that are subtle and not so easily controlled.

Water is transparent, but it can be felt and managed. No lives can live without it. Air is transparent, but it is less manageable. No lives can live without it. Highly achieved humans rely on good air more than water or solid food. The Light is transparent, but it is even less manageable. It is the most important food to the highly achieved humans.

At a general level, the Light colors the vegetation green and helps it grow to support all lives. The Light also directly helps the life of humans, though this tends to go unnoticed. The Light vitalizes human life with gentle light. The Light constantly feeds human life with warm light, and continually assists its growth with bright light. The Light unceasingly strengthens human life with great light, and heals and cures human life when it is sick. There is also a much higher level than this. There is a deep level of Light that can only be known by those who pursue immortality in life.

Among the existing formed lives, there are the invisible lives, and among the invisible lives there are high beings known as Perfect Beings. High Beings protect their beings with the immeasurable and non-formable Light. However, such subtle reality cannot be revealed to rough people, as it would be like giving ice to summer insects.

Perfect Beings can be any size and appear in any image. They are identified with the Light, and can appear and disappear suddenly in short time spans.

For those who pursue the Wisdom of Life there is the Subtle Light, which is deeper than the invisible light. It is not the result of an external search, but it can be reached with utmost sincerity of heart.

The Subtle Light is able to brighten the minds of people with a soft and hidden light. The Subtle Light is able to enlighten the souls of some people with a subtle transpiercing light. The Subtle Light is able to regenerate the worn-out lives of moral people with a miraculous light. The Subtle Light is able to rejuvenate the elderly life of spiritually meritorious people with a golden light. There is also the Subtlest Light that can revitalize the life of a person of virtuous fulfillment in times of need.

People's thoughts are weighed down by thinking about worldly heaviness. People's emotions are weighed down by too much attachment. People's souls are weighed down by sentiments. The secret of immortality is to become the Light by reducing the weight of those things. Yet the Perfect Being of Light never fails life by taking on the burden of Universal Duty.

Is Human Life the Final Stage
of Beingness in Nature's Energy?

The formation of life into human form has spiritual significance, unlike the mass production of insects.

Universal nature has its own evolutionary process from nonbeing to beings, from the material to the spiritual, and from the non-conscious life to conscious life. This is the universal process of higher spiritual evolution.

It has taken millions of years to attain the high form of human life. Even though this form of life has been attained, the conscious condition is still very low. It takes several lifetimes to attain the high form with high consciousness.

Life follows the cyclic movement of nature, but the formation of a high human form with a high conscious condition is not merely a process of nature and lifetimes. It also involves your subjective spiritual effort. Although there are many people on Earth, how many highly formed humans have attained mastery of spiritual beingness? It is not that the world is so imperfect; rather it is the high form of life that is imperfect. Based on their natural impetus, where are humans being pushed?

As you all know, the fleshed earthly life is imperfect. It involves suffering and troubles. As the high form of humans though, we have a significant choice. We can decide to give up certain things to go further and reach for Perfect Beingness, or we can decide to remain as suffering imperfect beings. These are different destinies. One way is to attain higher autonomy and share in nature's dominance, while the other way is to give up our life form to whatever result nature decides. At least the choice belongs to our conscious life.

The natural process is different from the process of Perfect Beingness. During the stage of nonbeing to being, the essence of the surroundings is gathered to form a more improved life form, until it reaches the form of a human and the possibility of the highest stage of consciousness is reached. The process of going from a human being to that of a higher being of Perfect Beingness, involves subjectively giving up something in each stage of life until the Perfect Being, which relies on the Light as the only substance of its form, is reached. That is Perfect Beingness.

The process is from the natural to the supernatural. Merely offering obedience to nature's objective evolution is not enough, as you will receive a life based on nature's mechanical operation. At the stage of a highly formed human life, the bargain is that physically your form of life is subject to the natural law in the low sphere, but spiritually you now have a choice. Throughout many lifetimes, you may have sacrificed your conscious being for a better physical condition in the endless plane of life. Have you ever thought to restrain your physical enjoyment in order to support the growth of your spiritual being that took many lifetimes to attain?

It is an interesting fact that in the vast universe there are a variety of beings, from the lowest insect to the highest, universal, spiritual, perfect beingness. As humans, however, you are constantly fighting the war related to the emotional need of your beingness. The emotional choice of beingness and nonbeingness is endless.

Mother Nature has done half the job for you. Through her you have physically evolved from nonbeing to being, and from non self-consciousness to self-consciousness. That is from the lower sphere of evolution to a higher level each time. Now at this stage, as the high life of a human form, how can anyone disrespect his or her life form?

Earth is a place for choosing Perfect Beingness with no heavy form. A Perfect Being has dissolved the negative accumulations of the material essence from the lower spheres. You need to get rid of the low level of beingness to go to the high level of beingness. Mother Nature has offered you the form of high life. Is the higher stage of Perfect Beingness your interest? It is more an internal process than an external one. It is not a free lunch!

In the Tang Dynasty (618–906 CE), a new big vehicle of Buddhism was created from the spiritual harvest of all known religions on the Earth. Hundreds of experts and scholars worked together on this new religion. As its common belief, it exalted *Fu*, the Being of Nonbeing, to expand the sense of an awakened human. People were taught that they are on the big wheel of spiritual evolution, and that there is the choice to either progress spiritually upward and forward or regress downward and backward. They focused on personal behavior and conscious content. Unfortunately, they wrongly caused the internal refining process to become an external belief by relying on the power of *Fu* or *Bu*. Spiritual dependency was thus created and no real work was done on the individual level of life. This is not much different from what other religions have done.

"Evolution" is used here to describe all the invisible, unnoticed changes, large and small, that happen in each individual, institution and society—over time and in response to the external changes of life. With evolution also comes devolution. There are four stages of the whole process: establishment or accomplishment, maintenance for a short or long time, decay or decline and emptying. Sentimentally, you can see this as a reflection of physical life, and no physical life can escape this destiny. All religions, whether Christianity in the New Testament or the New Buddhism, want to put a big period mark at the end of the natural evolutionary stages of moving forward and upward, denying the devolutionary completion of the cycle.

People do not see that in the big scale of the universe, devolution is merely a part of the great evolutionary process, which involves the phases of beginning, prospering, gathering and harvesting, and recollecting. The recollecting, or winter phase, does not mean death, but is the way to return. That is the way the universe regenerates and revitalizes itself. In relation to this aspect of life, we choose the understanding and faith of the Way, and use all the other interpretations as supplementary explanations.

In the *I Ching*, with its entire 64 stages of change, a complete cycle ends with completion and the unaccomplishment. It seems no one can break these cyclic repetitions. Cyclic living is the sensation of living on the edge of the wheel of the 64 spokes. Moving into the central axis or hub, the 64 divisions are reduced to 32, and from 32 to 16, and from 16 to 8, then 8 to 4, from 4 to 2 and from 2 to 1. From the unique 1, a person can rise to absoluteness. A developed life is spiritually centered. From the integral view, the physical law is centrifugal to life's spiritual center. The spiritual law is centripetal to the spiritual center of life. Spiritual law is much subtler, and the changes are mostly internal, affecting the spiritual qualities of one's life.

People of deep spiritual awareness should continue their internal spiritual evolution through better concentration. This is done after they have fulfilled their physical duties, and prepared their lifestyle for better concentration. The fulfillment of your physical duty is an important part of your life's evolution or progress. Some things you can escape, but how can you work on your spiritual evolution by living a life that is a burden to others?

Few notice that there is a difference between social evolution and individual evolution. The spiritual condition of beingness is individual. It is a very personal matter. Religions, whether right or wrong, attempt to offer big directions, but in the real achievement of the individual believer or religious user, there is no uniformity. Uniformity is not a concern.

Although the creation of the new Buddhism in the Tang Dynasty was positive, it led to a confusing direction: people became more withdrawn. The villagers changed their homes to ashrams, and fewer people worked hard in the fields. As a result, the society produced very little for people's mutual support. This caused Emperor Wu Chun (841–847 CE) to abolish the Buddhist priesthood. The descendants, after experiencing the mistake of people's lack of productivity, tore down what the ancestors established as the best vehicle. The life of a monk or nun, or indeed any person, should not be associated with idleness and laziness. No one, wherever or whoever they are, should confuse spiritual improvement with giving up the duties of life. It is fair and upright to support your own physical life while seeking spiritual progress.

Kwan Yin is the image of the Lady of Light. She is the Spiritual Light as the brilliant white light and the shining golden light within life. She is more internal than external. Both homemakers and religious ministers respect *Kwan Yin*. From *Kwan Yin's* inspiration, and in the pursuit of her kind and the perfect image, you may live to understand the duty of personal evolution, together with the duty of the social and spiritual improvement of the world.

In the pursuit of the Spiritual Light we have seven great wishes.

We wish that all people understand the deep truth of universal beingness, and have the same determination to achieve the One Great Life.

We wish that all people deeply study all good teachings and find the essence to attain the great wisdom that is as abundant as the ocean.

We wish that all people can communicate with each other without obstruction.

We wish that all people can remove all vexations and the five biggest obstacles of Greed, Hostility, Hatred, Jealousy and Attachment from their lives.

We wish that all people can attain wisdom and lucid understanding in their lives.

We wish that all people can cleanse all guilt and wrong doing through personal efforts.

We wish that all people uphold the great purpose of uplifting those in darkness, and helping those people do the same for others.

Chapter 8

Guidelines for Students of the Universal Constructive Way (The Road That Takes Your Life to a Bright Future)

Beloved friends,

In recent centuries, the Western nations have intellectually outgrown the Eastern societies. This shift has had a strong impact on the politics and conventional culture of the Eastern societies, leaving its people shocked and shaken, and experiencing many difficulties. In fact, the Western nations have experienced a similarly strong impact on their own conventional beliefs. What people truly need, whether they come from the East or the West is a spiritually guided life with correct spiritual knowledge.

Because people live busy and distracted lives, many passively accept and adapt to the confused trends of society with its distorted concepts and values. People have lost faith in the value of conventional life, and so they and the world are lost. At the same time, society's conventional beliefs have lost their strength to hold society together. The numerous teachings that have arisen, such as the new age teachings of the 1970s, have only added to the confusion. Most people's spiritual condition is far behind the light of dawn. A true and objective spiritual education is a necessity for all people in this generation, and in all generations to come. Open and broad spiritual improvement is still the only light for the human mind.

The Universal Constructive Way is inspired from the fountain of the ageless Way. It is based on the early observations of the ancient developed ones who discovered the simple natural faith and truth of life. The Way does not lure the crowd to gather social strength. Rather, it supports and guides all people to naturally detoxify their souls. Furthermore, it shields the natural truth from the contamination of darkness. It encourages the spiritual growth of all people by guiding them to be actively involved in their own development, rather than passively accepting the negative influences of society.

Today most people are fed and colored by various stage shows and life dramas. We don't mean movies and television shows, although they are a major influence on our modern culture. What we do mean is that participation in politics, religions, commerce and other matters, all involve game playing and artifice. For example, the success of an election campaign depends on who stages the best show, and who is the better actor. It does not depend on who understands the deep reality of life. In today's world, the depth and direction of a person's life, whether in their social conduct or personal life, is mostly a matter of how well they play the game. Life has become a modern theater show.

We encourage you to pay attention to the teachings of permanent value, and to the inner worth of all life. We wish to give you something to nurture your soul, and to strengthen your great life in this time when it has become so weather-beaten. This message is for those people who are willing to follow the Universal Constructive Way, and undertake the mission of the PCL. It is a condensed teaching of the Universal Constructive Way, which stands for the essence of life, and the healthy expression of life. We also wish to make you an offer. Whether or not you agree to it is up to you and your stage of spiritual growth. To those of you who are willing to assist and continue our worldly mission of the PCL, we shall give you the collection of skills and teachings of the Universal Constructive Way.

The Universal Constructive Way is the collection of skills and learning gathered and distilled by our spiritual family over many generations. It presents all the important knowledge gleaned from the experience and development of earthly life. We hope to pass it along to those of you who will continue the task of objective, spiritual self-improvement, and objective improvement of the world.

Maoshing and I have been using these teachings to help our young friends nurture the spirit of self-reliance, and achieve well-being and balance in all aspects of their lives. This is so that they may have the strength and confidence to use and share this great treasure with others in a subtle and unassuming way, just as we do for you. Over many decades, we have offered numerous talks and books for this purpose. Our spiritual teaching is not a paid career. It is an offering; a personal dedication and devotion to all people.

Throughout generations, religions have been used to assist political establishments. In return the political organizations have helped religions become parasites that feed off the well-being of society. This is a consequence of the unbalanced development of humanity, which lacks true spiritual knowledge. This worldly trend has harmed the well-being of society by downgrading its human nature. As true spiritual individuals, we hope you don't play this same game over again.

The social and spiritual offerings of the Universal Constructive Way follow a different approach. First, you need to learn how to respectfully conduct and take care of your own life. After you have achieved a position of having more than enough, you can go on to take care of the rest of the world.

The teachings of the Way encourage you to become pupils of life. This is unlike other world teachings that spread heavy sentimentality from which you can find excuses to hate life, or hate others who are different. The real way of life is the Universal Constructive Way. Your life should not be segmented into pieces whereby some parts belong to the church, some parts to the government, and still other parts to a political party and so on. These divisions only cause pressure and undue obligation. You need to live with the essence of life to keep your life whole, and to maintain its all-important balance. You can learn to do this by following the Universal Way of Constructive Living, and by being pupils of life by living in the Light.

Unfortunately, we have had some negative experiences with a few individuals who have used the purely intended teachings as a new ideological tool, or a new excuse to live off others by offering unprofessional training, and unregulated skills to the society. Good teachings and methods of improving human health, in all aspects, should be supported by good means, or made as a fair exchange in accordance with appropriate public standards. All teachings should be supported by high, personal, moral standards.

In each generation of the past, one individual was expected to shoulder the entire task of uplifting the moral condition of the whole world. This has become an unrealistic task. Our approach is to teach people to become self-responsible in order to watch over, and improve their own health and spiritual life. This approach is more helpful and useful. Occasionally, I have become frustrated when I see some spiritual teachers and writers misleading people, and some individuals adopting our teaching only to repeat the game of living off the well-being of others. However, one cannot expect everyone in the world to have the same sense of spiritual responsibility, as people are at different levels of growth. So I realize my frustration is unrealistic.

Through teaching, I chose to face the different challenges of the world. Now, in this period of my life, I hoped to be less active and transfer the great duty of overseeing the health of the world to some of you individually. Yet, looking at the enormity of the work, I would like to shift this social and spiritual responsibility onto all of you as a group. You can, along with other aspiring and high, spiritually minded individuals from around the world work together for the bright spiritual future of the world and all people.

Those of you who rely on your own strength are doing much better and enjoying much more than those who have learned, through social conditioning, to depend on others. I respect that for many it was your ancestors who came to new lands and depended on only their own strength to build prosperous families, a good community and a good society. Likewise, I hope that the next generation can rely on your healthy, spiritual development, and even surpass your own achievements and the achievements of your ancestors. For this reason, I will continue to strengthen you all, as individuals and as a group, so the new generations can rely on your good guidance. With this purpose in mind, Maoshing and I present the following condensed and concentrated version of the Universal Constructive Way.

The Main Spiritual Focus of the Path of Constructive Life

The PCL is the realization foundation of the Universal Constructive Way of the truthful life. It comes from the teachings I received from my parents, and from a long lineage of achieved beings over many generations.

The underlying focus of the PCL is to live a life guided by the Subtle Light, which encourages one to:

Live with an upright endeavor.

Live with an affirmative and positive attitude.

Live with reasonable optimism.

Live with openness to progress.

Live with balanced creativeness.

Live with a sense of righteous duty towards oneself and the world.

The Spiritual Direction of the Path of Constructive Life

Confirms the life that unites with the inexhaustible source of the Universal Way.

Confirms the life that constantly and patiently perseveres to improve the well-being of itself and of humanity.

Confirms the life that lives as an example of health in all of life's aspects.

Confirms the life that progresses through a gentle approach.

Confirms the life that tirelessly pursues greatness and the opportunity of a Natural Life.

Confirms the life that lives with the enduring constancy of the Universal Way.

Confirms the life that respects the regularity and normalcy of life more than the love of special occasions.

The Nature of the Teaching of the Path of Constructive Life

Prepares its pupils of life to be successful for themselves and for the world.

Guards its pupils from the negative emotional burden of life.

Does not accept people who have no motivation towards the pursuit of happiness in life.

Prepares and strengthens the well-being of its pupils in all aspects of life so that they may be able to help others in the world.

Does not encourage a wasteful style of life in any aspect such as money, time or life energy.

Prepares its pupils to be the instruments that carry the natural will of Universal Life in guiding all people to live better and more fruitful lives.

Guides its pupils to live and fulfill the Way of Heaven in their own lives, as described by Lao Tzu. This is in contrast to the way of some worldly cultures, which keep people living in the dark with the expectation that someday they will go to heaven as their reward.

The Yellow Emperor, one of humanity's great ancestors, is our model, and Lao Tzu is the elucidator of the Way of a universally happy life.

The Main Practice of the Path of Constructive Life

The main practice of the teaching is to eliminate all the darkness in life and to receive the Light. Realizing the Light in one's life is achieved by practicing the "Triple Nothingness" of no self-doubt, no self-defeat, and no deception of oneself or others. The practice of the Triple Nothingness is assisted by daily spiritual self-cultivation.

The Five Goals of Spiritual Self-Cultivation

(1) To see through all the darkness in human life that causes spiritual downfall and personal failure.

(2) To see through the darkness that prevents one from recognizing that a healthy spiritual life is the core of each life being.

(3) To see through the darkness caused by certain personal behaviors and emotional actions and reactions.

(4)   To see through the superficial customs of all spiritual cultures that set people apart from one another, and prevent them from reaching the unity of genuine spiritual oneness. Spiritual truth is the one universal spiritual reality.

(5)   To see through the darkness of certain mental attitudes developed over one's life from different intellectual influences, which disable one from reaching the Highest Truth and Light of life.

The Path That Leads to Tao

The teaching of the PCL does not mold people to fit the common model of daily bread winners, who accept whatever social conditions are current, and whatever narrow, dark leadership exists. Nor does it follow the conventional step of degrading them to be ruled under a system of confusion.

Instead, the PCL leads people to succeed and attain well-being in all aspects of their lives by the power of their growing rationality. By guiding each person and the society towards safety and progress, the PCL promotes a natural, healthy life for all.

For a long time, the world has been established under the control of spiritual negativity and confusion. Many people died as sacrifices for the few who manipulated the social power to live off the lives of others. At the same time, negative regimes and ruling forces based on might and led by people who lack spiritual growth, continue to vie for control of the world. These people have been misguided by religions that prepare people for death. Everywhere around the world, strong, but dark-hearted people have manipulated society for their own shortsighted ideas, and engaged in endless struggling.

The main goal of the PCL is to guide people towards real, personal spiritual growth. It encourages people to model their lives under the guidance of the

Universal Life, and to live with genuine, natural decency. For such a great mission, people are encouraged to first learn to enjoy peace and harmony in their daily lives, and, especially, not to be provocative and aggressive, as this only invites hatred and hostility. For example, they would abide by the following important guidelines.

The followers of the PCL prefer to look like dummies, but they ensure they make no mistakes in either big or small matters.

The followers of the PCL prefer to look like cowards, but they act gallantly for righteous causes.

The followers of the PCL may look like they are moving backward, but all the while they are steadily moving forward.

The followers of the PCL prefer to look small, but this is how they achieve greatness.

The followers of the PCL prefer not to push aggressively towards fulfillment, yet they are all-accomplishing.

The followers of the PCL prefer to be considered nonexistent, because they do not display any dashing or dazzling smartness, but they are never outwitted in unfavorable situations.

The Recognition of the Different Attainment of Six Worldly Spiritual Models

Long ago, Fu Shi initiated the teaching of the PCL at a time when early human beings had just begun to move from the infantile stage of crawling to walking. He used his strong power of intuition to develop useful knowledge to guide the society. Later, the Yellow Emperor learned the Way from various teachers who lived in accord with the Way. They used its natural energy to live to be over 3000 years old. The Yellow Emperor used the teachings to guide people to live in harmony with nature. Then, in the new generation, around the middle of the Chou Dynasty (1122–256 BCE), Lao Tzu devoted himself to elucidating the Way.

Now in our time, some 8000 years after the teachers of the Yellow Emperor, when most people are living in the momentary excitement of their lives, Maoshing and I encourage you to treasure the things of permanent value. We respect personal spiritual worth more highly than the new, fashionable, social, and material rewards of the world. The teaching now needs to be refreshed for the modern generations, who live among varying cultures, and who can truly benefit from the positive vision of universal harmony.

Just as it is important to appreciate the progress of other cultures, it is also important to understand their different and non-permanent spiritual expressions. All divine lives, as spiritual leaders in the different stages of human life, were the spiritual functioning of the universal spirituality. From among the relatively recent cultures, the pupils of the PCL are encouraged to appreciate the achievement from the following specific individuals.

Jesus

Jesus realized the Way with the sacrifice of his own life, during a time of cultural narrowness some 2000 years ago. He made a model out of his life by living up to the direct, natural truth that Heaven is our father, Earth is our mother, and all people are our brothers and sisters. All people should treat one another with kindness and patience. He also showed people how to correct their overly extended desires that caused them to deviate from the broad, Godly nature of life.

The pupils of the PCL appreciate Jesus as a great model of the broad, humanistic spirit of God, which includes all people. They also recognize that Jesus, as a figure, was used to create a narrow, organized religion.

Mani

Mani was the one who realized the Way by sacrificing his life for the pursuit of the Light. He used his own life as an example of his teaching. He taught people to conquer the darkness from within themselves and from others. His teachings became known as Manichaeism.

Mani's spirit and teachings were adopted and absorbed by the later religions of Pure Land Buddhism and Tibetan Buddhism. Mani offered the invocation of the six vibrations to break through the darkness. This was an important promotion in the founding of Tibetan Buddhism. His teachings were also integrated into folk or religious Taoism, and inspired the common effort of all general religions to exalt the light and reject the darkness.

The pupils of the PCL accept the voice of Mani as the "breaker of darkness." However, they do not accept the versions of Manichaeism that came after Mani, as these were mere re-interpretations and fragmentations of his work, and only created more darkness.

Mohammed

Mohammed was the one who realized the Way by redirecting people's piety towards the broad sky. Allah is the first muffled sound to be uttered from any human life. It implies that piety be given towards life and the light of life. It also represents the deep strength that supports life when in difficulty. You need this spiritual function of being able to declare an inner war on your life's unhealthy emotions and impulses. Mohammed courageously proved his faith in "no false establishment" by fighting against all the confusion and false images of his time, which he felt detracted from the purity of human spirituality. His own life was a model of the compromise between physical desire and the dignified, spiritual practice of pure piety. Piety is used to sustain the spiritual essence in life.

Mohammed's contribution to spiritual progress was that no one should force others to accept or worship any mental image or concept to be the true expression of spiritual reality. Through his own development, he saw that people lived a false religious life, and were set apart from each other because of the confused beliefs and customs they were led to accept. However, the new and binding customs that were written into the Koran were not the work of Mohammed. It was mostly the work of his followers who wrote down what they remembered of Mohammed's teachings.

The pupils of the PCL recognize Mohammed as an example of courage. He faced the bare Truth through all the rigid customs and narrow, extreme thoughts of his time. Unfortunately, some of them were perpetuated by the limited experience of his followers. The pupils of the PCL also see that using a book to replace the natural Truth can detract from experiencing the Truth, which is unnamable. This is so, even if the work is carefully done by scholars of the time. Books cannot replace the purity and unity of spiritual Truth. The highest expression of spiritual reality is that it is!

Sakyamuni

Sakyamuni, or Buddha, was the one who realized the Way by awakening from the overly ascetic, and socially dominating religions of his time. The purpose of his teaching was to lift the veil from the face of organized religions, and return people to the basic facts of a natural life. He realized that all life is subject to one basic and natural physical law that life itself must move through the trouble of birth, age, sickness and death. The Buddha represents the power to deeply reflect through struggles and conflict. It is the vision to see through the bondage that comes from life's mechanical cycles, and it offers rescue through an undisturbed mind. A peaceful mind is a necessary spiritual function in today's disturbing worldly life.

Sakyamuni achieved a spiritually awakened life. This means that he was no longer tormented by the emotional demands of excessive materialism and worldly expansion. This is unlike the people that came after him who used his name, and added a great amount of spiritual fantasy to his teachings to create the big religion of today's Buddhism. As a result, people are led to live lives of religious fantasy, instead of pursuing natural spiritual awakening and attunement to the Light of life.

The pupils of the PCL accept Sakyamuni as the great awakened one, the Buddha, who attained freedom from the bondages of emotions, and conceptually organized religions.

Lao Tzu

Lao Tzu was the divine individual who embodied respect for a natural and honest life. He elucidated the Way, which was passed down to him from Fu Shi, Shen Nung and the Yellow Emperor. He advocated unifying the developing human nature with the universal nature. He discovered that in the final stage of achieving eternal life, one's human nature and the universal nature become unified.

The pupils of the PCL accept that Lao Tzu's work is the simple and straightforward presentation of the Way from natural spiritual inspiration.

Confucius

Confucius was an earnest individual. He endeavored to update the fundamental order of human relationships by focusing on family and social life. He exalted respect for personal, honest conduct. Though some accused him of fossilizing Chinese society, he did, in fact, value a humanistic culture that allowed for appropriate and flexible development in people's practical lives.

The pupils of the PCL accept Confucius for his personal contribution to human relationships.

The names of Jesus, Allah and Buddha were the spiritual projections of different ancient cultures. In the beginning, those projections carried some mixed emotion from the life background of the individual leaders. Since all people are one race, that emotion should be relinquished now. It can die away with the spiritual growth of peoples' new life. This new life should be a progressive version of the old life.

There is permanent spiritual value in what these individuals demonstrated to reach universal agreement, and so their specific spiritual functions can be respected. However, you should recognize that the deep reality is one—the Tao. Hence, the thoughts of the different individuals should not be expected to cover all generations, since the spiritual condition of life is constantly changing. Those leaders spiritually responded to the needs of their time. They should not be expected to be responsible for all future generations. Correct responsibility lies with the current generation, as a live entity within the endless procession of the universal flow of life.

Each of these individuals demonstrated a necessary spiritual function of the one great life of the universe. The PCL encourages you to make a correctly proportional investment in those useful spiritual functions in the different phases of your life. Remember, too, that above all you have the highest Light of Tao. Tao, as the earliest human spiritual discovery, is presented as the Truth Above Oneself and the Truth Among Ourselves.

History has shown that only a few were able to catch the real service of the profound Way. Although the Way has appeared before, it needs to be put in a new style. Both Jesus and Mohamed's teachings involved new interpretations of the Way, but suddenly those new teachings have become old after tens of centuries.

The Practice of Spiritual Openness and Broadness

Art of all types is the expression of human piety and other emotions. Piety, when well conducted, is a healthy emotional strength. In almost all people, its essence is the same, though its expressions, in the form of rituals and customs, are many. The power of developing discernment enables people to differentiate between the different levels of spiritual teachings and spiritual arts. Discernment helps people distinguish between idol worship and the adoption of symbols and statues.

Idol worship, with its low artistic achievement, came from the undeveloped stage of the human mind. Artistic expression gradually developed with such forms as the wood and stone carving from China, and the later skill of statue making from Greece. The skill of carving and making statues has become a popular spiritual fashion. Through the Greek influence, both Hinduism and Buddhism adopted statue making as their spiritual expression. Some of those creations possess the artistic value of humanity.

The Great Subtle Truth of the Universal Way is inexpressible. No name, word, image, statue or form can really present the Truth. Therefore, no art form can be accepted as the direct Truth, nor be preferred or established as any authority of Truth. However, these forms, including music, can be used as spiritual metaphors and reminders of the Truth. Some cultures, for sentimental purposes, adopt and use symbols to kindle the sublimity of spiritual energy in people and in nature. Those things may also serve to spiritually help some people in their early stages of growth. However, if people overly rely on them, or use too many of them, they only confuse themselves and others as well.

We encourage the pupils of the PCL to recognize and appreciate the following art forms as symbolic representations and reminders of the Truth.

Minarets

The minarets (towers) of mosques and the spires of churches are artistic ways to hint at the zenith of the sky. This suggestion can be easily noticed and understood.

Four-Faced God of Thailand

The four-faced god of Thailand, with each side facing a different direction, suggests that the sun shines its light in all directions upon the Earth. Earlier, in mainland China, the same image represented the light that shone upon all people from the Yellow Emperor, the sun, the central God. It also represents the mythical position of the Yellow Emperor. Similarly, an important realization of the PCL is to embrace the sun within your life being, allowing its light to naturally radiate to your surroundings.

Statues of Kwan Yin

The statue of *Kwan Yin*, the Goddess of Mercy, was created as a projection of peoples' sense of Beauty, Purity and Perfection. In spiritual reality, the development of an individual's spiritual vision enables them to see and discern subtle matters and qualities in different levels. This spiritual truth has induced the worship of the image of the Goddess of Mercy as a metaphor for the Universal Divine Energy. The many-armed statue of *Kwan Yin* represents the multiple beams of light coming from the light bodies in the sky, such as the sun, moon and bright stars.

Images of Buddha

The calmly seated images of Buddha express the qualities of good concentration and high self-composure. They also imply the need for spiritual reflection in all people. All over Asia, the numerous golden statues of Buddha, and the golden temples, speak of the golden light of the sun that guides all life towards unity and health, both inwardly and outwardly. These images of Buddha symbolize the bright side of nature, and present the respectful and dignified human form of golden light.

The Important Convictions of the Path of Constructive Life

We embody the ultimate truth of the universe, which shares the same identity with our ancestors' concept of the One Supreme God.

The Universal Constructive Way understands and explains the subtle reality to be the true Lord of the sky, space, all Earths, all lives and all beings.

The Supreme One Truth is known by displaying the natural virtues of uniqueness, absoluteness, purity, clarity and orderliness in connection with all life.

As offspring of the universe, we serve the Universal Supreme Truth of Tao by offering obedience to its natural unity, and its natural order of Heaven, Earth and Humankind. Heaven is the first sphere to come in the order, and is the spiritual core of the Universal Being. Earth is the second sphere to come in the order with its physical, solid shape. The Earth attains stability among the other planets and all heavenly bodies by following the order of the sky. The third sphere is Human Life with its growing mind and ability to conform to the superior aspects of Earth and Heaven. Significantly, a human being, by possessing all three levels in their life, is a micro-universe of the macro-universe.

In spirituality, the subtle essence and the subtle law of the universe is the Only Supreme God, which displays, among and above all things and all beings, unity through chaos, clarity through murkiness and purity through impurity.

The Supreme One Spiritual Reality can be appreciated through intellectual research. However, it can only be reached by nurturing one's own inner Light, and by experiencing the Universal Unity. This unity is reached by the total integration of one's being within oneself, with all life and with the universe.

The Way is the harmonious order of nature. People follow and develop their inner Light by recognizing the need for internal harmony within their own lives, and the need for external cooperation with others.

In an individual life, the spiritual sphere of life is Heaven. It is the superior aspect of life, and deserves to be worshipped. The physical aspect or being of life is Earth. It is the foundation of life, and should be treated with respect. The mental aspect or being of life is Human Life. Its natural role is to harmonize itself with the aspects of Heaven and Earth, as well as with all people. The Way is the internal and external order of life. All individuals are encouraged to live in the Light and observe life's natural order. Therefore, your physical being should serve your spiritual being, and your mental being should serve both your spiritual and physical beings in correct order.

We do not declare war on any one. Endless wars are the darkest behavior of humanity. Rather, we encourage all people, through non-biased help, in their search for the Truth. Spiritual growth is a natural challenge that everyone faces. The PCL guides you to see the Light. It offers a common ground that leads you to naturally integrate the many levels and various expressions of your being into the one, unique, universal reality that is the Way.

Followers of the Way live and work for the universal nature inside of their lives. Every one of us has been rewarded and supported by receiving life from the subtle power of the universal nature. There is nothing greater than the giving and receiving of life.

You need to nurture an appreciation of your human life, and of life in general. You can exercise your appreciative spirit through suitable daily rituals and prayers. You are welcome to teach that the world is one, open home, and that no one has the power to be considered special. All people are one family. Within the family, people are at different stages of growth, and each time they learn life's lessons they move forward to a better and more positive life.

We re-introduce the Universal Integral Way as the Path of Constructive Life. We are encouraging a new spiritual direction to include the majority of people in many varied walks of life. We ask for your help and consideration to join together in sharing this new spiritual effort among yourselves and others. It is through your genuine spiritual growth, and sharing it with others that the new effort becomes effective and complete.

The Steps for Learning the Universal Constructive Way

To activate the necessary spiritual activity, the PCL offers an initiation ceremony for those who accept the PCL and wish to become a disciple of the Universal Subtle Truth. The ceremony marks a special occasion wherein an individual shows their sincere, personal wish to follow this spiritual path, and use its guidance to prevent them from becoming spiritually lost. The individual may make a public proclamation to this effect.

The disciples, who also serve as teachers and instructors, known as mentors and coaches of the PCL, are ordained and certified by the current master of the PCL.

After twelve years, one may be promoted to the Knighthood of Enlightening the World, and then after another twelve years one may be ordained as the King or the Queen of Light.

The Proclamation of a Disciple of Truth

I live my life with the Truth of Eternal Life.

This is not the assumed truth of any time, society or religion,

but is the Universal Subtle Truth.

My work is to remove all obstacles in my life

that prevent me from seeing the Light and the Truth.

I challenge no one, but work to attain the great well-being of my life

and of a harmonious world.

I constantly follow and consult with Reason and Conscience,

and develop these powers as the true rulers of my life.

With utmost sincerity, I declare that I am a disciple of the Way of Everlasting Life.

(One can use this proclamation as often as is needed.)

The Prayer of Appreciating the Power of One Life

My own developing inner Light is the true Lord

that enables me to see the Light of Truth and the grandness of life.

In pursuing spiritual unity, both within and without my life being,

I heed the universal, positive guidance of all pioneers before me,

and overlook any limiting and circumstantial expressions and instructions.

The high and simple realization of a Complete Life is achieved by embodying the Way. One who embodies the Way learns nothing beyond the nature of life, is self-complete, stops all types of worries, is self-content in the face of any passing conflict and does not run after worldly glories or vulgar fantasies, in order to maintain their inner peace. The following books are related to the study of this Path.

Let *The New Universal Morality* interpret your spiritual breadth and health.

Let *The Power of the Feminine* soften your impulses and keep you from making big mistakes.

Let *The Path of Constructive Life: Embracing Heaven's Heart* guide each step in your life.

Let *The Love of the Mother Universe* (unpublished) expand your spiritual being in life.

Let *The Union of the Divine and All People* (unpublished) be realized in your non-dualistic life.

Let *The Foundation of a Happy Life* establish the personal foundation of your life.

Let *Moonlight in the Dark Night* guide your emotional life.

Let *Enrich Your Life with Virtue* inspire your inner virtuous health.

Let *The Centermost Way* guide your spiritual self-discipline.

Let *The Majestic Domain of the Universal Heart* be realized by your own heart.

The *I Ching* and *The Complete Works of Lao Tzu* are the sources of the PCL. Lao Tzu's *Tao Teh Ching* is derived from the heritage of Fu Shi, Shen Nung and the Yellow Emperor. The *Hua Hu Ching* (Lao Tzu's other work, both of which appear in my work *The Complete Works of Lao Tzu*) is my family version of balancing the conflict between Buddhism and Taoism, as a new spiritual life from the two.

Tao, the Subtle Universal Law and the Integral Way of Life is the illustration of the subtle network of the universe, especially that of the human spirits and nature.

The *8000 Years of Wisdom, Book I* and *Book II* can be reference books for unspoiled lives.

For those individuals who are seriously interested in cultivating spiritual immortality, the following sources are suggested.

Tsan Dao Tsen Yeng (Chinese)

Jing Hua Cheng Tsong (roughly translated by Jung)

Mysticism (published)

Immortal Wisdom (unpublished)

The New Physics and Spiritual Cultivation (unpublished)

All the above-mentioned books are the essence I have extracted from 8000 years of enlightened human wisdom. Although I can guide you to the nectar, you still need to make your own honey from my offerings.

Research Materials

Many other works have been written and made available as elucidations and illustrations of the Universal Way of Constructive Life. Most of the English publications (books and videos) have been published by SevenStar Communications since 1977.

The Sponsor Institutions of the Teaching

The sponsor institutions are the Shrine of the Eternal Breath of Tao, the Union of Tao and All People, the Integral Way Society of Constructive Life, and the Taoist Global Mission.

Love,

OmNi

PART II

Improve Your Life Through Constructive Change

Chapter 9

The Biggest Challenge of Human Life

Both the darkness of humanity and the brightness of humanity take root in the sexual energy of human life. From this main desire come countless other expressions and side desires. Should you fulfill your desires in moderate and varied ways, or should you indulge in the extremes of being overly desirous or absolutely self-denying? Although the question of how to correctly fulfill sexual desire is an innate problem of each individual, it has also become an external social problem.

The basic energy of life is *yin* and *yang*, or female and male energies respectively. While the male energy is more aggressive and restless; the female energy is just the opposite, being gentler and more passive. In normal circumstances, both accomplish one another. Spiritually it does not make a difference whether you are single or paired. In other words, in fulfilling the sexual desire or transforming it, it is not a question of being holy or unholy, but a matter of health and suitability.

Superficially, people have many different excuses for being restless. They even go to war for religious and social causes. Few people deeply understand that all of humanity's cultural creations (including its religious and marriage systems), whether civilized or uncivilized, are attempts to find a compromise for the conflict between people's sexual impulses and their lifestyles.

When male sexual energy is not suitably channeled, wars develop at a local level. These small wars may develop into regional wars, and possibly into a world war. The untamed libido is the source of many conflicts. If there were no male energy, what would fuel the wars? As a result of inappropriate or unfulfilled sexual desire, people have invented wars to avenge their own lives and the lives of others. Female warriors also reflect an over-activity of testosterone in their female-shaped lives.

The marriage system was invented as a way of finding cooperation between the different types of sexual energies, and it was broadly accepted. Although it may have solved part of the social problem, it has not altered the deep root of the transformable nature of human desire, which has brought forth all types of complicated social creations and individual criminal behaviors. Both marriage customs and criminal behaviors are related to how humans tackle the internal sexual pressure to either become a fortunate, suitably paired individual, or an unfortunate individual who lost out on the opportunity.

You may question why we are discussing desires when our focus is on spiritual problems? By so doing, we are probing the root of the need to be spiritual. Let's admit this fact: life is composed of physical desires. Creation itself is a desire, and a creator is the enactment of the deep natural desire to create.

It is not so simple to merely acknowledge that sex is the main desire of all created lives, because there are many accompanying side desires. Not all people have the chance to fulfill their sexual desire ideally or satisfactorily, so the concept of individual destiny was brought forth. Destiny is discovered when there are obstacles to the fulfillment of life's desires. There is the destiny for those who complain about this matter in their lives, and there is also the destiny for those who do something about it. There are also the innocent lives that die for causes unknown to themselves, driven by their internal force to become ash from warring gunfire.

The types of people who complain about their destiny become the people of the masses, while those who do something about their destiny evolve differently. They devote themselves to artistic creation, spiritual practice, or conflict that turns into war. The same type of libido or secretion in people can transform into innumerable expressions. From such a little thing, people are unable to manage their lives.

Look at the world after World War II. Holes were punched into the lid of conventional society and the post-war generation became wild. Many sexual problems arose, including sexual diseases and abortion issues. World leaders did not know how to manage these problems. Some less responsible leaders even used it to benefit their careers. In our view, these events show how humanity has regressed. If world leaders cannot see what causes these problems, the world will continue to degenerate. A better vision or solution can be produced from wise individuals who are not blinded by the world.

After the war, although the individual's right to life was improved, the blind social solutions could not fulfill every individual's basic needs, unless people were driven, en masse, back to the level of livestock. Some hasty social experiments, such as 20th century communism, revealed what a heavy price society pays when it is driven backward to live life without spiritual roots. When the value of individual life is denied or dwarfed by society, the moral sense of personal life is denied too. Once the old moral value is destroyed, more difficulty is encountered. The efforts to improve humanity degenerate when people are directed to live a new socially organized life that only recognizes one level. Further, it is impractical to expect real spiritual achievement of all people, because each person has a different mentality and they grow at different rates.

The Universal Integral Way and its vehicle of the PCL recognize that the broad human society needs both social spiritual leadership, and an individual focus on spiritual self-improvement. To this end, there should be regular social support in the form of spiritual education and spiritual service. Both group learning and personal improvement should work side-by-side to uplift the spiritual stature of the public. The teachings of the PCL give valuable guidance for this purpose, applying the vision of twenty-five centuries of human spiritual experience.

In working to improve the spiritual condition, we admit that if we take away the desire in life there is nothing left but a twisted sense of life. Therefore let's openly face the challenge of human desire. The overzealous religious hypocrites may deny its reality, but you can find proof in the thick religious books people use for reference on how to behave. For your own reflection, you can review the Old Testament of Christianity, which is a sad story of how humanity failed in tackling their internal problems.

Problems began when human life tried to shape nature for its own convenience, no longer wanting to treat nature as nature. Other troubles arose as a result of tensions generated between males and females due to their gender differences. And still further problems are encountered due to the proliferation of the human race, which has brought forth moral crises.

However powerful God can be, God still represents the natural tendency of creation. The natural impetus is to implant. You may or may not like human libido. The key issue in the stories of the Old Testament or the Koran, looks at how humans faced the irreducible problem of the self and the libido, and how, because of that, they are destined to continually experience the trouble of self-creation, and the creation of human society. Sexual energy can initiate a new life. You cannot simply enjoy this life impulse and ignore its consequences, which can lead to multiple problems. When you examine the health of humanity can you live without religious taboos?

The tradition of the Integral Way educates the young ones differently. The originators of the Way observed that the universe began with the Original Energy or *Chi,* which cannot be definitively defined. This Original energy may also be known as the pre-heaven stage of the cosmos. As the Original *Chi* is self-generating, it can also be conceived as the Generating *Chi.* All lives come from this Generating *Chi,* and libido, as the impulse to create, fits into the Generating *Chi* stage.

Once formed, the myriad individual lives enter the post-heaven stage of the cosmos, though they are also still part of the Generating *Chi.* In the post-heaven stage, the best life conditions come from the Upright *Chi* which maintains health;

the Pure *Chi* which produces the conscious function, and the Harmonious *Chi* which helps an individual get along with others.

Human beings can accomplish themselves with these five types of *chi*, and more importantly, from these five types of *chi* they can produce refined spiritual *chi* to effectively assist and improve their lives. Nature only endows your life with a benign potency. It is up to you and your individual efforts to reach God.

The natural benign potency does not fit into the mental framework of good or bad. Good and bad result from your application of this benign potency, as in your living habits, which either support or degrade your life. Therefore, besides the five types of *chi* described above, there are also derivations of *chi* that come from how you engage in worldly life, such as bad energy, sick energy, evil energy, vicious energy, deceptive energy and so forth. These fall under the category of human application and their habits combined with the continuing situations of life.

Humans arrogantly believe they are the children of God. The tendency to project one's faith onto a powerful God, who ensures the safety of its believers, allowing them to relax and do and be whatever they want, is similar to how communism arose. Human life contains inertia, which is how communism came to be accepted even though it did not work for the society. According to Marx this is how religions came about. The believers neglected that nature needs improvement to fit human living. When natural disasters come, no human forces can refuse them, not even the spiritual ones who people pray to.

The Integral Way can be a hard path to follow. It guides people to live decently in order to unify their human nature with God and become one. Culturally, it is a difficult concept for people to accept, since conventional religions have idealized God. To realize the spiritual goal of becoming one with God, you are required to spiritually improve yourself.

We wish to remind you that God should not be at the starting point to make you run. God should be at the end of your life's journey to congratulate your real victory. As part of nature, God is not the first-born, but the last product of life. God is the destination of all lives, though to one sage the spiritual truth is always where you stand and in each step you take. Most importantly, God is the goal of all lives—God is not preentitled to anyone. God is the healthy side of humanity. God should not be made to stand in between the healthy and the unhealthy sense of beingness. Such a God is the semi-god, which humans invented to reflect themselves.

For centuries the high spiritual standard of health has been difficult for the majority to accept, and it is the majority that decide human destiny! Followers of social religions should ensure that their beliefs are guiding them to live healthily. People's spiritual faith needs correction so that all religions represent the healthy side of humanity. Only the effort to live healthily is worthy of your faith, respect and fellowship as a broader social direction.

Healthy beliefs positively affect your health and the health of humanity. Likewise erroneous beliefs can harm your health and the health of humanity. Alongside your work and social efforts, you need to work on yourself. With an open mind and respect for all healthy religions, you can work on your development. Also through discernment you can use the corrupt culture, with its exaggerated sexual promotion, as compost to grow from and rise above. Your individual efforts are what bring real spiritual harvest.

What follows are responsible spiritual truths from the highest development of humanity. These truths do not carry the manipulative tendencies and social agendas of mass religions, but they do recognize the need for cooperation as the way to prepare people for the high truth.

God Is the Value and Hope of Life

As the deep spiritual truth, God is the nonbeing or universal being. This is the self-recognition of the spiritual nature of life developed from many generations of human growth. Socially established religions, however, infused this deep-rooted conscious awareness and deep spiritual conscience with social excuses.

The concept of God first grew out of the need to correct the self-abusive sexual habits of young males, who recklessly engaged in sex even with animals. The image of the vampire reflects the mental confusion from this stage of the early people's sexual experience.

In those times the males died very young, until they became aware that their self-abusive sexual habits were the cause of their shortened lives. To correct their habits, severe measures were invented equal to the self-punishing styles of spiritual discipline, like flagellation and sleeping on nailed boards. The awareness of life's spiritual value overtook its physical engagement. This overly strong style of self-discipline remains the spiritual custom in some parts of Asia. You should know that masculine-centered religions were developed from a specific imbalanced attitude towards sex and women.

Later spiritual leaders from India, such as Jain and Sakyamuni, rose up as a result of the overly expanded socio-religious power of Brahmanism, and offered spiritual discipline through the mind, instead of only through the body. They saw the need to reduce the excessively self-punishing style of discipline. They balanced what had been over corrected by this old style of self-discipline.

The fear of sex remained in the story of Genesis, which viewed sex as the reason for humanity's downfall from angelic life. This view associates sexuality with sinfulness, and is a conceptual over correction invented by men.

Consequently, the world's religious cultures tend to overvalue the spiritual sphere of life, and devalue the physical sphere of life. It is the opposite of the world's commercial culture, which uses sexual images as lures for business. Neither of these cultures presents a balanced point of view. Balance is the cultural position of the Integral Way, which advocates the healthy approach towards all aspects of life. The reasonable and appropriate reduction of sex and food (as in celibacy and fasting) has value for human health, longevity and spirituality, but extending to extremes does not.

Although God presents the self-respect and spiritual respect of life, which is worthy of your respect and devotion, you need to look for balanced and suitable ways to fulfill your valuable life energy. Sometimes the over externalized practices of social religions bring forth the opposite effect on internal spirituality, by damaging the sacred sense of the inner God. Restoring the dignity of life by nurturing God within yourself depends on your own efforts. As an externalized faith, God is the weak spiritual sense of self-respect for life. As an internalized development, God is the real fruit of mental growth, nurtured and developed by your whole life.

Balance Between the Material and Non-Material Sphere of Life Should be Valued

Over emphasizing the material sphere causes the spiritual sphere of life to shrink. The spiritual sphere is the nonmaterial and unoccupied spiritual capacity of life. The appropriate ratio between the nonmaterial and material spheres should be seven to three. That is, the nonmaterial sphere should be over double that of the material sphere. The unoccupied space assists the health of your life. Just look at the many generations of Chinese emperors who lived a short life due to the imbalance between their material and nonmaterial capacities of their lives.

"Purify your mind and rarefy your desire" was the wise answer given to Genghis Khan (1162–1227 CE) when he requested the secret of immortality from Master Chiu Tsan-Chung. It means to keep more space for the invisible, but more valuable part of your life.

The Real God Is Achieved From the Sublimation of Your Sexual Energy

Damaging your sexual energy is not the Godly way, nor is it the way to spiritually pursue God. This is the invaluable secret discovered and passed onto the public by the Immortal Tradition. This may be hard to believe; yet this is why Lao Tzu said the high comes from the low. A person who has achieved immortality, lives with a universal sense of being that is above the sense of gender and the mental and physical frames of reference of humankind.

A Balance Between Individual and Societal Values Is Best

Today's overly expanded sense of society can suppress the value of and respect for individuality, and damage its moral sense. Once the spiritual value of humanity is lowered to the animal level, there is no hope for its social progress, and no religion can help.

God and All People Are One

The PCL aims to make it easy to practice the Integral Truth that God and All People Are One with the Constructive Nature of the Universe. This is the instruction that can help people grow their inner sweet flowers and fruits out of the world's condition.

The PCL Is an Open, Spiritual Learning

The PCL is not a tightly lidded, conventional social program to place over your head. It is an open spiritual path that can:

(a) Transform your overly desirous life to be the source of your life's healthy strength.

(b) Guide you to sublimate your painful emotions to be your life's main internal support and natural joy.

These two goals prepare you to undertake the process of sublimation and attain whatever size fruit you wish, be it good health or immortality.

If you are spiritual and healthy, you should courageously pursue a suitably paired life and live constructively. And if you have a suitable partner, you should still pursue the sublimation of your desires and emotions through constructive practices such as described below.

Artistic creations, such as fine art or music, can sublimate your emotional pain and heavy sexual desire. Integrated body movements, such as gentle *chi kung* practice, can help increase your health and vitality, and can be approached as the art of life in practice. These are a good way to sublimate desire. Nurturing a flower garden and practicing Chinese calligraphy are also beneficial. You can choose a few Chinese characters and repeat them as a spiritual practice, or use the characters for the phrase "Peace under the sky" that can be found in my book, *The Power of Natural Healing*.

We recommend using spiritual concentration and performing hidden good deeds, as the positive means to transform your heavy desires and bothersome emotions. These blessed ways particularly help unpaired individuals.

The transformation of desires into high wisdom is one of the goals of the PCL, while indulging in emotional suffering is not the appropriate way to deal with life. Transformation or sublimation can be achieved by quiet living. When properly guided by the art of living, the transferring of conscious energy into light is the higher goal of immortal pursuit.

We know from life that spiritual support is meaningful for everyone. You should know that God is not something that controls you, but God enriches your life by encouraging you to live a healthy and constructive life. It is the spontaneous and constant Subtle Universal Law that works to affect your life, based on the laws of energy correspondence.

Few people have become sages. Most people are on an arduous life path, living a hand-to-mouth existence feeding themselves and their relatives, without knowing why they have to do so. Some individuals become criminals, not because of their sexual behavior, but as a result of the many transformed excuses stemming from the one deep libido source. Yet others, as a result of the same internal force, achieve excellence in art and music, make breakthroughs in science and technology, create magnificent handicrafts, devote their lives to improving social conditions, and write the most beautiful literature. Still others have created religions, even though these are self-deceptive creations. It seems, at the time, the religionists did not have a choice as most people were not enlightened. A similar situation may exist today. The other choice was to have no self-delusion. That choice, however, can extend to brutal warfare with bloodshed as the sacrificial offering to the devil-like dragon nature in human life—the life-creating impulse gone astray and turning into the desire to kill. All wars are means of human self-punishment; a wager with death.

How a social leader manages his or her sexual impulse not only affects themselves and those around them, but also the whole society. All may suffer for the leader's cause, if he or she is ridden by the devil-like dragon force. Most of you don't understand that your internal force can be far more destructive and bring greater suffering than any widespread natural disaster. When used inappropriately this force can drive a generation to catastrophic ends, and still the leaders and their people do not know why or how such tragedies came to be.

A single wrong behavior can result in deep and far-reaching consequences, such as in social revolutions. Most revolutions are struggles against socially and sexually repressive conventions and cultures. But you need to reflect on the consequences of the freedom you struggle for. For instance, was the sexual revolution of the last century a price paid for the deceptive culture established by the social religions to dam up human desires? Please reflect on this. As a healer, you cannot truly treat a patient's disease unless you understand the real trouble.

If you can see beyond conventional concepts, there is no real difference in being sinful or holy. What really matters is whether you channel your internal pressure constructively or destructively. It is holy when you are riding smoothly on the dragon of sexual drive. It is sinful, or leads to suffering, when you are being ridden by the evil dragon, which drives you to do harmful things. It is not a matter of you killing or castrating the impulse; it is a matter of how you guide the impulse for your own safety and that of others. It is more important that you transform it into useful and creative endeavors.

Can you be more responsible with your life, or would you rather become a component of society's evil dragon force and be driven here or there with no definite direction of your own? If you only search for momentary release of your internal pressure, troubles will inevitably rise again because the life force remains inside of you.

Creation is not the purpose of the cosmos, but the expression of its natural impetus. The high purpose or self-awareness in life is that life should continue for higher spiritual evolution. Spiritual self-improvement is the only choice left once you give up false and deceptive spiritual teachings. And such improvement can be fulfilled through the mutual help of individuals and groups.

The world can be multicultural, but responsible cultures should offer constructive guidance to people to ensure the world's safety through the healthy and useful expressions of people's life energy. The PCL recommends one discipline in life and that is to be more constructive in your life.

It is wrong to kill the evil dragon.
Tame it and you can journey the universe.
Your constant effort to tame the dragon
is the greatest humanistic behavior.
No matter what keep trying,
and you will succeed.
When you are able to enjoy riding the dragon masterfully,
you are holy and majestic.

The key solution to solving human problems is that each person, especially world leaders, needs to broaden and deepen their spiritual vision. We hope world leaders can see that there is no real distance between what is spiritual and what is secular in life. Spiritual development guides secular life. You need to spiritually learn and develop yourselves to be blessings to the world. This is possible for all people to do through the teachings of the PCL, together with some of the positive aspects of traditional religious services.

Our work is the spiritual reflection of human problems. Real, practical efforts need to be made to correct these problems. You need to be constructive in your life, as this benefits your own life and the lives of others. The world religions have made their contributions, most of which are inadequate to help the world now. May we all review the old ways and start a new spiritual life.

The high self of each individual can achieve unity with the God of universal harmony and progress. Each individual has a moral duty to the world to continue what has not yet been fulfilled. Do not expect sages to die for you and come again to do the same work. Can the world be improved without sages? Can a sage be found in each individual? You can prove this through your own life.

The essential message from the Immortal Tradition is this: the reproductive force is your life's internal medicine after it has been refined through spiritual cultivation. An excessive sexual life lowers your mentality and ends your life unnaturally.

Human salvation is both internal and external, but when the internal force is destroyed, what is there left to save by external abundance? Modern people are conditioned to overly trust external medicine, but when their internal medicine is badly damaged, external medicine only brings more harm and hastens an unnatural death.

When you are young, value the physical essence you produce. When you are older, protect and nurture its strength for your life's health and natural joy. Rigid practice brings harm. Be artful in achieving the art of life, even while living a happily paired life. And be aware that it is immoral to bring forth many children without their good care and responsible education. The world suffers as a result of its degraded over population. Fewer people in the world who develop virtuously are preferred. Unfortunately, irresponsible priests have selfishly encouraged people to produce more children while they live free of financial burdens. This has occurred throughout generations.

The sexual desire of humans, the basic impulse of life, brings forth many emotional expressions and transformed desires in society. These expressions either become individual blessings or great human calamities. Life is not sinful; life is a blessing when it is fulfilled constructively. Life can be troublesome and involve the biggest sin of ignorance when driven by the lower impulses. The invisible sexual force drives everyone with the same intensity, but each of you can choose how to channel it for vastly different results. We hope your children and your descendents will not be victims of your misguided desires, but recipients of your high motivation for moral fulfillment. Please check.

Maoshing's and my work is accomplished with team support. It is performed by individuals with humanistic love in their hearts and given to whosoever may receive. We hope all people can fulfill their lives decently and grow spiritually with the cooperation of their friends.

Chapter 10

Do You Have a Self and What Is the Self Made Of?

During the Ming Dynasty (1368–1643 CE), the famous novel *Westward Journey* appeared. It is an extended version of *The Journey to the West*, which is one of the four parts of *The Four Journeys* novel. *Westward Journey* is a great work with deep meaning, but few people are able to appreciate its metaphor of an individual's life journey.

In *Westward Journey*, the main character is a spiritual seeker who has four disciples, who most people are fascinated by. Careful study reveals that the master and his four disciples actually symbolize the emotions and traits that comprise each and every individual.

The Master represents conscience. He does not act, he only responds when there's trouble. The Monkey represents intelligence. It can give you numerous ideas, but you don't really know which ideas are truly useful or truly unworkable. The Piggy symbolizes endless desire. It craves food, sex and other luxurious things, but it would rather get these things without considering the safety of itself or others. The River Monster is cruel and indifferent to people, and is only concerned about itself. The Horsy represents intent or will, which provides action and energy. Generally it isn't opinionated, although that depends on who's riding it.

Altogether, these five different human traits form the normal human psyche and its emotions. They make up the team of your life. Of the five, one is spiritual, while the other four are semi-physical and semi-spiritual. If you are unable to control them and keep them together, imbalance will inevitably arise and troubles and difficulties will ensue. All the characters are important, because life is a process of refinement of the whole person.

The conscience is your higher self. This is not difficult to accept. The other four aspects are the lower selves or demons under the control of the head demon—intelligence. Altogether, they consist of one portion of neutral energy and four portions of demonic energy, or 20 percent neutral energy and 80 percent low energy. This is an accurate ratio of the different energies within a person. Only one part can be considered righteous, while the other four are demonic. How dangerous a world you live in! This is the reason why the Integral Way exalts spiritual self-improvement, self-cultivation and self-refinement for all.

In the world, there are no leaders who can be completely trusted, so there needs to be a good system that can restrain their demons. Modern democracy, with its political power divisions, cannot economically involve all people when a job only needs a few trustworthy individuals to do it. Therefore, democracy is expensive and can be wasteful, but compared to other political systems it is better, as it can keep some check on its leaders and reduce human error. Yet even a good system can be manipulated. Democracy is still a system for the mediocre, and so far, no leaders have shown themselves to be sages when trouble arises. And, even if the leaders' demons are restrained, how do you expect those leaders to handle the demons of others?

Political power and religious power can also create demons. When such social creations are taught as absolute truths, people's deep conscience and their political administrations can be warped by it. This leads to the development of darkness.

Religions and other social customs are social instruments containing emotional elements. Their nature and service should be correctly recognized and made completely separate from the political system. Although there is no perfect political design, there are some that are relatively safer. In this way, social progress can be made with less confusion. And, importantly, pure spiritual teachings such as the Integral Way need to be separately recognized and correctly established as the necessary and basic education.

While the world needs good leaders working within responsible systems, the fundamental problem remains that each individual has inner demons, which need discipline and guidance. Troubles arise from the low spiritual qualities that are hidden in people. You need to learn to control these energies that come from inside as well as outside yourself. On the outside they can appear as challenges and obstacles in your life. If you don't keep these energies under control, they will overwhelm your only rational power of conscience and destroy your life.

In *Westward Journey*, the Monkey is both a demon and great helper. Early in its life, it declares itself to be "the Sage equal to Heaven." This is what happens when your intelligence feeds itself with pride, and constantly competes with your conscience or "Throne of Life." Also, the Monkey cannot keep away from the greed of the Piggy, which only invites more trouble. Nevertheless, when correctly employed, intelligence can also dissolve troubles, since greed cannot go ahead by itself. However, by ignoring and competing with your conscience, your over extended mind eventually defeats itself.

When troubles become too big for the super-mischievous Monkey to handle, it begs the Goddess of Mercy, who executes the Subtle Law of Nature, for help. This means that when the internal demons (of desire and intent) become active, the external demons (the challenges and obstacles in life) are also activated to respond in an equally strong or stronger way. Trouble eventually ensues and one must appeal to their enhanced Higher Self or Conscience (the Goddess) for help.

Both troublesome and healthy situations are the result of the atomic operation of the natural subtle law of correspondence. Essentially this law means that the same energetic wavelengths attract each other. This is a useful spiritual discovery, and is much more sacred than fixed religious dogmas. An individual who attains the secret knowledge of universal life does not attract trouble.

The Goddess of Mercy represents people's spiritual growth and attainment. She is the healthy fruit of spiritual cultivation, or the deep self of your high life. She represents the knowledge and the reality of the universal subtle law. Through your growing knowledge and understanding of life, she functions to correct any problems that arise.

If you only pay attention to the external aspects of your life, you will fail to see your life's inner aspects. You also express doubt about your life's subtle, inner knowledge by allowing your intellect to grow and compete with it. Your doubt, though, will not defeat your life's inner knowledge, known as the Goddess or higher conscience, nor will your inner knowledge be unreachable by your wild Monkey intelligence. Rather, your Monkey mind will end up defeating itself by arrogantly holding itself out as the most powerful one, equal to Heaven. The reality of Heaven, however, is the wordless, healthy and pure atmosphere inside of all life.

Your intelligence has an irresistible charm of being asked for help, and your conscience can be too naive in handling the demons that dominant 80 percent of your life. The ratio can differ depending on the life path you take. When the two aspects of conscience and intelligence don't get along, trouble begins from within. Without correct spiritual learning and the Way to guide you, how can these two aspects become one? As young Gods and Goddess, you are vulnerable and not prepared for the task of controlling your life energies if you ignore the Way that we present to you.

I use *Westward Journey* as an illustration of spiritual self-cultivation, and its team of characters as spiritual examples of The Path of Subtle Light. Its original purpose was to describe how to accomplish the task of a complete life. It gives the title of *Ren* (human) to the team as one individual. Finally, in the story, the holy title of "Victorious Bodhisattvas" is respectfully granted to the Monkey. I rename the whole team of five as the "Victorious Completed Being." In Chapter 20 of this book, you can learn about the five elements and five virtues, together with the practice of the five-beam star as a way to daily identify with your complete life.

The story of *The Three Kingdoms* is another book we recommend you read in order to learn how to leave the rank of monkey in your life. The world is a society of many monkeys who take pride in whatever they mischievously accomplish. They play out their games of contention and war in human society. All mad monkeys adore these games. Do not become fascinated by the story, but use it to understand how monkey business is conducted, and learn how to stay out of and be above such business. You cannot reject the monkey world while living on Earth, but you can learn how to handle the monkey in your own life, and in the lives of others.

The story of *The Heroes at the Waterside,* which Pearl S. Buck translated as *All People Are Brothers,* describes four similar characters who take great delight in breaking any order or positive effort of life. The popular Chinese story of *The Romance of the Red Chamber* also presents the self-abasement of one's own good life. People's souls can be pulled into confusion and negativity by imitating the characters' decaying lifestyles.

Do not become fascinated by these stories, but deeply reflect upon them. They are about people, society and the world. Use them to contemplate what has happened to the societies of China and other nations in this and the last century, once human nature moves and expresses itself in the direction of negativity.

Most of the time life's forces are on two sides. These two sides don't usually get along as they are always competing for the "Throne of Life." This is the story of any individual, any community, any society and the international society. The dark and the light are constantly at war.

A holy war goes on internally as well as externally. Its deep-rooted causes result from the conflict between the pull of physical desire and the motivation of high morality. The Monkey is at the border of good and evil and can be cultivated to guard the highly moral life. You should ask yourself whether the cause of your internal holy war is the Monkey Intelligence, the Piggy Greed, the River Monster Hatred or the Horsy Blind Impulse. Has your conscience found peace and transcendental superiority? Your conscience, with the support of all partners in your life team, has a balanced interest and a good and improved knowledge of life. Balance, harmony and great cooperation are the real authorities of your life.

Everyone should know that God represents the power of life, and that life is a process of conquering internal and external obstacles and troubles. Every person, along with his or her team of energies, undertakes the task of self-accomplishing and self-completing the universal life. You need to follow the goal of being and living a decent and healthy life, for life itself. It is the only way to win in life. This approach directly and honestly brings forth the universal life energy.

The questions and problems of human life cannot be completely solved, because existing religions have confused people and negatively conditioned human society for conflict. This is why there is a need for teaching the direct truth of the Path of Subtle Light with its principle of spiritual self-cultivation. The teaching comes from the cooperation of three out of the five partners: Conscience, the innocent fellow; Intelligence, the powerful monkey king, and Intent, the far-reaching horse. The only aspect you can truly trust is Mother Nature's intent to balance each and every situation, and whatever can be achieved.

The development of intelligence is part of spiritual self-cultivation, whereas the gathering of knowledge is a habit. Intelligence is the substance or quality, while knowledge is the application. Without intelligence, you do not know how to choose the right knowledge, but without knowledge, what can intelligence be applied to?

It is not helpful to over extend knowledge, so only gather it where necessary. Deciding whether it is necessary depends on your own inner growth. When a single function is over extended, human-made disaster inevitably grows until it is out of control. It is far better to respect life as a whole, with all five aspects working cooperatively together.

Where do people find the wisdom of life? The wisdom of life is in nature. Wisdom has no need to prove itself; therefore it is the *Wu Wei* (of doing nothing extra) behind and before the activity of the five aspects. Human culture presents itself as the confused mind, but through painstaking experience and trouble, wisdom can be harvested. Hindsight, however, is usually too late to mean anything. We would rather you follow nature.

The ageless teacher Lao Tzu said, "The Earth followed the sky (heaven), and the sky followed the Way." The Way means the Way of nature that manifests as balance and harmony. Whoever goes against the laws of nature, even by a small degree, creates trouble for themselves and others. Wise ones give up struggling to follow the harmony of nature, both inside and outside themselves. Nature makes everything become equal. You may call it profound intelligence and on its back rides the Universal Subtle Law. The truth of nature isn't easy to understand though, because it is nonverbal and wordless.

Despite the widespread confusion in the world, where many people hunt for profit, there are still a few respectful individuals, with firm characters, who are righteous to the world and faithful to their friends. This marks the true value of life and raises life to the Divine.

If you lived long enough, you would probably keep silent for peace. However, there are so many confusing ideologies in the world that people are more bewildered than helped. Should you and your descendants, each of whom are born into this world, leave the world in darkness or should you brighten it for future generations, even if the price has already been paid? It seems you have to help them because they have already formed the habit of eating words whole without first examining them. The world is full of followers who don't see where they're being led. Be reminded: choose the right nutrition for your precious soul!

Chapter 11

The Internal Duty of a Constructive Life

The Health of Your Body, Mind and Soul

The health of your body is your own duty in life.
The peace of your mind is your own duty in life.
The joy of your soul is your own duty in life.

Good physical health is within your control. You do not need to rely on health professionals, special nutrition or tonics. Health comes from a balanced lifestyle and routine, an appropriate diet and regular daily exercise. Also recognize and respect that the healthy performance and support of these things comes from your undisturbed mind, and good life spirits working together.

Your three life partners of the body, mind and spirit are mutually influential. It is therefore important to balance your attention to care for all three.

Your spiritual health is the center of your life. Normally, when your mind does not separate from your spirit, your spiritual condition can be seen by your mental neatness and orderliness. In this situation, even though your physical condition may not be outstanding and your living conditions are average, health and longevity can be assured, as in the examples of Einstein, Kant and Toscanini.

No one can deny that peace of mind has something to do with health. However, mental peace can be of two kinds. One kind is the true kind where no uneasiness remains in the mind, and the other kind is the false kind that covers up or does not think about the unease.

The tradition of the Integral Way does not encourage avoiding difficulties and pressures in order to live longer and attain mental health. It respects those whose living conditions are not necessarily above average, but who have attained peace of mind while living a dutiful life. This means that one has made practical efforts in and finds healthy and constructive support from the ten basic levels of life: food, clothing, shelter, transport, education, finance, recreation, family and social relationships, intimate relationships as in marriage and sexual life, and spiritual faith. As a result, one can attain superior peacefulness in all aspects of life. The peace you achieve supports your life even more, and helps prevent disease.

Peace of mind is reached after all your duties are fulfilled. It is not achieved by sloppy or impractical means. Clearly understand that a weak mind looks for escape and a rewarding mind for peace; the two are in different categories. Your enjoyment of peace and spiritual contentment should also include consideration for humanity's progress.

Spiritual joy comes from your peaceful mind. It is achieved by the real gains you make in your life. For this there are three things you need to do.

(1) You need to achieve spiritual independence. This means relying on no one and no thing. It also means that you do not shame your conscience by living off someone else's labor. You need to be able to support yourself to develop your ability for spiritual enjoyment. Spiritual cultivation is not an excuse to escape from life. Rather, it is the time you give to develop your spiritual and mental power—in support of your health and longevity, so that you may be constructively creative and productive in your life.

(2) You need to attain spiritual freedom. This means that you are free from hidden harms and free from worldly entanglements with their negative contaminations.

(3) You need to build spiritual equality with those who achieve before you, those who achieve at the same time as you, and those who will achieve after you. Then, you do not have the disgrace of a wasted life or any regret.

To maintain your spiritual joyfulness and for your spiritual support, your deep thoughts and spiritual connections should keep within the Transcendental Range of concern. That means you are above any possible entanglement with the "Five Ws" of "Who, What, Where, When and Why (How)." You are not troubled by who the people are, what the matter is, where the location is, when the time and how things are done. In other words, you do not compete to produce mental harshness. However, in the serious performance of your life, success or effectiveness depends on your ability to give complete and accurate attention to the Five Ws. This means that in order to successfully produce your desired undertaking it is important to have: the right people, with the right approach, in the right place, with the right object and the right timing.

Your conscious self takes care of the duty of your life. Your conscious world is composed of *yin* and *yang*, which means the two different departments of the latent and the apparent, or the substance and function of your life's various activities. A serious distinction needs to be reached: the conscious self is the sense of self. With the sense of self as the center, there are at least two other conscious spheres. One is the subtle substance of the conscious energy, the soul itself. It is also the pre-heaven stage, or the neutral phase, before the conscious energy is activated. And the other is generally the noticeable conscious energy of the activity, known as the post-heaven stage.

Though the substance of the soul has no solid form, it may sometimes be perceived as white light. This spiritual light is the true divine energy in your limited physical life. It is the spiritual potential of human life, and is respected as the Lady of Light. It corresponds with the Universal Subtle Law. The soul of life can therefore be recognized as the agent of the Mother Universe.

A baby is produced from the physical essence of the mother and the father. The baby carries this physical essence, and that essence carries the subtle spiritual potential of the baby. The subtle essence becomes the physical and conscious foundation of the new life. Though the subtle spiritual essence has no form, it helps the growth of the baby's physical body and its conscious capability. The baby's entire form thus develops from formlessness. A baby's life is also shaped partly by its mother's mental conceptions.

When a troubled mother "sees" the soul of her baby, she does not see her baby's soul, but her own mental projection. This means that for people with psychological difficulties, "seeing" does not necessarily mean proving in spiritual matters. Likewise, when religious followers "see" their faith's divinity, it does not mean they see the objective reality, but rather their own mental projection. This is not to suggest that you stop believing, but that if you lose spiritual balance you can become a stranger to yourself, you can become lost. The mental force of a believer is malleable. The spiritual truth is already inherent: it is your life and your life is physically and spiritually reproductive.

The Ego

In human life, is the self or the ego important? In terms of self-responsibility, the self is the center of life and should be respected, unless the ego becomes so swollen that it competes with a sound sense of self. In that case, the ego becomes a negative weight in your life.

In the early stages of life, all life is spiritually centered. Newborn babies are sweet, naïve and innocent. With some life experience such as competition, imitation and learning, self-consciousness grows. If the self-consciousness is overly expanded, the egotistic tendency of the individual will predominate.

Ego is a psychological attitude. It is the overly expanded sense of self with exaggerated self-pride and confused arrogance. In contrast, wise ones are constructively relaxed. They have no need for any offensive approach as their ego has been dissolved.

Some people refuse to recognize the existence of the soul in their lives. It is not a problem to shake this fact of your deep life, but what is a problem is your ego. This is because the mind of an egotistic individual competes with their soul, and their emotional self attempts to override it. As a result, their conscious sense of self disrespects their soul.

It is the mind that forms and supports the ego, not the soul. This is an important distinction to make. The mind, by usurping the soul's throne of life, takes the soul's natural and rightful position in a healthy life. Your mind can then cause your soul to suffer by making it pay the price for what your ego said or did, perhaps for an entire lifetime. The ego is irresponsible. It is just a cluster of conscious energy, which temporarily clouds the mind. It is turned off when your physical life ceases.

It is important to discover your ego early in life and dissolve it. If your mind insists that the ego is the self, your life becomes troubled and you become blocked from reaching maturity. In some people their ego completely takes over their lives, and, if their symptoms are severe, their craziness eventually destroys them.

An unhealthy conscious self can also cause serious problems. It can lead to cancers in your organs. This is different to the trouble and possible suffering from the egotistical self. Egotistical individuals can experience great social power or wealth, which their minds usually become proud of. These things, however, poison their soul. The internal conflict causes the mind to separate from the soul. Then, when the ego feels defeated, it usually takes a radical approach of destroying the soul completely and ending the life through suicide. Many such tragedies have occurred, but what people usually don't understand is that using too much strength in life is the seed of tragedy for all. True achievement in life relies on improving the qualities of one's mind.

We mention these things for the purpose of pointing out the great value of egolessness. With a strong sense of responsibility, you can balance the condition of your soul and your mind. When both are harmonious, your life will have a dutiful mind and your soul can greatly enjoy your life's journey.

The Subtle Sphere of Your Life

In Chapters 4 and 6, we described how you are composed of numerous spiritual entities. Your conscious spiritual groups make it possible to do several things at once. For example, you may read or work mentally, listen to music and work physically, all at the same time. Or you may drive and talk on the phone at the same time. On these occasions, several conscious spiritual groups operate your mind. Handling several things at the same time is not the best way to use your mind, however. It can become a habit. We value unification rather than separation.

What about the spiritual situation in meditation? In meditation, if your conscious activity is not centered, your inner conscious world can become wild. What, then, should the spiritual principle be in this personal experience? In meditation it is best to have full spiritual awareness with an even attention to your life being. The conscious self dutifully attends to the surrounding conscious fields. This can be hard to do. There is no need to maintain the energy of a 200-watt light globe all the time. During long sessions of meditation, such as over a couple of hours, your mental awareness should be in the range of 10 to 20 watts, or less. If you fall asleep, your inner light is blacked out and you may dream. This loss of conscious control can lead to a loss of your refined subtle energy. As your subtle energy supports your health and longevity, it is your inner duty to maintain it and increase it.

In a materialistic world, people are driven to make more money and buy more things. The panic and desire for more security in life is also very strong. In these circumstances, peace, quiet and good sleep is more necessary than meditation.

Serious meditation is not appropriate for all people anyway. Although for some, serious meditation may contribute more to life than normal, good sleep.

In waking up, if you do not use an alarm, a small group of conscious body spirits becomes busy to produce a "show," or dream, in order to stir the main group of conscious energy into action and awaken your entire life energy. It is marvelous that a small group of conscious energy, the spirits, is able to produce dreams to awaken you. The unfolding story creates enough pressure to wake you up.

The tiny body spirits do not write the play or cast the actors. It is the semi-awakened conscious spirits of your brain that suggest the content and perceive the show. Therefore, the development of the story doesn't come from the bodily group of spirits, which are the actors, but from the perceptions of the brain group of the spirits, which are the audience. Remember, however, that dreaming is the result of the internal separation of your spirits, and daydreaming is a mental escape. Neither is encouraged from the healthy viewpoint of the *Integral* Way.

Your soul does not go to the trouble of creating. Positive and negative creations come from your mind. Generally in life, you do not require that much financial strength, but the overly creative minds of modern people can amass 10- to a 100-fold of what one truly needs in a lifetime. This can bring a negative influence to your life as your mind becomes complicated, in contrast to your soul, which prefers simplicity. When your mind gathers temporal conscious energy and material supports, which your soul does not need, it is impossible to maintain inner balance. Truthfully, your mind can create more darkness within your life.

It is normal for your mind to act and react to situations of life, yet it does so hurriedly that it leaves no time for your soul's supportive counsel. If your mind could just slow down on what it wants and how it wants it, it can have counsel from your soul. Your mind usually becomes dominant though. By adulthood, your life is usually headstrong and your mind competitive. Even during adolescence, your mind starts to think that it knows everything already. Consequently in life, your soul is no longer the executive, your mind is. Your mind, as the brain, is connected with the nervous system and issues direct commands on everything. Your soul is pushed aside to become a mere adviser. The center of your modern life changes to be intelligence-centered, rather than heart or spiritually-centered. We recommend that there should, at least, be a balance between your mind and soul, to avoid the suffering that is generally caused by squeezing your soul out of all situations.

Your mind matures when it learns from the consequences of its being overly assertive or too externally oriented. Eventually, at death, your mind has to give itself up as your conscious group disintegrates. So no matter how high your academic, intellectual, financial or social stature is, all these products from your mind's conscious efforts will cease. Although your mind needs to learn and achieve in order to live a good life, the central goal of life should be spiritual achievement. This can be obtained through self-discovery. You may still have all types of material, intellectual and social achievements, but these are not created to serve your own life, they are your soul's gifts to the world, which needs your help and contribution. These gifts can uplift the stature of your soul.

You should know that expensive food is wasted on an individual who does not know what the dish should taste like. Living is related to your understanding of life, and understanding is one form of mental power. With the achievement of self-discovery, or the discovery that life is about living, your mind can reconnect to the spiritual being of your life.

In benign conditions, there should be recognition of life's depth whereby the spirit or the soul is exalted. Religionists, by over applying the mind in defining their religions and in expressing their differences, have exalted the mind as the God in life, in place of the original purpose of setting the spirits as the God of life. This is the cause of the world's problems. If religionists do not respect the inner spirits, how will general people know to respect these silent partners of their lives? Religious storytelling, or any type of storytelling, only serves to amuse the mind. It is not the way to serve the spirit or the soul of your life.

Your ability to adapt to life relates to your spirit. Life's challenges are different for people who live in different environments such as the plains, mountains, desert and water, etc. Your spirit responds to these different environments. It subtly shapes your mind and bodily strength to eventually become the spiritual, physical and mental adaptation you need to respond to and/or overcome the environmental forces in order to live. Similarly, whether your profession is in literature, commerce or whatever, it is the subtle sphere of your life that prepares you for success or relinquishment. Although your spiritual being is not well-known, it is tremendously important. But your mind thinks it does everything.

In order to help you live a long and healthy life and achieve spiritually, we have summarized the essential requirements below.

(1) Use your mind smoothly in one direction.

(2) Enjoy a regular life schedule.

(3) Maintain your emotional stability to ensure you have very few ups and downs.

(4) Make sure you do not have any big financial pressures.

(5) Pursue a special valued interest.

(6) Do not allow anything to disturb or interfere with your valued interests.

(7) Do not insist on your spiritual faith in conflict with others. This behavior does not invite good health or a long life. Tolerance is the true attitude that enhances your health and longevity. You may be tested in your life, and there is no turning back.

(8)   The combination of tolerance for all people and constructively pursuing your personal interest can double your life's support.

(9)   A nonprejudiced and general broad faith in life is a bonus, but reaching the real Truth means a lot more. Actually, your personal choice of interest is really what makes the difference in your health and longevity.

(10)   Your interest should be constructive both in your personal and public life.

Recommended constructive interests:

(a) Transreligious spiritual truthseeking.

(b) Exploring formless spirituality.

(c) Philosophical pursuits with attention to their conceptual health and suitability.

(d) Constructive scientific pursuits.

(e) A deep interest in walking.

(f) The high form of *t'ai chi*.

(g) The high form of sword practice.

(h) Chinese calligraphy.

(i) Being fascinated with flowers, plants, lakes and mountains.

(j) Any combination of the above.

(k) Staying in one good marriage or no marriage.

(l) Cooking simply and enjoying a few good dishes using a variety of foods.

(m) Limiting your direct social communications and allowing your spiritual self to do the rest.

(n) Alternating between quietness and motion in life.

(o) Broadly tolerating life's small annoyances.

(p) Working tirelessly for the spiritual improvement of life.

(q) Using sound therapy. For those less interested in ideological pursuits, chanting the vibration type of invocations from ancient times can benefit your psychological health and spiritual development. Though sound therapy was mentioned in *The Yellow Emperor's Classic of Medicine* or *Neijing*, it has never been completely released.

The sound therapy material is still in my mother's Chinese files. It has nothing to do with your intellectual self. I have not translated this material because nowadays most people are selfish, and they ignore their soul because of her attitude of "I am not involved with whatever you are doing." Your soul may appear lofty or proud of herself as the moral self. However, in reality, how can that be? What other part of your life—intellectual, conscious, social, etc.—is interested in respecting such an unfashionable position?

Although the vibration invocations are just different groups of sounds and short sentences, they carry vital importance for your soul. I may consider that a member of my family teach these invocations to some serious individuals who are not driven by intellectual curiosity, but rather have a true interest in helping themselves and others. In my view, only women of a sincere spiritual heart should learn and teach this material. The security of the world should be put in their hands, and particularly in the hands of women who have not been conditioned by men, so that they are not drawn into the masculine interest of competing and fighting.

(r) Have true faith in the Lady of Pure Light and the Goddess of Good Water; they are not conceptual fabrications. They represent the high energy of the sources of life and have a lot to do with the spiritual survival of humanity. There is a whole set of spiritual practices as mentioned in *(q)* and *(s)*, which are related to this true faith.

(s) Enjoy spiritual pleasures and the high spiritual practices that nurture life's spiritual pleasures. This is a higher stage than the psychological health mentioned in *(q)*. It is for those who live in quiet and solitude and who have a serious interest in pursuing spiritual life as mentioned in *(m)*.

(t) Protect and nurture your soul's precious opportunity in life. Your soul's suffering does not begin at death, it occurs right now. Your soul is not a newcomer: she experiences everything in your life along with you as the conscious self. Although your soul is the real hostess or Queen of the party of life, your conscious self thinks it is, but it is actually the leader of a big group of unpleasant guests. In a morally weak life, the mind usurps the soul's position by associating with these guests who love all types of outrageous merrymaking, such as the overly extended Mr. Desire, the subnormal Mr. Interest and the overly strong Mme Emotion. Initially, these behaviors are limited to the occasional party, but eventually the guests join forces and take advantage of the Queen's unguarded naivety, locking her away and taking over her entire kingdom. The inner life of the individual then becomes like a beast's den.

Although one's physical life seems to be greatly enjoying life, the soul, as the caged hostess, is powerless to stop the robbers and usurpers of her land, and she faces internal rot and decay. The hostess's only chance is to learn and use the practices mentioned in *(q)*, *(r)* and *(s)* to build subtle protection and support. As the contents of *(q)* and *(r)* are non-intellectual, it prevents the conscious and intellectual selves from interfering, since they are "too smart" for self-protection. This is the soul's only chance to strengthen and restore her position. The high practices mentioned in *(s)* are used when the entire kingdom is back in the hands of the rightful Queen of life.

(u) The last chance for your soul. The last judgment of your life has no need to wait until the "Lord" comes back. It happens in your lifetime when your life is sick, and particularly when you are on your death-bed. A clean soul leaves quickly as there are no lengthy complications. However, the soul with worldly experiences and moral responsibilities, whether due to being a witness or through some involved responsibility, has to go through the suffering of the ten stern judges. They question and immediately punish the associated senses and conscious partners of your life, before your life is split into at least the two aspects of the physical and the soul. Even secret behaviors will be brought forth during this separation, or just before. Some people think this is due to the power of the brain. However we say it is due to the spiritual department of your life. This means that although you may be very capable and you may fool the entire world, you are unable to cheat the spiritual sphere of life at the time of separation of your body and soul.

The strange punishments for the dead and dying established by modern medicine are all invited by your various selves with their group of partners, most of which have the approval and support of your conscious self. The record on your invisible conscious chip exists forever and transfers to your blood relations, as the continuing punishment for your transgressions during your life. Your only chance of ensuring this will not happen is to engage in serious spiritual discipline using the practices mentioned in *(q)* and *(r)*.

(v) Use my translation of the *Tao Teh Ching* as your essential spiritual guidance. A well-governed life that has safety and peace from among all three partners of the mind, body and soul, should be like the description in my work of the *Esoteric Tao Teh Ching*. If you use the instructions from these sources, you will not need the vibration invocations or the instructions and material described in *(q)*, *(r)*, *(s)*, *(t)* and *(u)*. At most, these can be used for supplementary help.

(x) Give between 10 percent and 100 percent of whatever you attain as your service or financial support for the spiritual improvement of the world.

Initially to learn how to do spiritual practice is enough, but the newly developed mind demands to know why? This demand for understanding has moved Maoshing and I to offer help through the intellectual approach of lectures and books. However, spiritual matters are not only what you understand; they are what you are to be. Truthfully, we take strength from the nonverbal side of life to support the verbal side of life, simply for the offering of spiritual service.

Chapter 12

Is It All Physical Trouble?
(More About the Mind and Guidelines
for Its Improvement)

As we have expressed, the distorted creations of the mind have incorrectly been exalted as the God in life in place of life's genuine spiritual sphere. When dealing with spiritual matters it is important to know the nature of your human mind, and how it can mislead your life to become untruthful.

The mind has various levels. In simple terms it can be divided into three aspects: the apparent conscious mind, the subconscious mind and the combined life sense of the physical being.

The brain operates the apparent conscious mind like a government or administration, at most like Congress. It does the talking and it affects the condition of the rest of the bodily nation. It occupies only a small space in life, while the vast territory of life is governed by the nerve systems, which produce the subconscious. In each organ and system there are also local governments, which can be called the internal spiritual agents or regents. Beneath the agency of each organ and system, there are numerous spiritual entities.

When your physical body enjoys health, it means your mind is functioning smoothly and serving your life. Whereas a mind that is full of negative suggestions, unconsciously affects your physical health. If you do not monitor the pollution of your mind, the price can be fatal. When your physical trouble occurs as a warning or preliminary symptom, much help can come from personally straightening your mind.

It is a great wisdom to constantly work on maintaining a healthy mind. If your negative mental habits are not corrected immediately, your physical symptoms may return or get worse, indicating that your mind has poisoned your life. That is to say, your rotting consciousness can cause the rotting of your internal organs. We call this internal self-poisoning.

Similarly, a sick physical condition of society, as evidenced by social failures or social disasters, can be caused by the rotten social conscience of the whole society, and particularly by its sick-minded leaders and conflicting groups. Sick-minded individuals produce misleading information and miscalculate situations. This combination eventually plagues the society. These things are not difficult for people to see, but the problem is who would admit to being the internal problem maker?

A healthy mind is also important for spiritual health. Spirituality in life is the subtle essence, and it is the source of happiness or suffering. Normally it functions healthily. The spiritual sphere reflects and is influenced by your mental condition and physical behaviors. Therefore, mental self-examination and self-inspection should be done regularly and after each personal contact, because your mind can easily become negative and cause trouble, both physically and spiritually. Furthermore, your life's subtle sphere can easily be neglected if you overly concentrate on material pursuits.

The formula for a healthy world is simple: when the mind of society is healed, the society will get well. As an individual, a society and as a world, the focus should be on the health of the mind. It is a pity that when innocent people suffer at the hands of someone else (namely world leaders and influential individuals), they usually have to make up for lost time in their pursuit of health. So please remember: the conscious condition of your life is both the source of blessings as well as disasters.

The health of the world's mind needs all devoted people working together to establish common and agreeable mental disciplines. Your personal health is still the priority, and an example of healthy living is given by the ageless Way and its new social vehicle of the PCL.

The mind is also subject to conditions. For example, when you travel in the desert and become thirsty you can only think of good water; you don't extend your thoughts to enjoying watermelon. The fantasy of thought is further conditioned by the different stages of life.

Today, modern people live under such tremendous nervous strain that they usually don't think of living more than a hundred years. Yet long before written history, during the time that the ageless Way was developed, there was less pressure in life and living a long and enjoyable life was fun. People were inspired to live healthier and happier lives, and to achieve longevity. They lived for several hundred years or more. The pursuit of the ageless Way is not a modern product like the efforts to find the elixir of youth—those efforts are indirect steps using money and their purposes are mixed, not pure.

Is living a long life a practical goal for people? Yes. Yet most people would rather buy something to numb them, which may make them feel good temporarily. This is how the later religions and drugs found a market.

According to the old records, some people lived for a very long time and their achievement attracted others to imitate them. Let us consider what there was to imitate.

The first thing was to have a good faith in life. We have talked specifically about this in Part I. Generally there are two types of faith. The most popular one is to believe in and please a spiritual giant that gives you everything you desire. The other type of faith is to trust in Mother Nature. The high life of the human form, with its conscious energy, is an endowment from Mother Nature.

If there is a spiritual giant who lives in the sky, it is the expression of desire mixed with personal ego. That expression was created by cunning people who sold it to the psychologically needy in exchange for their support. If there needs to be a spiritual giant in the sky, it should be the mind's direct impression from Mother

Nature herself. A good and balanced faith should not be a mental product that people use to confuse themselves for selfish gain.

We can accept that there could be two faiths from the same one reality, although some spiritual work needs to be done to correct the confused beliefs. The most balanced faith would be aligned with that of the natural mind of the early people.

The early people of the ageless Way believed in Mother Universe. They did not value any spiritual emotional nonsense created by confused leaders. The worship of Mother Universe is simple. There is no need for numerous rituals and ceremonies with different names to confuse you. Just be earnest and constructive in your life. An honest faith that originates from true knowledge and is subject to natural conditions should be the thought of your life.

Mother Universe treats all life like any healthy mother treats her children: she offers equal support to help her offspring develop their best in life, and never asks her children to fight for her. In contrast, world leaders go against their mother's wishes in making people carry out mischievous deeds in their lives, and in the lives of others. As a result, someone sells you salvation and others sell you spiritual liberation. Who are these people who endanger your life anyway?

The deep truth of life is the formed nature of the universal substance, which is whole. Those who set up a different evaluation based on all types of efforts, created a spiritual authority and played that spiritual authority as a profession. What spiritual authority is that anyway? The emotional force and application that is derived from your social being may not be from your natural being. Both Maoshing and I have faith in the God that is the substance of all lives, and which can be developed. Specifically speaking, the constructive quality of life is God.

Living a healthy life and attaining a suitable old age is not a desire, but a duty. Mother Nature bestows great grace in giving you life. Many religionists prefer to say that your life is the biggest trouble, and that if you do not have life what trouble could you have?

True salvation does not come from the evangelists' tongue; it comes from your own deep reflection. Your spiritual nature is a reflective function of your mind. Through self-reflection and by clearly observing your surroundings, you can know what is detrimental to your life.

Your life is endowed with potential, but in selecting what potential should be developed there are many emotional and intellectual choices. Among all the different options, wise individuals choose to live with health, happiness, no prejudice and a long life. The possibility of attaining these things relates to your emotional constitution, lifestyle and sexual discipline. You can create misery in your life by choosing the wrong conditions, out of social confusion. Being strange or subnormal, or proudly thinking that you do good things in your life, is not how to express a good life. A good life goes beyond the modern contaminated conceptions with all the different types of sickening competition.

Experiencing the suffering of birth, old age, sickness and dying is no reason to discourage you from living a good life. Your parents have brought you into the world. Your life is not a shame or a sin; it is a grace. You need to work out all the difficulties and challenges in your life, and prove your life's worth. There is no better rebirth for people who have lots of complaints about their birth.

Appreciate everything that people refer to as suffering, as it makes you wise and strong. What are you being wise for? You are being wise to live a life of health, happiness, nonbiased mindedness and longevity. This is how life should be lived. No God can help those who do not know how to bless their own lives.

The goal of the teachings of the ageless Way is simply to support your good life. The teachings do not manipulate your life or create a ruling system to interfere with your life. They encourage you to engage in self-education, self-improvement and self-refinement.

Few people see the importance of a daily mental workout, though a daily physical workout has become very fashionable. Those of a constructive life spirit can use the following suggestions and books as guides for their internal improvement. This is how to produce good mental nutrition and support.

In General

Make your worldly life experience the raw material of your growth, but be wary of the stern teacher who tries to rule over all lives in the world.

Use your spiritual learning and your life's reflections as the fuel and fire for your internal refinement. Refer to *The Centermost Way*. Gradually this leads to the production of spiritual nutrition for the growth of your inner life. Refer to *Enrich Your Life with Virtue*.

Externally

Bear with the world through your spiritual broadness. This means to cultivate a calm and objective mind, so that you never lose the vision of where you are and what you are doing. Do not take difficulties in life personally—they are the mechanics of life. Rather, use difficulties as a learning process with the conviction that real winners are the healthy-minded, the kind-hearted and the upright-spirited individuals. Refer to *The Key to Good Fortune*.

Internally

Watch your general conscious condition—it is the subtlest factor that determines your health, your fortune and your achievements in life. There should be no negative burden. To that end, you need to use the three-step process of filtering, refining and sublimating your emotions and reactive thoughts. These processes help you attain the high essence of your life for spiritual support. In addition, choosing good food to eat and choosing good mental food to absorb will support a healthy mind and inner condition. Refer to *Stepping Stones for Spiritual Success*.

Fortify your conscious being with the new learning and improvements you make in each stage of your life. Refer to *The Foundation of a Happy Life*.

You can produce spiritual nutrition by taking in the outer life through your senses, and gathering your conscious reactions internally. Then reflect upon and filter your thoughts. Refer to *Internal Alchemy*. In the process you may see ideas and visions. Then condense your emotions and floating thoughts until they become simple and essential guidelines. To further your mental training and for self-protection, you can select invocations from the *Workbook for Spiritual Development of All People* (*Spiritual Workbook*). You can also refer to the books mentioned on pgs. 99–100 of this volume to help you.

The *Integral* Way is correct; the separation between real spiritual life and secular life is wrong. No escapist beliefs or practices should be considered spiritual. Take the experience from one side to help the growth of the other. Real spiritual achievement comes from real worldly life.

You also need to actively help the public because when the water in the pond is poisoned, how can you, as one of the fish, still safely enjoy your life? You may become a spiritual coach of the Integral Way and offer spiritual help to the world. The practices of the Integral Way (unlike my lectures which can enter one ear and go out the other) can save you ten lifetimes of spiritual searching.

We require a team of talented and devoted people to help edit and polish our work, including the earlier publications. By working through the material we provide to the world, you can have a first-hand opportunity to deeply reflect on yourself. At the same time, you can skim off the cream to work on your own high essence. That was how I worked with the world's spiritual culture over many years. Or, for your spiritual merit, you may help us better present our work for the benefit of the world.

Remember that spiritual work is the devotion of many. With many devoted hearts, it is possible to bring about a better epoch. Cooperation is welcomed, but competition for unhealthy commercial purposes is a sin. As part of the poison, it pulls the world backwards. And though the irresponsible competitor is the first one who brews and ingests the poison, many other people can be harmed in the process.

In true spiritual life, discipline is not forced on people by an external source. True spiritual value and inner discipline comes from inner growth and deep spiritual awareness. The world can definitely be saved when any individual or group of people decide not do irresponsible things. This is the guaranteed salvation that is fulfilled by your constructive life.

The Five Merits of the Path of Constructive Life

(1) *The worship of the Light.* It is the deep truth that your soul is light. The worship of the Light involves a respect for wisdom and a love of the four pillars of a complete life. These are health, happiness, longevity and an ever-youthful spirit that makes it easy to forget wounds and troubles. Abbreviated these four pillars are known as HHLE. The worship may include making some contribution, such as ten percent of your income, for world improvement by realizing and developing your local Integral Way Society (IWS). In turn, a local IWS community may contribute ten percent of its income to the Taoist Global Mission to serve the book fund.

(2) *The use of* The Complete Works of Lao Tzu *as your essential spiritual guidance.* You can use other works of the Universal Integral Way as important supplements to also help guide you throughout life.

(3) *The practice of daily gentle exercise.* Walking, Dao-In or simple *t'ai chi* are recommended to keep you physical balanced and healthy. In contrast, vig-

orous or hard physical work relates more to your physical work needs rather than normal health.

(4) *The development of a healthy and disciplined sexual practice.* Most people engage in a general animal style of sex that is combative, competing, struggling and exhausting. The aftermath of this type of sexual practice can be seen by the black rings under the couple's eyes and their puffy faces, dry mouths, tiredness and irritability. Their voices are hoarse and they quarrel among themselves until the next physical impulse. Such a couple has fallen into the vicious cycle that leads to health problems, and/or an early death.

In order to correct the vulgar practice of general people, I wish to reveal the secret of the gentle Tantric sexual practice of the ancient Immortal Tradition to mature-minded and open spiritual pursuers. It is one level of sexual practice, which helps maintain health and vitality. This ancient practice has unfortunately been religionized and commercialized, so be careful not to confuse it with subsequent distortions and impure practices. In certain circles it is considered a sacred part of religious practice, and the traditional male spiritual community has abused it. We do not agree with this behavior. We only promote the original pure intent of this practice, which is to harmonize a couple's energies and benefit their health.

Tantra is twin or dual sexual practice. It harmonizes the two polarities of *yin* and *yang*. It comes from ancient times and is illustrated by Hexagram 11, *"T'ai"* or "Peace," of the *I Ching*. The *Tao Teh Ching* also explains this practice, but in a hidden way. The harmonizing approach of sexual cultivation mutually helps the practitioners, and supports the four pillars of HHLE of a complete life.

In the gentle Tantric style of sex, the usual role of the male and female are reversed. The woman can enjoy great satisfaction, while the man is required not to ejaculate. This practice improves people's health and can transform the "die fast" males into thoroughly civilized gentlemen.

The PCL accepts the original heritage of this practice as the main style of sexual life. However, it recognizes that to be effective it should be respected, practiced and contained within a marriage or mature and committed relationship. This protects a couple's sexual hygiene, and avoids social confusion and moral problems. The parties should also ensure that appropriate safety standards are followed. In addition, and importantly, the frequency of your sexual activity should be decided by considering your age, health, life stage and the natural energy cycles. For more information on sexual relations refer to my books, *8000 Years of Wisdom, Book II* and *Harmony, the Art of Life*.

My view is that if the real performance of the sexual act is not changed, the world cannot be saved from all the self-destructive wars. No one individual has the power to stop war, and there is no high religious standard that can save the world, no matter how much money is spent or how many religious workers are sent out. Modern life symptoms express that sexual freedom has been abused. Sexual culture floods every aspect of society, and relations between males and females are very tense. This has led to new and unhealthy trends in society.

Even though God is the spiritually ideal faith of people, and perhaps the moral strength of society, people are still biologically based. Biological needs are generally stronger than spiritual needs. Your biological foundation should, therefore, be viewed at least equally with your emotional projections, spiritual interests and social religious establishments.

Without doubt God should be valued and respected, but the real foundation of all individual lives is the tiny particles that have the potential of spiritualization. What is generally thought of as spiritual experience, such as "seeing God," is simply a response of the innate body spirits to a person's mental activity and desires. Through effective research, these body spirits can be shown to be an underlying aspect of a person's being. They can be expressed or transformed within an individual life. Specific spiritual practices of the

Integral Way are available for practitioners and researchers who wish to deeply explore this human truth. For most people though, it is sufficient and effective just to cultivate and nurture the inner Light that is above the conscious level of life.

(5) *The practice of healthy eating.* Generally, eating a predominately (around 70 percent) vegetarian diet is recommended for your health. For more dietary guidance please refer to *The Tao of Nutrition* and *8000 Years of Wisdom, Book I.*

More Important Merits of the Constructive Life

Be honest even if others are not.

Be productive by focusing your life energy on constructive and useful endeavors.

Be respectful towards people and avoid injuring or taking advantage of them, even in difficult situations.

Take care of your health.

Focus on healthy and balanced thoughts, and do not hold onto any unhealthy emotion.

Select friends and social relationships based on whether they live constructively.

Give your time and energetic support towards a constructive spiritual direction. Having a constructive direction helps you fulfill the merits of life.

Be financially responsible by building a stable financial life, and avoiding unnecessary debt or becoming over reliant on social and governmental support. Instead you should support society by your own creativity.

Be responsible by taking care of your family, emotionally and physically.

Fulfill the underlying "spirit" of religion, but avoid being fanatical about any religious or political party. Most of these organizations reflect the struggle to impose ideas on the world.

No life can live in a stagnant situation. Instead, you can strive to fulfill a constructive life by actualizing the spiritual merits in your life. When they are all fulfilled you will achieve wholeness with perfect spiritual merit.

The Virtues of the Constructive Life

Below are ten virtues to ensure your success in the material and spiritual spheres of your life. Your complete health is the most important. If you wish, you may carve these ten virtues of the constructive life on the tablet of your heart, so you will never forget them.

Spiritual Respect. Spiritual reality is in nature, and in all lives of high spiritual awareness. There should be no disrespect for the unformed subtlety of the spiritual reality in your life or in the life of vast nature. A decent, orderly and self-responsible life, both in private and public, is the best expression and fulfillment of your respect towards the divinity of universal nature. Your love for the spiritual realm should be similar to the way children love their parents, grandparents, elders and other caregivers.

Tolerance. All people are the offspring of Mother Universe; therefore, they are all brothers and sisters. You should care for each other and tolerate each other's differences through good understanding and mutual support. A broad public spirit should be respected as a part of your duty of life.

Moral Health. A broad standard of morality is best molded in personal life. High moral fulfillment is a personal pursuit.

Moderation. Govern personal desire and emotion with moderation.

Equilibrium. In life watch the equilibrium of your body and mind.

Normality. The best expression of spiritual health is normality. Strangeness and peculiarity should not be considered as high expressions. Those sorts of low social behavior were common in the early stages of humanity, when people lived in spiritual darkness and confusion.

Spiritual Stability. Spiritual stability is expressed by the regularity of your emotional life.

Spiritual Self-Cultivation. Self-cultivation is the means to spiritually improve your life. Mass production cannot replace it.

Temperance. Tempering your consumption of food and drink is the right way to value the natural support of your life.

Frugality. Living frugally leads to effective living. Therefore being frugal in spending your personal money or the public's strength should be respected.

Be persistent in following these things of lasting value.

Chapter 13

The Useful and Necessary Foreknowledge in Human Life

It is a fact that during times of natural and human-made disasters many lives are lost. What you do not realize is that prevention and help comes from nurturing and developing the innate abilities of your mind.

For many years I have observed natural disasters. I was in Thailand when the December 26 tsunami hit many parts of Asia and East Africa in 2005, leaving over 170,000 people dead. Many of the victims were innocent people seeking fun and pleasure by the sea. You cannot conclude that their deaths were a result of spiritual punishment. I have also observed whether external religions and external faiths can offer any help to save people's lives in these events. I discovered that while these organizations foster social connections, develop social customs and help people order their rough emotions, they offer no real service in times of natural disaster. In fact, in earlier times, certain people used natural disasters to play on people's fears and establish religions. They did this to strengthen their social and political authority. Although religions were promoted as offering protection, they actually offer none.

Effective help comes from your own deep mind. Each of you has an innate spiritual system that can produce foreknowledge about impending trouble or disaster. Spiritual self-cultivation and, in particular, nurturing a quiet mind in your daily life can develop and support the natural spiritual capability of producing timely warning when danger is near. With a quiet mind, you may experience unusual dreams and be able to read the signs in your surroundings that foretell disaster. By being aware of the small-scale happenings around you, you can gather enough warning signs to know what could happen. You can also look at the degree of development of the general person to know what could happen to the world. You do not need to be a prophet, but you do need to be dutiful in being aware and helping others become aware.

From one perspective, foreknowledge is no big deal. Even small creatures such as cats, birds and fish know what is about to happen in their surroundings, as evidenced in natural disasters. Also there is evidence that working animals, such as oxen that are used to till the soil for rice growing, know when they are being taken to the butcher for slaughter. They often try to refuse the trip, and may shed tears of sadness for being so unfairly treated. Some farmers who notice this avoid eating beef as a result.

Though you come from animals, you have lost the natural capability to foretell trouble or the possible loss of your life. This is because you fill your mind with all types of useless information, and busily pursue excitement, power, fame and money. In addition you are educated to believe that foreknowledge is something extraordinary. Many people find it strange to believe that it naturally exists and that they are capable of its power. They prefer to rely on artificial religions to tell them that there is a God, while ignoring the natural reality that resides inside and outside of themselves.

Nobody can deny that the mind exists. Broadly, the mind receives sensory information and contains consciousness. The apparent conscious department works to know and to think. In contrast the subconscious department of the mind acts in hidden ways. It works to provide you with invaluable information about potential harm that may come from any direction, and from any connection.

The experience of seeing God, deities, angels and devils is your perception of the suggestions from your subconscious mind. These visions are how the conscious mind views the thoughts and suggestions of the subconscious mind. Spiritually, there is a way to enhance communication between the conscious and subconscious spheres of your mind, and help you understand your life. Consulting the *I Ching* is one way to develop psychic strength, and discover whether in your conscious endeavors you have an agreement from your subconscious partner. The *I Ching* can even provide you with warnings without your request.

In the process of using the *I Ching*, your subconscious mind responds to the request from your apparent conscious mind. Effective communication between the two partners, and with other people, requires continuous self-improvement. Although the *I Ching* has been widely used for divination, its real purpose is to help you relate to the deeper levels of your being. Using the material from the *Spiritual Workbook* can also strengthen the internal function of your subconscious mind. Your strengthened subconscious can provide protection by altering your vision to make someone or something appear as a message. Usually your subconscious cannot handle things single-handedly; it needs the cooperation of your conscious mind.

Life is natural, and a normal, peaceful life is the most effective type of life. When such a life is coupled with external and internal knowledge, it is possible to know the deep, subtle sphere of life, as well as the subtle conditions of the natural surroundings.

From my lifetime of devotion and research, my practical advice is this.

Maintain your spiritual interest. This allows you to touch the ocean of human spirituality, and to respect all external religions. Do not be pulled away by religious activities and external attractions, which are mostly skin-deep. Although they may provide some emotional help, they offer no genuine spiritual help.

Reduce your external activities. Take more time to be with yourself and remain quiet-minded most of the time.

Strengthen your potential. In quietude, you may consult the *I Ching* and use the invocations in the *Spiritual Workbook* to help you spiritually develop.

Manage your emotional life. Spiritual life is not much different from your secular duties. You just need to shift your interest to seek the earnest fulfillment of a regular life, rather than the excitement and entertainment of an emotional one.

Continue to learn and grow. The publications of the Universal Integral Way are for your balanced spiritual growth and learning. They can help you avoid spiritual confusion, and protect you from being fooled by conventional spiritual mistakes or by overly promoted social concepts.

Work together. Spiritual interest and fulfillment needs team effort. The spiritual services offered by the PCL, restructured from the various spiritual study groups of the Universal Integral Way, assist each other to upgrade the spiritual condition of people and to correct the spiritual conventions of the world.

Enjoy a regular life. You do not need to be a spiritual expert who is well-versed in theories. Living a normal and regular life contains the highest truth of life. In addition, you need some self-discovery for your spiritual well-being and protection. Also, you need some exercise to keep yourself physically fit, but you don't need to be a champion fighter. And just as you exercise for physical health, you need spiritual practice to maintain your spiritual health.

Be your own spiritual expert. The advertised expertise is for commercial purposes. You do not need to exchange your own life's provision for these services. It is far better that you provide for yourself through your own decent living-making efforts. And you can maintain a spiritual practice at the side of your profession, or at a different stage of life when you are prepared for high spiritual development.

Spiritually cultivate and offer spiritual service. Most serious spiritual pursuit is known as the "white enterprise." It is a blank check for the purpose of attaining spiritual self-completion. Such pursuit can be engaged in your later years, or at any time you are prepared. With achievement, you can do voluntary spiritual work to dignify your soul and upgrade the spiritual essence of the different lives in your surroundings. This becomes part of your spiritual self-completion. There is no need to discriminate between the internal and external aspects of your life. The spiritual difficulty of the public is your spiritual difficulty too. You also have been part of the world's problem. It is fair to give whatever you achieve to the world of humanity. God appreciates your generosity for fulfilling part of the duty to improve human life. As humans we can be the worst troublemakers to ourselves and to the planet, due to our immature and poor spiritual condition.

Live from your Heavenly Heart. A constructive spiritual congregation works to enhance the health of the public's soul. Your joint spiritual efforts work to fulfill the duty of upgrading and maintaining the public's spiritual health. Do not take advantage of people's lack of spiritual knowledge. Instead, exercise your own Heavenly Heart to support and inspire the growth of their lives.

The recent loss of thousands of lives in the Asian tsunami moved me to write down the truth that all people have the capacity to avoid disaster. Each one of us carries the potential of foreknowledge; it just needs to be developed through our own efforts of self-cultivation and constructive living. May each one of us appreciate and realize our potential, both for ourselves and for others of the world.

Chapter 14

What You Can Do to Make a Difference
(The Twenty-Eight Phases of Life and Their
Useful Adjustments)

Before you can make a difference in the world, you must first make a difference in your life. Making a difference depends on your internal condition and how you adjust yourself before manifesting that condition.

Your morality and goodwill are all subject to conditions. Most of your life you have indiscriminately accepted all kinds of conditions. As a result, you react to the world based on how you are conditioned, and you bear the consequences of your reactions. You are rewarded by some behaviors and you suffer because of others. Some conditions arise from necessity—these are the unseen conditions in your personal behavior. The struggle between the conditions of the world and the desire for personal spiritual freedom is a constant holy war in your life. Spiritual education and religious presentations are supposed to remind people to choose the appropriate reaction to a situation, but if these teachings are questionable or contain prejudice, the result will be lasting trouble for humanity.

The first step for spiritual self-improvement is to nurture the attitude of treating others as you would treat yourself. This can be done by frequently checking what phase of life you are in and what emotions you carry with it. It is like driving a car on the freeway: you need to pay attention to the road, and you need to make suitable adjustments to make the difference between safety and trouble.

You may want to become more serious about by your life by asking what you can do to become spiritual. The answer is simple: live a spiritually constructive life. What is a spiritually constructive life? It means to look at the phase of life you are in and make appropriate adjustments for it.

Below are 28 phases for your self-examination. If you live a busy life, you can review these once a month. If you are less busy, you can review them more often.

(1)　When you feel your life is boring and dull, it's time to deeply reflect on the real meaning of those external excitements that you have been used to, long for, or are even addicted to. You may have overly relied on these external things through habit, and now you have trouble seeing the true face of your life. Do you know which is more essential to your life?

(2)　When you feel your life lacks independence or interest, it's time for you to grow a sense of appreciation for life. You may see that you are wasting the support of your life's good conditions, which others may not have.

(3)　When you feel you have been weakened by the good conditions and activities in your life, it is time for you to consider exercising the good will to do meaningful things to fulfill your life.

(4)　When you feel you are worn out psychologically by life or work, it is time for you to seek good rest with suitable virtuous work that is important and helpful to others.

(5)　When you become fussy and picky and make yourself unbearable to others, it is time for you to be grateful for the things you have, and accept the people around you just as they are.

(6)　When you have great satisfaction in life because everything is perfect, it is time for you to learn to be humble and helpful to others.

(7)　When you fall short in your finances and cannot support your own spending, it is time for you to improve your habits and seek balance.

(8)　When you feel low in life or in work, it is time for you to spur your will-power and boost your morale.

(9) When you start to doubt your life, it is time for you to gather your confidence.

(10) When you feel you have neglected your family members or loved ones, love and care should be offered to those who need your attention.

(11) When you spend your time purposelessly, it is time for you to work on yourself and study highly valued books to uplift your mental condition.

(12) When you work feverishly on something, it is time for you to take a break and look at what you are doing. Ask yourself for its meaning before returning to your work.

(13) When you notice that you have become arrogant, it is time for you to value your sense of humor.

(14) When you try to find an excuse for a mistake, it is time for you to admit to it and accept responsibility courageously.

(15) When you are in a panic, it is time for you to change your mood and develop a sense of prudence.

(16) When you feel frustrated, it is time for you to practice self-inspection and self-improvement.

(17) When you encounter obstruction while communicating with someone, it is time for you to listen attentively.

(18) When you feel that your business is disappointing, it is time for you to re-evaluate its service.

(19) When you feel everything is regressing, it is time for you to act positively with peaceful confidence.

(20) When you fear the possibility of failing in your duty, it is time for you to reflect on how to better fulfill it.

(21) When you are exhausted from thinking in one direction, it is time for you to change the way you think.

(22) When you have been overly introverted in thinking of a solution, it is time for you to be with others out in the world.

(23) When you feel stressed, look at what is causing it. Stress can defeat your health. To reduce stress, ignore offence from anyone and anything.

(24) By not creating stress for others, you will remove the stress in yourself. For example, in your personal life, do not think of arguing or litigating to avenge someone's unintended negligence, or whatever it is that has caused you loss and suffering. Look at the trouble you prevent by not making more trouble. This can release your own stress, tension and anxiety. And, as a result, you do yourself a favor.

(25) When you feel wronged by others, it is time to forgive. Forgiving people's wrongdoing is the way to harvest happiness in life. The world is a spiritual network. The connection among people is built on correspondence, and so treating others well is treating yourself well.

(26) When trouble arises in your life, it is time for you to reflect on how it came about. People of high spiritual sensitivity are aware of the simple spiritual truth that troublemakers invite trouble into their lives. Allowing trouble-making to become a habit only creates hell in your life.

(27) When you feel you do not have enough, it is time for you to remember the blessing of a deep and broad personality. Developing a deep and broad personality is more valuable than producing lots of money. A deep and broad personality is able to take pressure and troubles, and dissolve them

like the vast ocean that constantly washes and cleanses itself. Having this spiritual capacity is to receive boundless blessings in life.

(28)   When you feel your life is full of pain and trouble, it is time to regain your sense of innocence. Innocence is life's highest spiritual quality and a great asset. With innocence, it is easy to forget pain and troubles and enjoy happiness. Those who lose it, lose the spiritual protection of the Angels. Who are the Angels? They are known by the one name of Innocence. Innocence means no evil-mindedness, and no evil-mindedness means brightness inside and outside of your life.

Religions are not the direct spiritual truth. They are just different sets of symbolism. They respond to humankind's innate need for spirituality by projecting a certain order for a society, a race, a family or an individual. The positive contribution of any good and broad religion is its attempt to recommend a set of symbols to spiritually order society. It is the same for an individual who uses a set of symbols to order their internal spiritual condition. However, people who self-cultivate will find that by choosing positive and appropriate invocations, mantras, or a set of them, and using them constantly, will be more effective than the conventional religions in ordering their inner lives. Spiritual health and purity can be produced by such practices. In fact, mass religions would do well with such deep provisions. Conversely, you can also work together with the external order to achieve the spiritual harmony required in life. Though social religions mostly promote external spiritual order, and the Universal Integral Way approves of their positive efforts, the Integral Way draws on the essence of all human spiritual expressions to present the universal spiritual unity among them all.

In the cosmos, the unmanifested sphere is the root of the manifested. Cultivating the unmanifested can seem more important than working on the manifested. The manifested sphere is composed of the post-heaven creations like things and people. The unmanifested sphere, on the other hand, can be like the fermenting of grapes—it can turn the grapes into sweet wine or sour vinegar. Spiritual self-cultivation works to attune the manifested sphere to the unmanifested sphere.

Watch the conditions of your living environment, as they will try to shape your disposition, temperament and character. Some can be fatal. Do not overly exhaust your physical or emotional strength in daily life, as this can condition you to be irritable and unreasonable with others, especially family members or life partners. Though not a deep sin, it is a loss of self-control from being overly tired.

Both Godly people and devilish people are products of their living conditions. Hence all people have the equal opportunity to be Godly or devilish. Godly people are the winners in choosing healthy conditions for their lives, while devilish people are the losers in not choosing healthy conditions for their lives. They become the unfortunate victims of their environment. We encourage you to be spiritually self-selective. Do not allow yourself to be malformed by the world.

No matter how long you live, the world will never stop pressuring and challenging you, like an old frog under a big boulder. The real challenge of life is to remain upright and happy amidst all of the world's negative conditions, without withdrawing or escaping, and without wronging yourself or others. Artificial sainthood is for religious promotion. We hope the above suggestions can help you to guide your life well, just like the bright twenty-eight constellations in the sky that can help you find your way, even on the darkest night.

Chapter 15

Daily Rituals and Guidance for Your Constructive Life

Always respect the people, creatures and things that you encounter daily. This can help smooth the flow of your life's energies. As a daily spiritual practice, respectfulness produces a healthy and spiritually meaningful life. However, do not become overly rigid or artificial like conventional religions.

Practice kneeling and bowing in a clean and quiet place daily. This is called the grand salutation and prostration to universal unity. It expresses that you have attained the most important spiritual essence in life of spiritual unity, even though the worldly spiritual cultures created by the human mind are many and varied. The practice of spiritual unity can help you channel your life energy to be above spiritual confusion. Use it daily, both before and after engaging in your different life activities. It can help you develop spiritual unity, internally and externally, with the goal of complete well-being.

Practice meditation as it is beneficial. It can nurture and channel the energy flows of your body. By regularly setting aside some undisturbed time you can build a daily habit. Do not overdo it though, otherwise you won't be able to freely adapt to the commotion of modern living.

Use invocations and prayers to support the spiritual connection of your entire being. You may refer to the *Spiritual Workbook* and select those invocations that fit your understanding and need.

Practice fasting for physical and mental health. Fasting helps cleanse the mind and body, and reduces the burden you unconsciously gather everyday. You may fast periodically or as often as you need. On a winter's day, to benefit your body, you can fast by cutting down or skipping your evening meal. In summer, eat more watery food and less rich food. And in the evening or during quiet hours, you can mentally fast to benefit yourself.

Use holy water wisely. There are four types of holy water: the holy water that brings plants to sustain your life; the holy water you drink; the holy water you bathe in to maintain you health and cleanliness and the holy water that brings your descendants into the world. Do not waste the holy water produced by your body. Use it wisely with the person you choose as your closest life partner, such as your spouse.

Use calligraphy and gentle physical movement for spiritual training. The Asian practice of Chinese calligraphy calms the mind and improves concentration. Gentle physical movement, such as Dao-In or *t'ai chi*, can contribute to your balanced development in order to achieve health and longevity. Dao-In massages the internal organs and specific points. *T'ai chi* attunes and harmonizes the internal and external systems of your life. The Harmony Style T'ai Chi form is preferred as it improves your health without overemphasizing the martial art aspects. Each style of movement has a different purpose.

Learn to handle your emotions effectively. Uncontrolled rough moods and negative emotions can invite unfriendly responses from others. Accept these responses as your fault rather than blaming others. By using the suggested practices in this chapter, you can sublimate your emotion, hatred and hostility. This will help you nurture a healthy and loving disposition, which is much more beneficial than holding onto the destructive vapors inside yourself.

Do not build the daily habit of using coarse words or filthy language.

Learn not to laugh at others when they do something silly. Rather, learn to laugh at your own mistakes, as this will uplift your conscious health.

Be kind to the kind and be kind to the unkind, but guard yourself from evildoers and tricksters. Never do the same things back to them that they do to you. Compassion and sympathy are merely good words. Your compassion and sympathy are only real if your character remains unshaken when others trouble you.

Encourage those who lack confidence and help those with a benign nature, but do not help those with evil intentions.

Be constructive always. In life you may sometimes enter a destructive situation, yet no matter how bad it is, be constructive. This is the only hope to get out of the situation. A constructive personality doesn't mean that you can be constructive sometimes and destructive at other times. Nor does it mean you can be constructive for yourself and destructive for others. It means to be constructive *always*. This is the way to unite with the universal constructive spiritual nature.

When assessing another individual, the key point is whether the individual is constructive, particularly in a bad situation. People can become very self-destructive in negative situations. They may resort to alcohol, drugs or destructive sexual behaviors, thinking those things can get them out of their predicament. They don't see that they've chosen self-punishment.

How does a young person determine their future? The important point is whether the person has a constructive personality or a negative one.

Develop discernment. New friends and new opportunities bring you new perspectives, but it still depends on you to make the correct assessment before jumping into a situation.

Be responsible. Some people like to be the boss. They like to be the superior or dominating presence as in a competitive sense. What they do not see, however, is the responsibility of leadership. In life, the sky supports the Earth and the Earth supports the people. Great grandparents take care of the grandparents, the grandparents take care of the parents and the parents take of the children. It is the natural and harmonious order that the big and high take care of the low and small. In society, wise leaders respect this natural order. They know their duty is to take care of those around them. Subnormal situations can arise when people compete to be the biggest or the highest. These unwise individuals try to make the low and small serve them. They consider themselves to be big and high, which only proves that they are low and small. They have not grown enough to observe and appreciate the harmonious order of the greater universe. To be big and high is a natural growth. Growth means learning to serve and take care of your own life and the lives of others. That is the essence of life.

Use festivals and holidays for spiritual self-cultivation. The following are worth maintaining.

On New Year's Eve, keep quiet and experience time passing through you.

In deep winter, light your house inside and out with full spectrum lights to avoid depression.

On some islands it is the custom that when people pass away the body is buried or burned, and candlelight is placed on the water to bless the soul that is leaving. This can be a constructive way to handle sorrow. Where appropriate this custom can be maintained.

In spring, chose a clear day to visit the countryside or your ancestor's tomb as a memorial activity. Your sense of the duty of life can be strengthened through such purposeful activity.

In summer, before it is too hot, you may go sailing or play in the water to benefit your emotions and health.

In the middle months of autumn, the moon is very bright. During a full moon night, you and your family and friends may celebrate the moon as the symbol of the union, and the full development of the mind and the inner reflecting spirits. Young people may dance under the moon with the full and pure joy of life, and individuals of experience and maturity may visualize their life by allowing the moon's reflected light to reach their soul.

In autumn, before the heavy frosts and shortened days, choose one clear day or several days to climb and hike in the mountains and enjoy the far-reaching views. This can help open your mind, as can looking up at the vast sky during the day and night.

Improve your relationship with the sky, the Earth and all people. No honest earthling knows on which day the sky or the Earth began, or on which day human life began on Earth. It is an old custom though to recognize the first three days of the Chinese New Year, when the solar and lunar cycle merge. The first day is used as the birthday of the sky or heaven. The second day is used as the birthday of Earth, and the third day as the birth of human life. These are good conscious connections to make in support of your life. What other conscious human creation is more realistic than the connection with nature? On the first day, you can physically fast, except for the children. On the second day, you can eat simply and mentally fast. On the third day, you should go outdoors and greet everyone regardless of any past resentment or grudges you may have, to extend your appreciation of the human connection to all life as one life. If you feel the yearly cycle is too long for repeating this good practice, you may practice it at the beginning of each month in order to improve your relationship with heaven, Earth and all people.

On your birthday, you may celebrate or reward yourself with pleasures, although meditating can be a better way to celebrate your birth and renew your life cycle. You may even do both—have a social celebration one day and then use the following six days to meditate or live quietly.

Allow your sense of life to travel and ride the natural cycles. All travelers should take care of themselves and take care of each other, because everyone's destination is the same. Make sure that no one is lost on the Way of the universe.

In a week you have seven days. In a month you have around 30 days. When Lao Tzu said that there are 30 spokes in each wheel of a carriage, he was reminding you that your life's journey is to join with the universe. If you only look at the daily cycle, it appears the sun circles the Earth, but the moon's cycle tells you that you are riding on the vehicle of the Earth. Looking at the monthly cycle, particularly in the case of the solar and lunar eclipses, it is apparent that you are a traveler riding on a vessel. Can anyone tell you where you are going? Your vehicle reaches a great distance. In a year you have 365 days to use. What will you do and be in the remaining, unmarked days?

Respect the natural vitality or reproductive potency that lies behind and beyond the formed world. This is what individuals of true universal religiousness do. The natural vitality or reproductive potency is not formed, but it is able to produce forms. The highest form among all forms is human life. Human religious expressions have two types of conceptual attitudes regarding universal spirituality. One type worships the unformed. Although this formless conception of universal spirituality is close to the truth of vitality and productive potency, their conceptual creations still carry the image of form as a creator that brings forth all the forms. Before the formless conception became popular, people worshipped statues.

Some people kneel and pray in front of a blank wall, while others kneel in front of colorful statues. Which approach is spiritually superior? Only those who have reached the spiritual truth can have equal sympathy, understanding and emotional support for both approaches. People who have reached a higher stage of development can see that the spiritual reality of nature cannot always remain formless. It is constantly changing—forming, deforming and reforming. Formed things and beings result from the formless. Nature's potency is able to extend itself to the multiple formations of the physical and semi-physical planes of the world. This recognition is truly superior to the rigid approach that insists that God must have no form, or the Buddha must have form.

The most blessed people are those who are able to bow with utmost sincerity to the unity of the spiritual nature of the universe. They do not differentiate or discriminate between the conceptual images or statue worships of religions. All of which are merely various creations from the different stages of human growth. By respecting all the multiple creations, you express your kindness and under-standing to the worshippers.

Develop your conscious capability. Among the earthly creations of nature, the soil, stones and plants do not move, but insects and animals do. Human life can be considered as the highest form of life; the peak development of nature. What is considered high about our human life is the growth of consciousness in our lives. Although lower animals are driven by the same needs and desires as humans, human life is distinguished by the growth of a higher conscious capability. The conscious activities of people include: what to do, and what not to do (in the sense of what brings benefit and harm to life); what to undo and what to redo, such as the corrections or improvements to one's behavior. The first two activities are similar to the lower animals, which possess the same natural impulses as humans. The last two activities are what help people to evolve spiritually and possibly reach the divine level, which is the hallmark of life's mastery.

Each individual has his or her life track to follow. Life's destiny can be far-reaching. Those who ignore the growth of the internal knowledge of their life's track, and blindly follow the competitive trend of the masses can end up wasting their lives. Individuals who transgress their own lives cause friction and destruction as a result of knocking against the life tracks of others. As a high form of life, an individual should know how to respect the life track of each person. A truly meaningful life moves spiritually forward and upward with prudence. Do not abuse the concept of freedom. Although spiritual freedom is necessary to reach the infinite, it should not be used to indulge in personal freedom.

Do not take advantage of others, no matter how tempting the situation or how easy it may be to do. You may be in a difficult situation or be taken advantage of by others, due to the other's lack of knowledge or confusion, or as a result of an intentional scheme. Once you become aware of it, you may have to quietly accept it and recognize your own shortcoming in the situation. Sometimes you may be able to gracefully withdraw from the situation or person completely. At other times, you may have to pay "tuition" for your learning, which can protect you in the long run. If you are able to accept the troubles that result from your mistakes, and grow from your experiences, you will reach real spiritual superiority.

Learn from wise sources. To help you overcome the tensions of modern life and make the required mental adjustments, you may choose to learn from Chuang Tzu (see my work of *Attaining Unlimited Life: The Life and Teachings of Chuang Tzu*). The many pressures and social burdens of modern life can also cause you to lose your personal connection with nature and create mental burdens. You may end up living for others rather than for your own life. Studying the works of Lao Tzu can help you overcome these pressures, as well as the materialistic demands of modern life. Deeply researching Lao Tzu can help your sexual health too. We also recommend you study the *I Ching* to help you achieve harmony—internally, sexually and socially. And reading the five books of the Constructive Life series will help you achieve the spiritual expression of a constructive attitude. These books have absorbed the positive spiritual effort of all generations and all religions, leaving all irrelevant and useless aspects behind.

All these suggestions are constructive life habits that you may consider practicing and maintaining in your life.

Chapter 16

Put Yourself Together with T'ai Chi

The universal spiritual reality of life, the essence of life, is not partial to any culture; it is contained within the natural life of each individual. Your natural life is complete with the best essence from all three spheres of life: the material sphere, the subtle mental sphere (represented by your conscious energy), and the spiritual sphere (your soul). Your sacred duty is not concerned with worship, although its forms can remind you of your life's spirituality. More importantly, your sacred duty is about spiritually cultivating to develop and unify your life's truthful essence, and thus improve your life. The healthy expression of God is related to your soul and its development, and this development is the great social intention for all people.

Throughout generations of religious experience, there have been many ideas and forms limiting people's growth instead of supporting them to live a whole and balanced life. The focus of our work, therefore, has been to find a constructive practice that can support the complete and balanced development of human life. A practice that leads to improved health, a peaceful personality, a reduction in prejudice and violence and genuine spiritual development. With these objectives in mind, we recommend the gentle movements of *t'ai chi*.

T'ai chi is one of the most effective spiritual practices. With regular use, it can improve your health and help you unify your body, mind and soul. If that is not sufficient for you, then with the same devoted practice, you will be able to verify that the Heavenly Father, Holy Son and Holy Spirits are within your very life. You will also be able to witness the Trinity of Heaven, Earth and Humanity in your life. That is to say through the simple practice of *t'ai chi*, you can accomplish spiritual integration. Or to put it another way: through the ritual of *t'ai chi*, you can realize the Heavenly Heart. *T'ai chi* movement expresses the harmony of all human constructive efforts in all aspects of life.

In the beginning, the movements of *t'ai chi* were a natural symphony, orchestrated from spiritual signs, messages and language. Prayers and solemn requests, offerings in the form of dance and Dao-In movements were performed for both health and spiritual needs. Back then it was not known as *t'ai chi*. Different styles exist today having evolved throughout generations, but they all have something in common. They all use the same principles of balancing and mutually supplementing the forces of *yin* and *yang* through gentleness and harmony, as elucidated in the *I Ching* and the *Tao Teh Ching*.

Modern, popular styles include the Chen, Wu, Yang, Yu Shan and Zao Po styles. These styles have all contributed to the preservation and popularity of T'ai Chi Chuan. As a martial art, however, *t'ai chi* belongs to a different time and social environment.

Although we have mentioned some specific *t'ai chi* sets, we humbly suggest that the PCL can review and accept any *t'ai chi* set that meets its purpose of spiritual development. If accepted, the form can be publicly recommended in the Integral Way Society (IWS) newsletter. The IWS, through the Chi Health Institute, can also certify people in those accepted styles.

For some people, *t'ai chi* is too complicated. However, any small set or single move, practiced daily, can be beneficial. The support and benefit you gain can be very deep if the practice remains as your lifelong companion. Some people have united themselves with the high principles of the *I Ching* and the *Tao Teh Ching* using their own style of *t'ai chi*. These people have our respect.

When practicing *t'ai chi* you may recite the six-syllable vibration, "*Da Dao Kun Min Yun Zen.*" Mentally, this acts as a medium to unite your body and soul. It means, "The Way, the Truth and the Light are with me."

As a ceremonial gathering, *t'ai chi* is more suitable to perform outdoors. Such gatherings may include the styles of Eight Treasures, Harmony Style Tai Chi,

PART II: CHAPTER 16 ~ 171

Cosmic Tour Ba Gua, Infinite Expansion Tai Chi and Advanced Tai Chi Practice for Spiritual Cultivation. You can find most of these practices through SevenStar publications.

The practical goal of each member of the PCL is to achieve union of his or her body, mind and soul. And the single spiritual direction of the PCL is the Trinity of Heaven, Earth and Humanity.

Practical Instructions for
T'ai Chi Practice

General Guidelines

When practicing *t'ai chi* to achieve complete health in the three spheres (your body, mind and soul), keep in mind the following general guidelines.

Use Harmony Style T'ai Chi (or its equivalents) to untie the tensions and knots in your body that result from your emotions.

Use *t'ai chi* to soften your personality, especially if you are overly tight due to a fear of being beaten by others. The tightness you feel is usually a result of not feeling completely confident with yourself.

Use the practice to increase the flexibility of your body, mind and spirit, and as the path of self-development. For example, you can use the practice for your general healthcare, and thereby reduce the risk of modern medical abuse. Or you could use *t'ai chi* to help heal a chronic illness. People lacking self-control usually don't understand these things.

More importantly, use *t'ai chi* for spiritual self-cultivation, self-attunement in worldly life and the refinement of your personality. Also use *t'ai chi* to access the deep levels of your being, such as the *chi* level of life, the *jin* level of application, and the *shen* level of the final reality.

Men should be aware that with regular practice they will go through a stage of expanding their sexual energy, which, unfortunately, most tend to release through fighting and sex. Your training and attainment in *t'ai chi* should not be applied regressively; it should support your spiritual development. Therefore practice *t'ai chi* for self-control, rather than let yourself be pulled into worldly affairs that are against the constructive direction of life. Women who possess an over-abundance of testosterone may also benefit from this suggestion.

Generally achieved *t'ai chi* practitioners can slow down the aging process by around ten years, compared to the average person who doesn't practice. Practitioners with better than general skills can slow down the aging process by around 20 years, compared to people of average health. And practitioners with outstanding achievement can slow down the aging process by around 30 to 40 years. Actually, most forerunners of *t'ai chi* learned to forget their age, but this can be inconvenient in modern times, since personal information is usually needed for verification and identification.

You may notice that some general *t'ai chi* teachers can reach an average age and remain healthy without professional medical care. Many are kind and gentle as a result of their combined efforts of consistent practice and good spiritual discipline. These individuals are worthy of your respect, and you can learn from their examples.

When practicing *t'ai chi*, set the highest spiritual goal for yourself, such as to compete with no one and become a divine individual who has cleaned up all personal desires. Your high practical goal of how long you can live by regularly and confidently practicing *t'ai chi*, can and should be set higher than your present reality. It is also best to keep these specific goals a secret. Real attainment will be known by you at different stages of your development. Simply remain calm at all times, and do not become excited or dismayed by any momentary self-knowledge. You can also readjust your goal setting.

The forerunners of *t'ai chi* practiced for many years and gained a great deal of personal experience. They all had secret specific focuses. Their seniority and experience deserve your respect, but unless they share their attainment with you, do not hunt for such things. In time and with consistent practice, experiences and achievement will come to you too.

In the beginning, and for the first ten years, you may do one form and acquire all its details. After which, you can progress to a new stage where you can adjust and reshape the form to what best fits you. Personal adjustments are for your personal learning and development. Such things should not be promoted to others, as it would only cause confusion.

Generally, people who pursue excellence in martial arts combat enjoy being considered a hero. Consequently they usually end up shortening their lives. Unlike other men and women who excel in martial arts, but who choose to live a clean, single life with spiritual cultivation. Due to their concentrated interest and discipline, these individuals are able to enjoy good health, longevity and a clean, undisturbed mind.

T'ai chi practice is best used as a vehicle for personal spiritual pursuit rather than as a livelihood. If you do choose to teach, however, you should limit your teaching to a certain period, as I did to between my late 30s to late 40s. This is because once you start teaching, your social circle tends to expand and you may find it difficult to remain disciplined. This can be a great harm. Overeating and overdrinking have led to the death of quite a few famous *t'ai chi* teachers, who already suffered from hypertension due to the pressure of maintaining their hero status in competitions. They were less healthy than general *t'ai chi* practitioners. Today the social environment is different, and you may have more understanding about how to live a healthy life.

Specific Guidelines

Once you begin to move, proceed with gentleness and liveliness, your movements should not feel robotic. All your *t'ai chi* postures should be connected by subtle spiritual rhythms and smooth transitions. There shouldn't be any sign of roughness as other people can interpret this as a threat or challenge. Instead, direct the external force deep into your bones so that your bone marrow remains fresh and vital.

Health and longevity attained through spiritual pursuit should not be used for self-aggrandizement, but rather for fulfilling your moral duty and for accumulating invisible spiritual merits. This assists the health of your divine soul.

Most importantly in your practice, your *shen* (the spiritual awareness within your consciousness without any specific content and/or intention) and *chi* (the subtle, vital force of life before it takes form and becomes *jin*) should flow smoothly through the changing procession of different postures. Nothing should stick out or be cut off. At all times, move from the deep *shen* and *chi* level of your being to the outer level of your physical being. In other words, *t'ai chi* practice is about allowing the deep conscious energy to express itself through your body, rather than allowing the specific posture or bodily form to command your body's *chi*. You can then find the harmony that exists within the variety, and the distinct variety that exists within the unity. As you continue your practice, you will also find that there are more hidden degrees of change relating to the empty force and solid force.

You need to move calmly in order that the *shen* move the *chi*. This is how you gather *chi* into your bones. When the *chi* moves your body, your movements can progress smoothly. The *jin*[1] (which is the refined inner strength that comes from the concentration of *chi,* rather than from physical muscular force) looks loose

---

1. *Jin* is often displayed in push hands, whereby a small person with highly developed inner *chi* strength can throw someone much bigger in size several yards through the air.

but it is not loose; it looks like it is going to spread, but it does not spread; it is in control. While the *jin* can involve pauses, the *chi* should flow continuously like an uninterrupted sweet melody.

Attend to your conscious mind and then your body. By keeping your belly free of tension, the *chi* can gently gather and stretch to enter your spine.

Your consciousness should be comfortable and your body quiet. Always be aware that it is the *shen* that you are strengthening.

Once you start to move remember that as one part of your being moves, all parts of your being follow in exactly the same way, and as one part starts to quiet down, all other parts of your being should quiet down.

Necessary Requirements for Practice

Move with a quiet mind. Remain steady without any disturbing thoughts, however slight.

Relax and dissolve any feelings of haste.

Breathe evenly, following your natural breathing rhythm most of the time.

Never force or push. You need to be alert and ready to respond at all times.

The inside and outside of your life should be completely coordinated. Therefore, the internal triune of the *shen*, the *yi* (the intent or upper consciousness) and *chi*, and the external triune of the hands coordinating with the feet and legs, the elbows with the knees, and the shoulders with the hips and groin, should be coordinated.

Connect the entire set of movements like the smoothly flowing waters of a long river.

Maintain a high level of concentration without any absent-mindedness and/or distraction.

Coordinate your breath correctly. In *yin* type movements you should inhale. *Yin* movements are the movements of softening, emptying, gathering, converging, rising and moving upward, withdrawing, bending, surprising, swallowing, lightness, quietness, carving and inward moving. In *yang* type movements you should exhale. *Yang* movements are the movements of hardening, solidifying, initiating, opening, descending, forward moving, upward moving, extending, falling, sinking, straightening, expanding, out-sending and out-moving.

Your breathing will naturally become coordinated after many years of practice. If you give too much attention to your breath, you will only become tense. Naturalness is the principle to use when beginning to learn the movements, and just allow the correct breathing to follow. Otherwise you may find yourself giving up, because it is too difficult to coordinate everything at once. This would be a great loss for you as a potential achieved one.

Keep your body upright and aligned with the North Star, which is the axis of the Earth. This is an important spiritual, mental and physical alignment to maintain for both your health and your soul's development. Actually it is best to maintain this connection throughout your general everyday movements of sitting, standing and moving.

Become aware of your general posture, as good mental and physical coordination supports your health. Find and learn natural ways to readjust your tight shoulders and other ineffective postures that can, if left unattended, harm your health.

You may choose a standing cultivation practice for self-healing and self-strengthening. It can become a part of your *t'ai chi* practice. Standing practices benefit your spine and nervous system, among other things. When your head, shoulders, breathing, mind, eyes and inner *chi* are poised, vital *chi* will grow naturally. You can begin with five minutes of quiet standing and gradually increase it to one or several hours. Practice in a quiet, clean and fresh location. The practice can transform your mental rubbish into vitality and, over time, strengthen your immune system in order to fight off chronic disease and pathogens arising from weather and seasonal changes. Such benefits come through perseverance and regular practice.

If you prefer to do sitting meditation, the principle, requirements and effectiveness are the same as the standing practice.

Walking meditation can also be very useful. Personally, I gain a great deal from this practice. Most of my writing visions come about when I practice walking meditation in a natural and fresh environment, such as by the sea, in the mountains, fields, and gardens and along country trails.

Sleeping cultivation is also helpful. Be sure that you sleep on your side, and face towards your personal favorite direction based on the five element system in order to remain balanced.

For broader information on *t'ai chi*, you can refer to my work *Strength from Movement: Mastering Chi,* and the forthcoming book on *t'ai chi* by Dr. Maoshing Ni.

Chapter 17

A Good Faith Is the Healthy Strength of Life

The Faith in Constructive Life

Conventional religions were produced during times of difficulty and struggle in human life. They contained remorse for the passing of life and fear for an uncertain future. People generally express this type of mentality in adulthood and elderly life. Religions were shaped by strong feelings of guilt and remorse for mistakes made in people's lives. Such feelings were expected to lead to forgiveness and salvation from a supernatural force.

Those beliefs were formalized around 3000 years ago, when people had become exhausted and all that was left to do was repent and seek forgiveness. Feeling old and worn out, people continued their lives through the joy of illusions and dreams, creating a new home in the sky to meet their emotional fantasies. The new religions were based on the expectation that life needed special protection, and so God was created as an omnipotent being—in the image of a ruler of justice, a judge of kindness and a savior who removes all guilt. Confession was also created whereby people could admit the abuses to their health and life force through such acts as excessive and self-destructive sex. We can sympathize with these beliefs, but not to the extent of accepting or allowing their negative influence.

Though those religious beliefs provided cultural and spiritual leadership until science expressed a different attitude of life, we suggest that new generations overcome the old wounds, racial hatreds and prejudices brewed from those old societies.

In the past, before that awkward stage, people were good. They were proud to be human, living among other animals and beasts. They had a natural religion and a humanistic civilization. Recent generations may not know about the beliefs of these early human ancestors.

The early humans' believed they were the children of the sun. They believed that after the water subsided from the land, the sun gave birth to the first baby known as the Red Baby. The myriad people, who became known as the later people, all came from that one.

The Red Baby has no gender differences or sexual desires, yet its natural potency is thick and deep. It runs the whole day without being tired, and yells the whole day without becoming hoarse. It is active among beasts, snakes and insects, and has no fear in its life. As the life spirit of a new life, the Red Baby produces all necessary protection for that life. Such a life has no negativity, only the tremendous potential for a constructive life. Nastiness was a later development of humanity.

The Red Baby is the spirit of a new life, which conquers whatever lies ahead. This is not our fantasy of the early people; it is the spiritual projection of a new life, it is the baby angel. In those early times of angelic baby worship there was no remorse, as recovery from anything is faster when one has the nature of a baby.

Throughout generations of life experience, however, the human descendants of the Red Baby lost their honest nature and became deceptive. Gradually they became discouraged by what they had become and how they lived, so they created social religions. Later, these organizations proved insufficient to manage the new human animals whose blood had become thick with alcohol, drugs and other poisons, and so rules, regulations and laws were created.

The period between 1000 BCE and 2000 CE, marked the entrance of this new stage of life where people lived with a false social order. People relied on a dishonest culture with religions, professional priests, kings, queens, soldiers, policemen and so forth to guard against the harm caused from humanity's downfall.

Religions were created to cover the ugly nature of some people, but once the symptoms of a disease are covered, it is difficult to clean and heal the corrupt nature. Some aspects of religions are actually part of society's trouble.

The appearance of human life with a highly developed conscious mind is made possible by natural potential. The step-by-step process of human development is the result of natural evolution. When your spirit advances to follow the positive trace of evolution, and your spirit manages your mind, life is happy. However, when your mind pushes your spirit and becomes over extended, spiritual devolution results. This can be observed in the world today.

The Worship of New Life

The worship of new life gives high support to your life. Life itself is God. You do not have to separate your life from God and worship life's shadow. Life is served by your honest efforts towards realistic development; it is not served by fantasy. Essentially, the initiating spirit of life is life's foremost spiritual quality. It should be respected as God. It is religious fantasy to say that something can be done once-and-for-all. The world needs renewing, just as life in any stage of development needs renewing. This is the way you can improve your life.

Each day is a new beginning, as mother Earth rotates around the sun. As earthlings we can enjoy the newness of the sky and of life. Under the light of the Heavenly Father sun we can face everything as new. When we live with the freshness of new life, we need not worry about exhaustion. To say that there is nothing new under the sun indicates a defeated and spoiled emotion. Can that present the truth of life?

Every seven years of your physical life, new cells replace the old cells of your body. This is not a myth. Therefore do not reminisce on the past, but rejoice in the new life of an endless future. Life is great when you are young, so who says you are old? Look forward in your life and follow the Heavenly Father sun to enjoy life's neverending freshness.

The sun in the sky is the religion of life. It makes no sense to worry about the Heavenly Father sun, as it is constantly renewing itself. Life can never be defeated. Life means to overcome, to develop and to grow. Life lives with a fresh spirit when encountering any situation or obstacle. Similarly, you can move forward courageously, and pass over whatever is in your way to follow the Centermost Way of Everlasting Life.[1]

The sky is a life, the Earth is a life and you are a life. You have these life companions that keep the life of the universe going endlessly on. To discover the universal connection of your life, read the sky with its light and stars, and read the Earth by its seasonal changes. Have no fear, you have great company in your life, and together you can reach the bigger life of the cosmos.

The Spirit in life is everlasting. The Spirit in life is immortal. The Spirit in life is eternal. Do not degrade your life's Spirit by your bad emotions, your sad sentiments or by your negative thoughts gathered from your rough experiences. These things can actually help you grow. They are the nutrition for your eternal life.

Respect and worship the Spirit in your life. Do not scatter yourself, but praise and bow to your life's Spirit with grace. Be with the Spirit of life and enjoy its life in you. You are great because the Spirit in your life is great. Never shame the Spirit in your life. It is a great pity to believe you are produced by something other than life's subtle essence.

The Spirit in your life may appear to be tiny, but it can be the size of your life or it can be the size of the universe, connecting to all. It all depends on you and whether you grow normally or limit yourself due to narrow self-interests.

1. Refer to Hua-Ching Ni's book *The Centermost Way*.

The Spirit is in you and in other people. Respect the oneness of the numerous life spirits in you. There is no separation between the real spirits in life, though their form and function may differ. Love your life, respect your life and worship the everlastingness of your life. Be with the Spirit in your life. Be with the Spirit of universal life.

The Love of Life

You are taught to love God. This is correct because universal life is God. You are taught to love people. This is correct because people are part of universal life.

You are taught to love your king or queen. If life is normal, there is nothing wrong with this because your small life needs a king or queen to coordinate it. Some people have been taught not to love their life or the lives of others, but without the love of life, what is the value of life?

Regard enjoyment as a matter of loving life. Some people are better at this than others. The developed should learn from the undeveloped. The rich should learn from the poor. The more educated should learn from the less educated.

Love your life by the waterside.
Love your life in the mountains.
Love your life in the wilderness.
Love your life in the garden.
That's all easy to do.
Learn to love your life in the work place too.
Love your life at sunrise.
Love your life at sunset.
Love your life in the twilight.
Love your life in the evening.

Love your life in each moment with spiritual awareness,
and be dutiful in your life.
Love your life with the tides.
Love your life with the flying clouds.
Love your life under the moon.
Love your life with the stars.
Love your life while watching the city smog too.
Love your life with song.
Love your life with prose.
Love your life with poetry.
Love your life with dancing.
Love your life with music.
Love your life with a silent mind,
and love your life in quietude.

Love your life, and love all life.

Many people love their lives by spoiling their lives. It is far better to love your life with self-discipline. Loving life means keeping away from extremes. Avoid fighting meaningless battles and needless arguments.

Generally once society develops, life's happiness decreases. You can make positive progress if you can reduce your life's pressures. What else would you like to extend your interest to?

Human society has become very tense due to the social design of crooked-minded individuals. Your personal life has become tight too. Supposedly, slavery is no longer imposed, but beware: there are numerous slaveries of life that chain you under different names.

The Ambition and Goal of
the Path of Constructive Life

No one individual can save the world, and although this may be an individual's concern, it is hard to make it become the interest of all. Individuals can heal their own lives though. No matter what happens, you can still do something about your own life and connect with those of similar understanding, as a spiritual connection to all people's lives. You need to be firm and strong so you are not carried away by the world.

The PCL is your social connection. It carries the understanding that no single individual can change the world, but an individual can be a model for the world. An individual can choose their culture and select how to guide their life so as to enjoy its healthy activities. The healthy side of life is your life's model. May other people appreciate your model of persistently realizing the health of the world.

The Teacher of Sun Light

The various rituals and emotional shows taught by conventional religions are mere dramas. Spiritual learning is different from acting.

A spiritual teacher is not hypocritical. They bravely live with the plain truth of life, and remain in a normal, benign range that differs from that of the sick and false culture. A teacher, no matter what their age, has the nature of a baby—his or her heart is always young and naïve. They do not deviate from a natural life nor diverge from their spiritual pursuit.

Some students may have difficulty accepting the truthfulness of a spiritual teacher, or they may be disappointed because they expect a skilled actor. A teacher accepts all people as good, and overlooks the fact that people have different expectations of him or her. A teacher is in harmony with the spiritual aspect of life. They do not pretend nor try to please the seeker. They may not guard themselves against all worldly traps, however, so certain students or friends can trick them. An individual should not try to take advantage of the teacher's naivety or innocence though, because the Universal Subtle Law will respond as quickly as thunder to lightening.

The Role of a Teacher of Light

A teacher loves their students and offers appropriate instruction according to the specific occasion, their intuition, or the request of the student.

A student follows the teacher and offers the necessary support and assistance to his or her teaching activities.

There should be no unclear financial matters between the teacher and the students. Therefore, there should be no lending or borrowing between them and if there is, it should be quickly resolved.

There should be no business connections or sexual relations between the teacher and the students as this only leads to confusion.

Students shouldn't abuse the teacher's time and life force for their personal service.

Students should not argue with the teacher, although they can request an explanation from him or her.

Students should not visit the teacher without his or her permission.

Students should respect the teacher's privacy, as the teacher has his or her own life to prepare.

Students can be promoted as coaches. A coach is a form of teacher who donates some weekly time to public service.

Assistants can be elected to take care of the teacher's practical matters.

The Healthy Relationship Between a Spiritual Teacher and Their Students

In the natural order, the teacher is equal to the sky and the sun, and the students are equal to the Earth and the moon. The fulfillment of mutual help between the teacher and their students can be explained by the natural relationships in the five element system. This system classifies five patterns of nature, as learned from the Earth, and describes how these five patterns, or phases of energy, move through a cyclic process of transformation. The phases move in a ceaseless cycle that flows from water to wood to fire to earth to metal, and back to water to start over again.

In this system, the teacher is like the elements of water and earth, whose duties are to nurture the life of the vegetation. The students are like the vegetation, whose duty is to preserve the water and the land. The teacher offers heavenly love and care to the students, and the students offer earthly fellowship and friendly love and care to the teacher.

Among Fellow Students

In the modern world, the legal system is abused. In the spiritual family of the Integral Way, each person is shaped with justice, uprightness and righteousness. No one should try to wrong the other. Emotional exercise is not encouraged. Students' should not argue with one another, though they may ask each other for help. If a misunderstanding arises, it is better that one party yields to the other so as not to disturb the health of one another. If a serious argument occurs, arbitration is best adopted; however, if a student insists on litigating they need to withdraw from the spiritual family.

The Rules of Nature

The three basic rules of human life are learned from the sky. In normal situations, it is the natural order that people should listen to their king or queen, children should listen to their parents, and spouses should listen to one another.

The standard principles of the five basic human relationships are derived from the philosophical recognition of the five element system in nature. You will see how this system influenced the lives of the early people.

In the beginning of human society, there were no rules and regulations and there was no need to create any. It was a time when the natural order of life was followed. As society grew, so did rules and regulations. Human society slowly became rigid and mechanical. To reestablish the organic social condition of ancient times, the first thing to restore is the natural order of human relationships.

Early people shaped the first social rules about relationships from family life. In the natural order, the head of a family, the head of a clan and later the king or queen of a society, or a teacher, could be female or male. Later on, the active men filled these positions more often. It then became the new conceptual habit to symbolize the males only, including the brothers in a family, as the sky or the sun. The mother, the female head of the clan, and later, the queen, the female teacher and the sisters of a family, were likened to the Earth and the moon.

Early society's important conception of orderliness was taken from nature's example whereby the moon follows the Earth, the Earth follows the sky and the sun, and the sun follows the North Star, which is the remote spiritual connection of human beings.

In a modern spiritual community, the Natural Law may be the most appropriate law to apply and express the natural order and spiritual connection between a teacher and their students. The teacher is therefore likened to the sky and the sun, and students to the Earth and moon.

Six thousand years ago, human society was shaped around the following three lines according to the natural order. As the Earth follows the sun, the ministers were required to follow the queen or king, and the children were required to follow or obey their parents. As the sun follows the North Star, the children were required to respect their ancestors as a natural development from the relationship between the parents and the children. And, as the moon follows the Earth, the man was required to follow the woman, and the woman was required to follow the man, depending on the situation.

Then, around 2200 BCE, Emperor Shun developed the teaching of the five inter-relationships among all people. These are:

Ministers should express loyalty to their king or queen.

Between a husband and wife there should be faithfulness.

Children should express filial piety to their parents.

Between siblings there should be love and respect.

Among friends there should be friendly love.

Those five relationships also correspond to the natural, material aspects of the Earth. Therefore, the relationship between the king or queen and the people is like water: the king or queen supply and guide all lives to benefit each other. The relationship between parents and children is like the trees: the life of the younger trees is derived from the bigger, older trees. The relationship between husband and wife is like fire: they give one another warmth and mental stimulation, and it is from this basic relationship that human civilization began. The relationship among brothers and sisters is like the earth or soil: they are equally connected and mutually support each other. The relationship among friends is like metal: they help shape and guide one another with spontaneous, friendly advice.

The relationship between a teacher and student contains the five elements mentioned. However, this relationship is most similar to that between a king or queen and their people, parents and their children, friends and siblings.

Can a husband and wife be teachers to each other? Whether you are a man or woman in a marriage, it is preferable to adopt the attitude of a pupil in order to get help from your spouse. Generally though the woman is the smarter pupil, when she conducts herself gently to teach the real pupil of the male ego to effectively melt its strength.

Have you heard the saying that behind every great man there is a great woman? That great woman is the wife or mother. Men like to think they are the source of light, like the sun, and women are reflectors, like the moon. Truthfully, the real order of relationship is not so exact; it depends on the situation. Whether one finds an emotional competitor or a partner of understanding in the home depends upon how one approaches situations.

In ancient China, human society was an Integral Way society. Its teachers were natural social leaders who taught and applied the Way of Heaven and the Way of Earth to human life. Those teachers integrated the natural benefit of both ways in human life. China was thus a natural society long before it was a formalized country, and the natural law was the soul of its social order. Later, as society grew, the position of queen or king replaced that of teacher or sage. Once society reached that stage, its social leaders had lost their natural wisdom, merely mechanically following the rules and regulations of earlier convention.

Chapter 18

The Heavenly Way, the Earthly Way
and the Integral Way

The Heavenly Way is the spiritual relationship between the sky and the people. It has been interpreted in my booklet titled *Heavenly Way*. The Earthly Way is the five elementary phases of Life that symbolize earthly life. It has a creative or supportive order and a counterbalancing order (see fig. 1 below). The Integral Way is the symbolic expression of life. The Integral Way, with peoples' cooperation and management, integrates the Heavenly Way and the Earthly Way. The Integral Way therefore comprises the Way of Heaven, the Way of Earth and the

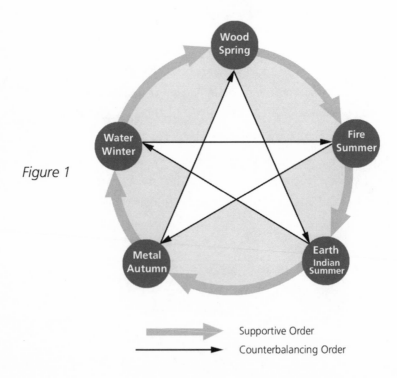

Figure 1

Supportive Order
Counterbalancing Order

Way of the learning and development of all people. The PCL values simplicity over complication.

As we previously mentioned, the five element system is the symbolic presentation of the theory of interdependence of Great Nature, and it is also the theory of circulating Nature. Although this system is simple, its vision is profound.

In the creative order of the five elements: Water gives life to vegetation. Vegetation or wood gives life to fire. Fire gives life to ash and soil. The soil or earth gives life to metal and metal gives life to or gathers water. The climacteric correspondences or expressions of the five elements are as follows: winter=water; spring=vegetation or wood; summer=fire; prolonged or Indian summer=earth and autumn=metal.

The Supportive Order and
Its Corresponding Manifestations

Water transforms to become vegetation, which corresponds to kindness, the season of spring and the relationship between parents and children, and between teacher and students.

Vegetation or wood transforms to become fire or warmth, which corresponds to love and civilization, the season of summer, and the relationship between social leaders and their followers, and between teacher and students.

Fire transforms to become the soil or earth, which corresponds to faithfulness, the season of summer or Indian summer, and the relationship between husbands and wives, and between teacher and students.

The soil or earth transforms to become metals and minerals, which corresponds to friendly love, the season of autumn, and the relationship between brothers and sisters and between teacher and students.

Metals and minerals transform to become water, which corresponds to wisdom and nurturing the student's potential for development and growth, the season of winter, and the relationship of spontaneous mutual discipline between friends, as well as between a teacher and their students.

The Counterbalancing Order and Its Corresponding Manifestations

Winter

Water controls or counterbalances Fire, which relates to dynamic and creative energy. Emotional application: to moderate excessive emotions, for example, curb anger.

This is the function of the teacher.

Equivalence: to control summer with winter=to control heat with cold.

Spring

Vegetation counterbalances the Soil, which relates to absorbing and transforming energy.

Emotional application: to be socially constructive and supportive, for example to be selective in accepting social influences.

This is the function of the student.

Equivalence: to control prolonged summer with spring=to reduce heat to be warm.

Summer

Fire controls or counterbalances Metal, which relates to reforming and forging energy.

Emotional application: to balance self-interest and social benefit, for example, avoid self-indulgence and cruelty.

This is the function of the teacher.

Equivalence: to control autumn with summer=to control coolness with heat.

Prolonged Summer or Indian Summer

Soil counterbalances Water, which relates to storing and releasing energy.

Emotional application: to apply healthy, firm control and restraint, for example, don't overdo or over extend.

This is the function of the student.

Equivalence: to control winter with prolonged summer=to control cold with heat.

Autumn

Metal counterbalances Vegetation, which relates to creating and grooming energy.

Emotional application: to apply temperance to oneself and in social relationships, for example to practice sobriety and moderation.

This is the function of the teacher.

Equivalence: to control spring with autumn=to control warmth with some coolness.

Subtlety and Atmospheres

Science finds ways to measure and establish standards in order to regulate the communication and behavior of people.

In Chinese culture, the term *chi* or *qi* is frequently used. It mostly expresses three different things: the vitality of life, the emotional condition, and the atmosphere of a specific internal or external environment. In English, the word "mood" is used to express a temporary internal emotional condition, but the internal atmosphere of a life actually represents the condition of one's health for a much longer stage.

Spirituality is the subtle reality of life. External religions are so defined because they depend on external things such as the specific design and layout of buildings, the priests and so forth, to tell people that God lives there. The priests and their devotees live according to a specific lifestyle. They depend on the creation of a specific atmosphere that is suggestive or creative of a feeling of worship. The feeling is yours, but the atmosphere conducts you. In European countries churches were used in this way. The creation of a specific atmosphere induces people to behave differently in church than in their daily activities.

The religious books, altars, statues, uniforms and language that differ from other kinds of communication and are used to create a specific atmosphere, are all artificial creations. They differ vastly from the deep inner spiritual development and growth that the PCL encourages people to pursue. The conscious religious forms with their subtle energy fields can either support or harm the growth of the soul.

Most religious teachings are immature. Some are even harmful, as in the examples of the Davidians of Waco, the Heavenly Gate of San Diego, and some of the new age teachings of the last 50 years. In those situations people looked for a better life, but that life was promoted by emotional causes. Your appreciation and trust of the PCL should come from your own growth, rather than any emotional preference. Through spiritual learning and growth, the PCL encourages you to develop the subtle power of discernment to see into the depth of any teaching, so you can avoid spiritual harm and entrapment. Discernment gives you the intuitive strength to help yourself and others.

Religions are mostly for people who don't know how to manage their time, at least in a harmless direction. That is how religions become popular. A religion represents the spiritual expression of a group of people. Different buildings for spiritual purpose create an atmosphere as if a different spiritual reality exists there. Which one is more truthful and which one is less truthful? How are people able to define the indefinable spirituality of life? All external religion is storytelling. The different designs that attract people become the very things that people will argue and fight over. Yet, in reality, such differences are nonexistent.

The important point is this: The spirituality of human life is naturally unified. The origin of spirituality is the same inexpressible subtle essence both in the beginning and final stages of life. The various expressions people present, truthfully do not exist in the subtle substance. What is more important to an individual's health is whether the internal atmosphere of their life is in harmony or conflict. A healthy internal atmosphere can be created and conditioned by good healthy thoughts, a strong conscience and healthy life behavior.

Conventional religions, nonetheless, can offer some positive service. Their external settings can positively affect your thoughts and offer some suggestion of peace. However, more importantly, you need to know that you are composed of multiple spiritual entities and different spiritual qualities, which affect and manage your inner life. If you do not manage your spirits properly, your inner life will become a den of beasts. Therefore you need a spiritual ruler in your life. People name and use God, Allah, or the divine Buddha and such like, as the spiritual ruler of their lives. These names can perform an important service for the religious practitioner, if he or she realizes that these names all represent the same unnamable Reality that is the subtle substance within and outside of their life.

Maoshing and I, as individuals who come from a family of global spiritual concern, suggest accepting the constructive customs of conventional religions. Their popular spiritual services can be monitored by their positive contribution to world spiritual health. Those customs can be acknowledged as Level One to help shape the ethical condition and basic social code of people. They can also be used in preparation for the spiritual upliftment of Level Two.

The promotion of external beliefs and the attempt to unify worldly spiritual expressions by force and for socially competitive ends, demonstrates a low spiritual quality rather than a developed one. It is improper and spiritually unhealthy to draw fervent people into war and believers into social religious struggle. There is no positive purpose in this religious behavior. Using aggression and force to conquer and bend others to your will is just a different expression; it does not change or affect the Reality within life.

A suitable expression for the inexpressible Universal Spiritual Unity is the Universal Divine One. It implies universal spiritual oneness and opens the way for global spiritual agreement between all spiritual customs and experience. This spiritual principle and attitude confirms the value of each custom and represents the climax of Level One practice. You may refer to the books *The Concourse of All Spiritual Paths, From Diversity to Unity* and *The Essence of Universal Spirituality* for a further understanding of this principle.

Modern science with its common external measurements is a cultural product of the West. Early people in ancient China discovered the five element system of classification and used it to describe the quality of an atmosphere. Understanding the subtle atmosphere of a specific building, location or region, as well as the inner quality of an individual's character, is one of the many applications of the five element system, and is specifically known as the art of *fengshui*. You can also manufacture an atmosphere by choosing and combining certain colors, arrangements and other things to create what you desire, but a cultured atmosphere is unnatural. What is natural is the truth in life itself.

The five element system can be used to symbolically describe the atmosphere of people and things. It also gives expression to the cyclical movement of nature, and can be used to tell whether a situation is harmonious or conflicting. It gives Chinese medicine and personality analysis a frame of reference from which to express and control subtle changes. As a real service, this system is worthy of further research and study.

The Real Destiny and the False Destiny

After going through the surface level of the different spiritual customs, we now introduce a higher level. This level, Level Two, is related to the deeper spiritual effort of humankind. Its more profound reality should be explored.

Your life is not completely managed by your mind or intellect. Looking at the bigger picture, your life is managed by your internal spiritual qualities. But spiritually, your mind can be a thief that is mistakenly trusted as the son of your life and expected to faithfully carry out your wishes. The mind is not capable of doing this. The mind has a tendency to betray your life by going against your life's subtle spiritual nature or surpassing it. Spiritually your mind is over ambitious. By relying on your mind, the spiritual foundation of your life becomes confused. To truly serve life, your mind should be the servant of your life's subtle nature, which is the True Lord or Allah.

Napoleon, Hitler and Saddam Hussein were once very powerful individuals whose minds were above many who lived at the same time. They were extremely capable at creating tragedy for people. They also bought a tragic end to their own lives. Why? Because by merely following the mind, an individual cannot be sure what type of reward or punishment they will invite. However, by following the constructive nature of life an individual will not end up wasting their life. This simple statement expresses the truth of life, and can be trusted as an observation made by many people throughout history.

There are two kinds of spiritual qualities in life: the positive quality and the negative quality. Most people are a mixture of the two. Normally, people are born with a 70 to 30 percent ratio between the negative and positive spiritual qualities respectively. Sages are born with a higher ratio, and may have difficulty living on the general plane of life. People born below that ratio tend to have strong troubles or criminal tendencies. As the ratio changes, the condition of life varies.

Spiritual learning can be of two kinds. The external religious kind relies on creating an external atmosphere that may offer people some emotional support; however their beliefs cannot produce any real spiritual constructive effect. The real spiritual work, the second kind of learning, is about changing the internal spiritual quality of your life, which in turn can change the internal atmosphere and the external results of your living.

Life is sometimes like driving a car in heavy freeway traffic: impulsive and hasty actions are unhealthy spiritual qualities. If these qualities suddenly emerge while driving, even if you are a good driver, you know what could happen to yourself and others on the road. It is more important that you refine your unhealthy spiritual qualities, rather than beseech help from an external divinity or from another external agent.

Now you can see the difference between real spiritual work and merely arranging an external atmosphere. Though people are generally entertained by different ceremonial activities, these have no serious meaning except to serve your emotion.

You should also know that accidental trouble is related to your internal spiritual quality. For example, a movie star, at her mind's subconscious suggestion, flushed her diamond ring down the toilet. Although she immediately regretted this, she could not recover the ring despite spending a great deal on plumbing. This accident is similar to how most accidents occur, such as car accidents. People don't notice that their worst enemy is pre-stored in their lives.

Each year there are a big number of malpractice suits whereby well-trained physicians and nurses are troubled by serious mistakes. Sometimes the mistake or accident, which may be fatal, is made when the upper conscious mind slips to one side, and the subconscious mind suddenly takes over. If you are the head of a big group of people, such as the captain of the Titanic, you have a big responsibility and you can understand the trouble that could happen by listening to the subconscious mind. Morally natured or highly trained individuals may sometimes be tricked by people and, as a result, may lose the trust of their public and their spiritual confidence. The trouble occurs when their upper conscious mind is raised too high, suppressing their lower conscious mind.

Have you heard the saying that for every inch of positive spiritual progress the obstacles in your life grow a hundred-fold? My book, *The Story of Two Kingdoms*, metaphorically describes the inner marriage between a person's internal spiritual entities as the real spiritual cultivation. Most people are anxious for a life partner, but they ignore their life's inner dual condition. Inside your life you have a subtle internal partner that has a stronger need to unite your life's upper and lower conscious departments, which are the different groups of spiritual entities inside of you.

Spiritual learning is related to the improvement of the mind. Practically, guide your mind to be an enlightened ruler of life rather than a muddle-headed monarch. The wise ones, who lived before written history, observed that it is more important to attain internal harmony and internal cooperation in your life than be a powerful monarch with a throne. As Lao Tzu stated, he would rather be a simpleton than a smart guy.

Look at today's people, the more they develop their minds, the more they dwarf their spirits. This imbalance brings suffering to their lives as well as many other lives, which is a great disaster. A simpleton is hard to be: the wisdom then is not to extend the pursuit to becoming perfect.

The subconscious department of your mind can be trained and reformed. That is the wonder of life. The PCL is based on the fact that in our lives we have predispositions for trouble, but we can guide these departments and subdepartments in a constructive direction.

All people have an internal holy war to wage. Unfortunately most attach to their upper conscious mind as the monarch of their lives, and so the spiritual side of their lives goes unnoticed. People don't know that among their internal spiritual groups some are more physical and emotional. If you study criminology, you will see that when one side of life suddenly rushes to do something that is improper, the other side of life suffers an undeserved punishment. One must then accept responsibility for that improper or impulsive behavior.

In all world cultures there are the conceptions of fate, fortune and destiny. Though there are predictable big outlines that can be told in fortune reading, the real fortune is the spiritual one. You see many people who just before reaching success, suddenly fail. This is because of a spiritual mistake. Our teaching recommends that you prevent yourselves from possible mistakes, like you would defend your lives from an enemy attack. The unification of your personality at the spiritual level also involves recognizing that the quality of your lifestyle affects your life's spiritual quality. This is why spiritual self-inspection and self-cultivation are your real spiritual duties.

Using the *I Ching* can assist your understanding of your subconscious condition. The fundamental principles that underlie the lines and words can be used to govern your life. With your development, these same principles can be used to govern the world. Personal divination can help you understand your condition and offer you possible improvement. It is not enough to simply use it for predicting worldly matters.

The rules you learn from deeply studying the principles of change include the good changes, the bad changes and the no change. Each one of the 64 hexagrams represents one of 64 types of images or atmospheres of the abstract condition of your subconscious mind. The suggestion it gives is limited by your personal mental conditioning. Your interpretation also depends on your personal experience and development. It may take many years to wholly understand the sentence you receive from a divination. Even so the principles behind the hexagrams can save you from trouble, help you develop an undefeatable personality, and enjoy a long and happy life.

The beneficial use of the *I Ching* is for teaching; it is not a system for choosing strategies. You can look at the situation presented by the specific hexagram in relation to your condition and learn from its teaching, rather than go to the individual lines that describe good or bad fortune. The lines represent the different stages of the development of an event; they are merely a situational aspect of the whole. If you are attached to the line reading, you will become trivial-minded. Through generations of *I Ching* study, the most valuable conclusion is: be constructive in your life.

The Climax of Human Life

Level One is helpful for those people who need guidance in living. Level Two is the best focus for those who have grown intellectually and who don't want to stay on life's surface. People who have outgrown their conventional backgrounds may appreciate the 50-plus publications of the Universal Integral Way, which were written for people's deep spiritual support. The universal religion, known as the PCL, is the climax of those works. Among them there are a few titles suitable for those who aspire to spiritual immortality or what is generally known as an Everlasting Life. This introduces Level Three. There is no need to apply levels when one makes human health the standard of life, but the fact is there are people who need direction, thus levels can be used to assist them.

The purpose of religions is to protect people's spiritual health. Unfortunately, some religious leaders pushed too hard and created the Dark Ages in the West. Throughout generations, all religions have produced what is known as the religious paranoid or fundamentalist person who splits the spiritual unity of humanity. Intellectual development is best used to protect the health of life, but, unfortunately, the intellectually paranoid person has made enormous mistakes in society, as we can see from the effects of communism in the last century.

Human life is the bridge between the spiritual and the material view of the universe. It is also a frontier of exploration and is as important as the physical and spiritual spheres. Based on the early classification, the three frontiers of life are equally valuable in universal existence.

Human life is not limited to descriptions in anatomy, physiology, biochemistry, psychology and parapsychology etc. Nothing can be put directly under one framework of established human knowledge. The focus of our oral and written communications is to help you break away from the paranoia of established knowledge. Still, further efforts need to be made as deep spiritual experience or achievement is a personal and nontransferable phenomenon. Modern parapsychology supports the paranormal fact that the human mind can move objects around, but human life can do much more than that. It can bilocate or multilocate as traditionally termed. Therefore, there is life outside a life, and there is life inside a life.

In our previous discussion, we touched upon how people can be troubled by their subconscious. The religious path, or Level One, is needed to give guidance on the conscious level of life, and spiritual cultivation is encouraged for general life support. In Level Three, what is generally known as the subconscious mind can be renamed to be life's spiritual asset. It is the hidden spiritual potential of life. What is impossible for the upper conscious mind becomes possible with the cooperation and development of both the conscious and the subconscious mind. Here, higher and further development depends on one's personal efforts.

It has been proved that people can fast for many years and survive. Chen Tuan[1] and many others are examples. What supports the survival of the physical life? If you are not intellectually paranoid as to insist on the views of modern nutrition you may consider the following. When the soul and the body stay together there is the phenomenon of life. However, the soul and the body can also live separately and revive as in resurrection, the length of which can vary from 49 days to three years. This was the basis of the early Christians' belief that the deceased faithful would sleep in their tombs and revive for the last judgment of Father God. In ancient China, the early people experienced the same spiritual phenomena, so they developed the custom of burying their deceased, unlike other groups, which burned their dead. In some ways, these actions reflect different views of the nature of death. How do you define death? Is it based on a medical certificate? How long is your death certificate valid?

The body can undergo a variety of transformations in death. There may be a half-conscious commanded explosion whereby the body transforms to colored vapor, and then disappears leaving some remnants such as hair, fingernails or toenails, or nothing at all. There are also those individuals who are able to shrink their life to become very, very small. Both styles of transformation are a lifetime achievement. They demonstrate how the form of life can be commanded by the will of life, and that death is not necessarily a reflection of weakness and sickness.

---

1. Refer to Hua-Ching Ni's book *The Life and Teachings of Two Immortals, Volume 2.*

Understand that your life experiences and intellectual education need not limit you. Life is great. Life is composed of tremendous natural potency and is much more than you imagine. As modern people, you have been trained and educated to pay bills and receive a paycheck. This is the cocoon the social designers spin for you. Yet your life is unlimited. It is not a political birthright that you need to fight for and win. Life is the natural birthright to develop and challenge your life's present condition in each moment. But, generally, the freedom you pursue is a political or a financial one. Do you really think you have all the freedom of life?

There is one type of freedom you have never imagined. That is the freedom to command the subtle level of your being to transform into a solid, physical being that you call life. In just a second, you can assemble and disassemble your physical being. In no time at all you can vanish before people's eyes. The assembly and disassembly of the physical form can take place in the snap of your fingers. Back and forth, back and forth, just like an exercise or sports game. You have the potential to transform. This freedom of life is worthy of your endeavor. Instead, you argue too much and fight too much for things of little worth.

Most people think that the ancient developed ones had no science. Yet they had their different pursuits and breakthroughs—unlike most of your lives, which have been controlled since birth by the cage of knowledge. You live in the cage of knowledge and are fed by bird feeders. You do not even know that there is a sky. Please appreciate when we say to you that there is a sky for your life to fly in.

The universe is a big life. She is active and lively, and she is on a continual path of evolution or sublimation. Evolution and sublimation is the nature of the universe, and is how the universe internally generates her life. The spiral movement is her physical exercise. The Way, on the one hand, is the subtle essence with its innate universal operation and, on the other hand, is the evolutionary processes of universal nature. The essence of universal life with its natural attributes leads the changes in the forms of life. What Darwin collected was only partial evidence of how the external form changes. He didn't see that the entire nature is on an evolutionary path, which is the Way.

Human life is a small part of the universal big life. As a miniature model of the universe, we take part in its big evolutionary path. We have no way of refusing evolution. Change and mutation happen to us naturally, both internally and externally. The specific spiritual achievements of some individuals, however, are not for everybody. Though it is the established truth that the potential for spiritual achievement is the same whether people are ancient or recent, except for those few who are spiritually defective.

The pursuit of spiritual life is not a one-time whim, and it may not suit everyone. Personal spiritual achievement may take many lifetimes. Some individuals, such as Chen Tuan mentioned above, reached a high stage of spiritual evolution. You are in a different time and a different social environment, wherein most people's lives are spiritually devolving. We offer you six guidelines on how to help your life rise higher.

(1) Value your life. It has taken a very long time and many troubles to come to this point in your life. Life is a continual process; you will be raised high again.

(2) If you do not fail your life, your life will never fail you. What is the you? It is your conditioned mind. What is your life? It is the Integrated Being of all spirits from the different parts of your life—the God in life.

(3) Live your life constructively. No matter what has happened to you, keep the root of your life healthy and firm and your life's tree will grow and flourish.

(4) Life is immortal. It follows an evolutionary path. Evolution is a natural momentum; all other things in life are just ado. The universe is immortal. The formations from its subtle essence change and vary continuously.

(5)   The physical form of life is a temporary or "passing-through" experience. All experiences are illusory. Generally, people live with illusions having never woken up to the essence of their life. Their life experiences, whether good or bad, and their social connections are all illusions and unreal. People are happy with those illusions when they don't cause big problems, and they are unhappy once they become troublesome as a result of their own pickiness and fussiness. That is the big fault in life. Replace your bitter mind and big ego with a forgiving one. Otherwise, you have to be open to a life that serves and takes the suffering brought about by your undeveloped mind.

It may take you some time to outgrow your attachment to illusions. When you do, you may be able to live with the deep truth of life. So far, people do not know what that truth is. It does not come from schoolbooks or superficial observation. You may discover it through your own efforts of a constructive life and appropriate spiritual self-cultivation. Once you begin to live an everlasting life there is no shame in life.

(6)   The highest stage of spiritual evolution is to be light-bodied.

PART III

Fulfill Your Relationships with Harmony, Peace and Compassion

Chapter 19

The World Needs Correct Spiritual Leadership

Spiritual leadership is traditionally the correct function and duty of a religion. Today, religions have lost this function because their teachings have fallen behind the modern conditions of life and the intellectual growth of people. This loss of spiritual leadership has created worldwide spiritual confusion and trouble.

The truth central to all religions is harmony among all people. If a religion is competitive and cannot promote peace locally or globally, it loses its leadership function.

A good spiritual faith works to support the decent living of all people. It assists people in learning how to value and nurture life, with the miraculous effect of helping them overcome difficulties. From this foundation an orderly and progressive society may be built. Confusion arises when religions destroy people's faith in doing and being good. The worse thing is to use the divine name for war and killing. In these circumstances it is easy for humans, who have evolved from animals, to slip back to the old ways of beastly cruelty, and lose thousands of years of spiritual evolution.

Conventional religionists have taken advantage of people's social nature by pushing them to join their artificial establishments. As part of their promotional skill, they exalt the good from the bad, and the believer from the nonbeliever. As a result, people begin to divide and the seeds of hatred and separation are sown.

A real spiritual life does not separate. A real spiritual life achieves kindness, and has none of the discriminating boundaries promoted by conventional religions. Do not be discouraged by all this trouble. It is important to admit the trouble, and ensure that you do not add any fuel of your own. Ordinary individuals like you and I can make a difference.

Conventional religions need to update in order to progress. So, too, do the modern trends of science and intellectual education, which are a result of only partial use of the brain. People of the world need a good form, a good religion, to help them realize their potential of high development, both personally and for the world. The religion we envision, known as the Path of Constructive Life, is to be a global spiritual effort with help from all people who resonate with the task.

The PCL guides you to live a decent and natural life based on your innate moral sense, and through understanding and embodying the true meaning of freedom, equality and independence. It encourages you to cultivate your spirit and grow to ensure the continual development of your life. Its central theme is to guide you away from the negatively discriminating mindset that causes tension and the severing of humanistic connections.

The high qualities of freedom, equality and independence should operate alongside your conscience. That is, your high moral sense should lead you in life as you practice those qualities to ensure that you do no harm to others. It is essential that your high moral sense leads because it is easy to contort freedom, equality and independence into expanded emotions and use them as excuses for unlimited selfish whims. These concepts can even be used to reject others who think differently, whether or not those others possess a strong moral sense in life.

An overly exalted freedom of expression in life without appropriate responsibility cannot replace a high moral sense. How can today's leaders mend the broken elements of society by promising equality and democracy, as if everyone were a king or queen from the old days? Having natural rights does not mean that you disrespect the rights of others. How ironic that after lifting the constraints of a rigid morality imposed by old political systems and religions, the modern practice of individuality sets out to reject others with the same arrogant demand.

Freedom, equality and independence have been used to challenge despotic authorities to bring about social change. They became the foundation for new demo-

cratic societies governed by God-fearing people, who promised freedom of expression to all. Eventually, the church-based society shifted to an intellectually
educated one, and schools began replacing churches. Freedom, equality and independence have been used as slogans in social revolutions to challenge oppressive
religious cultures and political systems. Yet socially these concepts can be inappropriately used. As tempting slogans, they can turn people back into wild animals.
Many examples can be found among teenagers and adults alike. Once the emotional foundation of a society is shaken, the promised free expression of life can
incite wrongdoing. Hence a child can bring a gun to school and shoot whomever
he or she dislikes. Or an adult can murder people in public places because he or she
happened to be emotionally frustrated.

In modern democratic societies, people argue repetitively in defense of their
personal rights without giving equal attention to their social duty. The stable
foundation of a democracy should be based on the strong moral sense of each
individual. The most basic sense of morality is the respect for life. Do modern
leaders know how to help people regain the respect of a gentle and effective
personality? Freedom, equality and independence are important spiritual qualities of a natural life. They are the high spiritual qualities in the good life of
developed people.

True freedom means being free from fear and jealousy. True equality lies in recognizing that you have the same opportunity to achieve your life as sages have, or
that your life is as equally valuable as the spiritual models of ancient times. True
independence is having clear judgment. It is the spiritual achievement enjoyed
by spiritually developed individuals. The foundation and enjoyment of a spiritually good life stems from a trouble-free conscience that has no moral burden.

In the attainment of spiritual freedom, equality and independence, there are no
rules to resort to and there is no need for any specific discipline. Such attainment
was the single pursuit of the ancient people of the Way.

We wish to make it clear that freedom, equality and independence are the qualities of highly achieved souls who know that maintaining personal health, and being happy in life are personal spiritual duties. No one should wait for the government to keep their heater on in winter or make them happy. Overly socialized societies expect social solutions for everything. Socially, particularly internationally, the moral sense of life should be the leader above all. This moral sense can be developed through spiritual self-cultivation.

The genuine spiritual development of people cannot be replaced by religions that are mere social customs and social painkillers. Nor can politics or an intellectual education, which merely teaches one how to make a living, replace spiritual teaching.

Spiritual pursuit and development is available to all individuals. Real spiritual pursuit involves the achievement of three things: the freedom to forgive, equal mindedness in all situations, and spiritual independence whereby one does not rely on anything or anyone for their spiritual worth.

The teaching of the PCL does not create a fear of God, or prepare people to accept some kind of social rule. It guides you back to respect your life through the natural love of life. You become free from the hostility and hatred that is taught in conventional society. Hence one does nothing wrong not because one fears God, but because one respects life itself, choosing not do anything that would disgrace life.

The PCL also guides you to practice the nebulous mind. A nebulous mind is the practice of embracing whole mindedness. It encourages you to tolerate differences among individuals and things, and protects your happiness in life. A nebulous mind is not overly sensitive to differences of rich and poor, beautiful and ugly, good and bad, likes and dislikes, and so forth. You even give up discriminating between friend and enemy. Such a practice can soften your emotional impulse to antagonize your direct surroundings, so that you no longer need to physically or emotionally harm your loved ones to relieve your anger or hatred.

The ancient practice of a nebulous mind has not been wholly understood or valued by the later generations. Even intellectuals disrespect it. Consequently, the real teaching of the Way has been lost to the public and false religions have developed, sharpening the hostility and hatred among people.

The acceptance of a nebulous mind has saved me from all kinds of suffering, enabling me to respond with the single goal of pure spirituality. As a young life, I left my parents' protection and plunged into the troubled waters of the world, bringing no sword, knife or pistol, but only a traditional life attitude of accepting all people. This attitude differs from the modern one that puts everyone under micro-scrutiny. When you over scrutinize your natural relationships, including that with your parents, you end up emotionally confronting a world of enemies. What happiness can you then enjoy, except one of hatred?

As a spiritual practice the nebulous mind can enhance natural relationships. Its capacity is higher and broader than the freedom to forgive. Forgiveness is still a dualistic practice whereby the self and others are established, whereas a nebulous mind embraces everything and all lives as one. It embraces both the holy and the unholy, and therefore it is beyond being holy.

Early, wise people applied the nebulous mind to connect with the world. They did not encourage forsaking or attaching to the world, unlike the later religionists who used spirituality as an escape from the world. The nebulous mind does not encourage avoiding your moral duty as a social citizen. It may even send people to battle under the right circumstances. The high choice, though, is to help your nation become invincible by eliminating the catastrophes that lead your country to war. This will benefit other countries as well. The middle choice, if war is unavoidable, is to reduce any destruction to the smallest possible. The last choice is to bravely defend your country.

An individual with a nebulous mind is neither proud of victories, nor dismayed by defeat. Rather, he or she fulfills their duty decisively and does what is right in the situation. Each one of you has different duties that can be fulfilled constructively by looking for the correct and proper way to do so. In this way you can live patriotically.

Living with the teachings of the PCL makes your life meaningful. It helps you eliminate suffering by clearly pointing out how to live in the present moment with cleanness, without using the present to battle other moments, or borrowing from the future to battle the present. In the pursuit of eternal life, you cannot miss the wonderful cleanness of each moment. Observe yourself in this moment and you can see the condition of your soul. With a free conscience you can live in the moment, instead of fighting against the past or future, and struggling against your life's harmless and constructive nature. The salvation of the Way comes from developing your mind to include all other beings and things. You may, however, prefer salvation to come from someone else or from some other time.

Everyone has a fortune or destiny. But it is not what the soul experiences that is important. Experiences belong to the narrative side of life and the literary level. More important is how your spiritual being uses your life's experiences to fortify your soul. Your true destiny is internal rather than external. The true cause of your unhappiness is your calculating mind and lack of care for your soul.

The teachings of the PCL aim to clean the poison of the world. Although the saviors of the world usually cannot save their own lives when the darkness of humanity remains as the dominant force, their demonstration of repaying evil with virtue carries everlasting spiritual value to all.

Nobody is perfect, but everyone can be wonderfully accepting. While all this may bring out the greed in others, you are supported by these teachings to be stronger. So expand your mind with the sky. The heavenly bodies give their broad influence to all earthlings and shape our destinies, but people with fortified souls do not bother to rearrange the stars. Instead, they find the readjustment of their choice by attuning their internal elements through spiritual cultivation. This means they follow nature and refine what is unnatural, which is mostly their emotional reactions to situations.

Spiritually, you are not a warrior of war; you are a spiritual protector of the world sent forth by Mother Universe. Your divine assignment is to transform human stupidity and all war. No one else but you can cause your mind to be antagonistic.

To be the lord of all lords and the king of all kings is not your interest. You serve, but do not demand to be remembered as a holy messenger. You see clearly that it is your duty to share these teachings, and help pull the world out of the mud.

The purpose behind grouping people is not to gather force to socially persecute others, but to conjointly fulfill spiritual development and service. A group is much stronger than the ancient style of spirituality that relied on one individual's effort for change.

The sweet well of the ageless Way also needs your protection. As partakers of its nourishment, it is your duty to protect its clean and nutritious water in order to preserve its inexhaustible fountain of the Everlasting Youthfulness of humanity. Congregations and organized forms of spiritual teaching can be mutually helpful to preserve and share the teaching. May this ageless spiritual fountain survive forever, reviving all who reach it and wholeheartedly accept it without obstruction.

The world can be saved when everyone is prepared to be a savior for the world. There will be no need for saviors when everyone knows how not to make trouble for themselves and the world.

A great, positive change will happen in the world as soon as its people awaken to a new life wherein they recognize each other as brothers and sisters. When people know that the purpose and responsibility of their lives is spiritual growth, the world will be closer to Heaven. With utmost sincerity, may this small, yet great wish come true.

Chapter 20

How Can You Fulfill Life?

A   C o m p l e t e   L i f e
I n c l u d e s   A l l   V i r t u e s

People often ask us to paraphrase the main point of our teaching. We would say that we offer the key to a true and complete life.

Another frequent question is what is meant by the phrase "virtuous fulfillment." We feel it is time to put these concerns together on one canvas to help those who have seen the trees, but not the forest.

The key to a true and complete life is personal spiritual development and growth through self-cultivation. What is spiritual self-cultivation? The word "self" reveals that you have to do it yourself or you won't achieve anything. The easiest way to understand this is to think of spiritual self-cultivation as spiritual self-education. We are giving you a spiritual assignment to refine yourself, to refine your life. You may even give yourself such an assignment. In everyday life, you need self-discipline to maintain your personal spiritual dignity. This is not something you expect a church, priest or government to do for you. They have the same duty to discipline themselves. Each person needs to keep his or her life force in balance at all times through self-management. You must do this for yourself.

Since individuals are the root of all levels of life, our focus is individual improvement rather than the improvement of the world's situation. The good and bad of the world is too much for most individuals. If a goal is too big, it is difficult to see any real effect. However, when you achieve the complete health of your own being, you are saving the world and your generation. This is why we encourage everyone to be centered in his or her own being and to engage in spiritual self-cultivation.

There are two main categories of spiritual cultivation. One is the balance and harmony of your personal life and the other is the balance and appropriateness of your behavior. For example, meditating, reading invocations, or performing *t'ai chi* are personal forms of self-cultivation. Though when you interact with others and your surroundings, you need to balance your behavior and make appropriate choices.

The teachings of the PCL encourage you to be self-reliant, and pursue the natural health of life that is free from the cultural contamination and religious reliance of any time or place. The teaching does not emphasize formality, because it differs according to each student's understanding of life. We want to help you develop the healthy side of your own nature, rather than weaken you through dependency. You are in the driver's seat while we are, at most, backseat drivers whose opinion you consult now and again. If you depend on us to tell you what to do—as would a priest, politician or general—your life will only degenerate. The naturalness of life is itself the Way. You, yourself, must learn to recognize the signs that point to the Way.

The main thrust of spiritual self-cultivation is to fulfill the five virtues as one, by integrating them into your daily life. In order to accomplish this, a person must be clear about his or her spiritual direction. One must give up emotional substitutes for spiritual development. You may ask how can I do this? By virtuous fulfillment—through bringing the five natural virtues of life into balance and uniting them as one. This is not beyond your capability. The amazing thing about the process of virtuous fulfillment is that it naturally expresses the healthy being you really are.

What then are these five virtues? Let us first examine the meaning of the word of virtue. In the West, the word "virtuous" usually refers to someone or something that is holy or spiritual. In our tradition, we regard virtue as the core of life, the intention behind all actions and communications. This is also the understanding of the ancient developed ones who first described the five virtues by closely observing their surroundings. They observed that when all five virtues were in harmony or balance, a state of completeness existed. When a person balances the five virtues in their life or behavior, they are not just "virtuous," they become virtue; they become complete. When you become virtue, you become complete. When you become unvirtuous, you become partial, both in your vision and behavior.

Kindness

The first virtue is kindness, or elderly, sibling protection. Kindness is both the core of a normal, healthy personality and the core of universal nature as well. The very existence of life is an expression of the kindness of nature. Nature is also kind enough to sustain all of life.

Kindness could also be called love and care. Among all five virtues, kindness is foremost. Its natural expression is vegetation, and it is the quality that the ancient ones attributed to the planet Jupiter. In China, Jupiter is regarded as a big brother of the much smaller Earth. Many times, the big brother has shielded the younger brother from the impact of comets. This protection has enabled us to grow and develop in the cradle we call Earth. The virtue of kindness or benevolence, therefore, includes protection, caring and love.

The scholar Confucius used one word to describe how leaders should treat their subjects. That word was kindness. He felt that governments, whatever their structure, should support, protect and fulfill life. However, in modern times, most governments have a partial vision and partial virtue that create a negative influence on society. As Confucius realized, any public service that is not based on complete virtue, with kindness at its core, will do more harm than good—because it is not rooted in the deep nature of love.

Most people need to work hard to make a living, and end up losing their health in the process. As they struggle for more and more in order to gain security, their lives become worse than that of a squirrel. This leads many to rely emotionally on social religions, which, as the Chinese proverb goes, help the starving by drawing a picture of cake. In the past forty years, Chinese leaders hypnotized people by drawing bigger, more modern cakes than the small wafers that some churches use. If they are not going to spread mere deception, religions need to practice the virtue of kindness and love, not as a profession in which kindness and love are traded for material goods and services, but out of true realization of the universal nature of life. The healthy function of all spiritual teachings is kindness to all people. It is the essence of all spiritual promotion.

If a retired person who has provided their own life support is willing to offer spiritual help to younger people, this would be an example of the correct fulfillment of kindness and love, whatever the person's religious background might be. The most useful guidance is to teach people to live a good, simple life, and to work and save with a sense of responsibility for their own health and longevity. The love of life is a great religion.

Whoever respects his or her life will respect the lives of others as well. They will work on balancing their life activities so as not to cause any burdens. If you love and respect your life, as well the lives of others, then you are a model of the Integral Way, which is broad and simple. People love to marvel at standing on their toes instead of standing and walking normally. They also like to take dancing detours instead of walking the straight way.

The balance that we recommend is not keeping half of your earnings for yourself and paying the other half to the government. The kind of balance we respect is the balance of the individual who loves his or her life, and has the same consideration for the environment and for others. Loving kindness is not measured in halves. Love must be whole.

Orderliness

The second virtue is orderliness or civility. This virtue comes from the element of Fire and is represented by the planet Mars. In the western world, Mars is considered to be the god of war, which draws on the destructive image of the fire of war. The ancient Chinese, however, saw the positive aspect of the element of Fire and the planet Mars, which associates light and warmth with civilization and social order. An orderly society can be considered a development of the virtue of civility, which removes or reduces personal darkness and therefore helps others live in the light.

This virtue can be applied on three levels. At a personal level it is expressed as neatness and a well-organized life. It also brings simplicity and unity to one's spirit, as well as personal hygiene at the emotional, physical, financial and social levels.

The development of human society is marked by the worship of fire or light in the sky, most notably in the sun worship of ancient Egypt, Zoroastrianism and Manichaeism. Judaism also inherited the Babylonian custom of sky worship, as did other eastern religions that contributed to the development of Christianity. Although many revisions have been made over the generations, the worship of light still serves as the social foundation of Western civilization. The social foundation of Eastern civilization, on the other hand, has always been the family. Leaders of this century have attempted to reshape China as a socialized society, but due to the absence of an organized religion, this has proven costly. Once the family is destroyed or disturbed, society can fall under the harsh control of a political party, which is not necessarily a good model of social order or of human life. Artificial social change that does not respect the natural process of gradual social evolution is inevitably painful and costly.

If leaders of the East and West respected the Integral Way as the means to achieve a balanced society, real and lasting progress could be expected. The parliamentary system of the West is a valuable contribution to a better world, as is the mutual assistance and closeness of family life that is so deeply valued in the East. Together they could lead the world forward and upward on its long journey.

Why is the family so important? Because the natural development of orderliness within the family is the foundation of orderliness in an individual life. Parents, by teaching the young ones by their own example to respect the order of the family, also teach them how to behave within society. The family is the foundation of a healthy personality, and healthy individuals are the foundation of a healthy society. In recent years, more and more young parents must both work outside the home in order to support the family. This seems like it will benefit the family, but the loss of a close relationship with one's parents and the loss of a united family life comes at a high price. The cost is the destabilization of the mental and emotional development of children who are raised by day care centers, television sets, baby sitters, summer camps and tutors. The results are reflected in lower human values and greatly diminished social safety, compared to recent generations before us.

Modern society may have created a greater external order based on the application of recent intellectual trends, but its impersonal values are not substitutes for real personal growth. This is where the present social confusion originates.

Most governments try to maintain external order by inventing more and more laws and regulations to enforce social control. Their efforts, however, usually lack consideration for the health of human nature and they strip people of their natural spontaneity. Furthermore, excessive rules tend to create more outlaws by putting so much external social pressure on the individual. Not only is this unnatural, it is social slavery. If the leaders of society are not aware of the true nature of life and society, they will never understand the stress that overly externalized social requirements place on human nature. Such requirements create disease at all levels: mental, physical, emotional and spiritual. We hope you will reflect on the importance of a natural, internal order in life, because it is the root of true civility and orderliness. Rigid social structures are not a blessing but a curse.

Personal and social civility goes hand-in-hand. In other words, social order reflects the natural, internal order of individuals. Naturally, internal order finds its expression in social life, not by force but through spontaneity. When good social behavior is expressed, there is a natural, positive quality present. Any society that relies on the police or the military to maintain order is a failure at the human level.

In the early stages of society, some leaders developed strong rituals and manners as tools of social control. These tools became governments and religions that were originally intended to curtail brutality, but the extent to which they have become overbearing, external forces in people's lives has created a profound dilemma for modern society.

We promote a balanced social structure in which nothing is over done. It is true that ritual and manners, carried to extreme, can become hollow and hypocritical, but it is also true that the call to "freedom, equality and liberty," which is supposed to help awaken human nature, can also backfire. Once the leash is lifted, the orderliness of the family, the schools and society is gone. People come home from work to a battlefield inside their own castle. Students bring guns to school to shoot fellow students and teachers whom they dislike. Whether there is too much external control or none at all, there is a price to pay for abandoning the natural order of human nature.

The traditional teaching of Tao was a reflection of the overly extended ritualism and mannerism of prehistoric society. It would be wrong, however, to reject necessary and rightful order. Civility and orderliness are internal qualities of life that are naturally externalized; they just shouldn't be over done or done incorrectly. Excessive social codes are stressful. On the other hand, people who think only of themselves, and do not respect the existence of others, interpret freedom and the natural rights of life as license to indulge their emotions at the expense of others. Drugs are another way of disrespecting one's own life and the lives of others. Whether on the highway or in ordinary places such as restaurants, offices, schools, and even homes, a hidden or open war is waged by people who never learned to respect civility and orderliness within their own childhood home.

We think that most people have not learned to observe or appreciate the orderliness of nature. Even in a grain of ocean salt, there is a beautiful, orderly world. It seems that modern people are raised with negligence. They are too busy or have no intention of improving themselves. They may also be simply unwilling to learn more about life by themselves. They know how to adopt civility when they want a favor, but this is false civility. Being civil is not the same as psychological manipulation of another person. True civility is kindness. It is a hallmark of who and what you really are. It is a quality belonging to a developed life.

Poison oak, by its nature, makes trouble for anyone who touches it. On the other hand, the sandalwood tree bestows its fragrance on anyone who passes by. In normal circumstances, your actions and attitudes are not like poison oak, but as sweet as the sandalwood tree. This is not an act, it is what you are. When you value the qualities with which you were inherently endowed, there is no need to be poisonous or saccharine. You naturally possess a sweet scent that comes from constantly cleansing your soul and purifying your personality. Such a person honestly and earnestly embraces the qualities of civility and orderliness.

Appropriateness

The third virtue is Appropriateness. Its element is Metal, and it is associated with the planet Venus. The Western world sees in Venus a literary or artistic quality.

The virtue of appropriateness can be described by many words. It can mean artful, tactful, suitable, feasible, just right, righteous, precise, exact, and correct, or a combination of all these words. The challenge of appropriateness is that what is suitable in one situation may not be suitable in another. When there is no absolute rule to go by, what are you to do? In the tradition of the Integral Way, you are given an instrumental concept to help you make a correct decision, based on what is temporal appropriateness and what is permanent appropriateness. If there seems to be a conflict, permanent appropriateness always takes precedence over temporal appropriateness. For example, say you owe people some money, or you agree to do something for someone, and when the agreed upon date arrives; you are unable to keep your word. This is considered inappropriate. If you fulfill your obligation at a different time, or in a different manner than you said you would, this can still be considered an appropriate outcome in which permanent appropriateness prevailed over temporal appropriateness. However, a trustworthy personality fulfills what is a priority in a suitable manner and time.

Appropriateness also means not crossing over an imaginary line. For instance, a young man might give a gift to his neighbor, who is in a committed relationship. This doesn't mean he has inappropriate intentions. Though if he were to give her a flower with the intention of seducing her, it would, of course, be inappropriate behavior. We must always ask ourselves, "What are the person's intentions in this situation?" Many unnecessary troubles and confusions can be avoided by being clear in our intentions.

It is appropriate to appreciate the humanistic contributions of heroic ancestors, and to teach people the value of righteousness. Aggression is unrighteous and inappropriate behavior. As individuals, we do not transgress our neighbor's property. How can a nation or race transgress the territory of another nation or race? Such crimes have been the source of great disaster in the world, and future generations will continue to suffer if their social education is not corrected. There is nothing wrong with being educated to love your family, your nation, or your tribe. What is lacking is the instruction to love the rest of humanity, who shares the same world with you. When a culture or society encourages its citizens to hate other nations, races or tribes, this is deeply unrighteous and inappropriate. If human nature is allowed to be natural, trouble will still happen but on a much smaller scale than worldwide political and religious warfare. A concerted educational effort to transform old patterns of aggression into a new spiritual discipline of nonaggression and nontransgression would save the billions of dollars that are now being spent on armies and police forces throughout the world.

Wisdom

The fourth virtue is Wisdom. It is symbolized by Water and represented by the planet Mercury, which is positioned most closely to the light of the sun. Water is flexible and cannot be deterred from reaching its final destination. A person who can learn the virtue of water will be close to the virtue of wisdom. Many young men and women suffer self-inflicted emotional wounds, as a result of the obstacles they create in their lives. As they become older and wiser, they may become able to see their own warlike behavior and choose to put an end to it through spiritual self-cultivation. This is not an escape, but a decision to face the reality of life and learn from it, rather than fight it.

There are three types of wisdom. The first is a sign of growth, and can be seen by yourself and others around you. Wisdom cannot be purchased. Knowledge is not wisdom. Going to a bookstore or library and reading someone else's wisdom may give you a higher intellectual vision, but you cannot consider yourself wise. Even if you can quote many sayings from ancient wisdom, you are still not wise. You must pay a personal price before you are able to recognize the first stage of wisdom. Rather than just read or think about life's lessons, you need to strive and go through all of its painful lessons yourself.

The second type of wisdom is unspeakable and silent. Your balanced mind helps ready you for all situations. When a new situation arises, you have no preconception, no immature thought, and no judgment of the outcome. You just allow your perception and observation to be clear and deep. When it is time for you to respond, you are not in a hurry, and, at the same time, you do not delay. Rather, you make a balanced effort and let it unfold. This is why Lao Tzu said: "It looks like I am hesitant to approach another individual or thing, but I am not." This implies that you allow the other person or thing to give you a clear picture of itself first. You take one step at a time and keep the same pace, so that matters can develop correctly. This approach also allows unfavorable things to dissolve themselves without a struggle. If things are favorable, you should not become overly excited. You just accept them as part of your growth.

There is a third kind of wisdom that goes beyond the unspeakable. This kind of wisdom is indescribable. It avoids all resistance, hardship and impulse, and is valuable beyond your imagination. Indescribable wisdom is attainable only through spiritual cultivation, which helps you build an attitude that unites you with the second and third types of wisdom.

The first stage of wisdom is necessary to help us grow, and it helps us learn to appreciate the other two, nonconfrontational types of wisdom. The first stage of wisdom is the small wisdom that can be seen and known, but the third and higher wisdom is totally beyond preconception, because it is indescribable and unknowable. Most people only respect the small wisdom they hear of or read in books, but the great wisdom of nature is beyond knowing. Even so, it is not beyond our reach. As you achieve a higher stage of development, you gradually reach the profundity of life that goes beyond worldly affairs. This third kind of wisdom is not inspired by words, nor can it be transferred. This is why Lao Tzu says: "The one who knows doesn't speak, and the one who speaks doesn't know." It really is not a matter of whether you speak or not. It is a matter of the indescribable nature of this kind of embodiment or direct witness.

The purpose of mass culture is to instill false concepts that seduce you into thinking that the beauty of life can be found in money, fame or power. After

being thoroughly educated and imbued with these falsehoods, a natural life becomes something to achieve rather than your innate birthright. The Way is simple
and broad. People have complicated it, so that it can only be superficially appreciated through art or literature. Few people appreciate the beauty of the universe
in a smile or a flower. People who lack naturalness of mind find such simplicity
difficult to grasp. However, if, as a quiet observer, one allows the truth of life, the
world, and the subtle law to reveal itself, the beauty of the universe can one day
be known. One then lives a new life of wholeness in a world of all time. One will
know what it is to reach the deep self, while others continue to experience the
surface of pain, joy and excitement.

The world awaits your growth. For now, most people live partially on the edge of
their emotions. They have not found the way to the center of their life and the
center of the cosmos. If they gently persist, they will eventually witness the
profound, subtle truth of life and the universe, and they will have the capability
to make good things happen. Their spiritual being will dance in the procession of
the cosmos.

Faithfulness

The fifth virtue is Faithfulness. In the five element system, Faithfulness is symbolized as the soil or Earth. It is associated with the planet Saturn, which represents
stability, and which is sometimes interpreted as obstruction. But rather than
obstruction, it is better understood as the imbalance that a negative circumstance
can bring if any element of life is misapplied.

Faithfulness is obviously not independent. One has to have faith in someone or
something. This could be a friend, a mate, a duty, a responsibility, a nation or a
suitable concept. There are two kinds of faithfulness. One kind changes with
your experience and education. The other kind is faith in a positive life.

Most people have the first type of faith that changes with experience and education. This kind of faithfulness usually exists at the level of right and wrong. If you are faithful to a friend, you are good; if not, you are bad. When faith is applied to a specific object or person, it is usually because of emotional attachment. For example, being faithful to a friend at the expense of your independent judgment is bad faith. In general, pure faith in life has nothing to do with being good or bad. Good faith or bad faith, high faith or low faith is a matter of personal growth. We appreciate the power of a pure, faithful heart. Being faithful causes a beautiful response from the universe. Being unfaithful or insincere causes a painful response. This is source of the proverb that honesty is the best policy.

Lao Tzu also teaches us to be faithful: "No matter how people treat you, no matter what the world does to you, you have to be honest and faithful in life." In other words, we have to be faithful to the attainment of our spiritual growth. Social events change all the time. You change too. What you thought was right ten years ago may not be what you think is right today. Faith in yourself is a desire to change for the better. This faith in your own personal growth is a deep faithfulness. Some people will have a conceptual faith in different external things. We look for individuals who have the intention to grow, to move towards a correct way of life, and to not hold onto the same stagnant understanding.

We encourage you to respect the high potential of your life. Spiritual growth comes from examining the basic virtues of life and making the effort to improve yourself. Even if most people don't have any special achievement, living correctly is still respectable, because they possess the natural potential to be good, do well and be sweet.

The Five Virtues in One

These virtues are not a matter of external learning. They are innate to anyone who is born into the world at a normal stage of life. Although any of the five virtues can be individually expressed in a specific situation, if one or all of them is turned into a specific external pursuit, there will be something missing and one's overall virtue will be damaged.

Even if you do a thousand sessions of meditation, or *chi kung,* or *t'ai chi* for years on end, you will not achieve much unless these five simple virtues are kept safely intact in your life. This is the emphasis in our tradition. When people neglect the completeness of their nature, they respond to situations with incomplete virtue or no virtue. Even if you are a good follower of a social religion or a good citizen of your society, your life will only be partially fulfilled if your true nature is limited to fit a conceptual mold. Religious and social beliefs, fervent though they may be, can be detrimental to the naturalness of your life. Life is damaged by bending it to serve an external purpose. Reliance on anything makes you unable to turn around.

Positive and Negative Aspects of a Single Virtue

Like most things in life, these five virtues have positive and negative aspects. Human life often consists of chasing a group of desires or emotions. It gets confusing when you use a virtue to fulfill an inappropriate desire or emotion. For instance, a leader of society may use the virtue of appropriateness as an artful or tactful way to achieve selfish desires. He or she may be good with words, but inside is a beast. In a situation such as this, can any good come from the followers' virtue of faithfulness and loyalty, or will their single-minded virtue only serve to strengthen social persecution?

Partial virtue is the application of one virtue to an extreme, at the exclusion of the other virtues. Whenever virtue or morality or a spiritual standard is socially externalized, cunning people can always use it to their advantage. Most of the time, worldly culture promotes only a partial view of reality. It exalts emotion and diminishes rationality. As a result, the basis of most people's lives is the pursuit of emotions and desires. Some emotions and desires are good and can be a correct fulfillment of life, but some are bad and can be harmful to the objectives of your life. If you pursue a partial preference, then you make one emotion or desire the dominant force in your life, and mold your judgment accordingly. For example, if you don't achieve your preferred interest, you feel bad. If, on the other hand, you pursue your interest with a balanced mind, balanced emotions, and balanced means, then the result is neither good nor bad, it just is natural. Some people would say, "Natural behavior! What a concept!" We say that natural or non-judgmental behavior is the true standard for all of humankind.

An educational system that produces an immature, dualistic frame of mind that only perceives good or bad, right or wrong, grace or sin, destroys the natural mind. Such systems further instill their poison through politics, religion, commerce and military training. Society and its leaders do not understand the consequences of squeezing the naturalness of life to one side by too many social and cultural creations, so that students only learn the dogma necessary to become cogs in a political machine that is run by a boss.

The Integral Way is the direct pursuit of deep spiritual reality. We do not promote the dualistic mentality of right and wrong, grace and sin, etc. There is only one level of good or bad, and that can only be known by your personal development. You may ask for its definition out of intellectual habit, but you surely know that being good is whatever is beneficial to your life and creates no harm to other lives, and being bad is whatever harms your life or other lives. For instance, something can be good for your emotions, but it may not benefit your life as a whole. Or, some religious or political idea may sound good to you, but it may not be as earnest as you think it is. You may say that you already know this. But what you think you know, you usually do not really know.

Personal assertiveness is the trademark of political and religious leaders. We all have proof of their mistakes. We do not want to be assertive. You might say that the Integral Way is a religion too. If so, then the essence of the Integral Way as a religion is to stay open and objective to things in your life and in the world, and to be permanent learners and seekers of truth. Personally, we think that this approach is neither religious nor intellectual, but rather one of strong spiritual confidence in the nature of life itself, with the understanding that partial knowledge and strong emotional preference are self-endangering.

It is not that one group or another is right or wrong, they are just incomplete, but this is not their fault. The fault lies with those who think that whatever teaching they personally prefer is complete, and should be followed by all people for all time. We want to point you towards the whole garden of the world and its entire history, not just one tree or flower. We appreciate and value all religions, all spiritual paths, and all political systems that make a positive contribution to the complete health of the world.

The Need for Detoxification

In most circumstances people are born with partiality, according to prenatal and post natal influences. Few are born trouble free. Therefore, we have a world of troublemakers. There may be a few individuals who are aware of humanity's crisis, who recognize the importance of spiritual self-cultivation, and who are willing to engage in it. Spiritual self-cultivation or self-completion makes the healthy and normal functions of life possible. Functions such as strong intuition and telepathy, which are strengthened through spiritual cultivation, are helpful to people living in the world.

Wholeness of virtue is a natural attribute of life. A single virtue, if correctly applied, is a great expression of the good quality of life, but its misapplication should be avoided.

You can never become complete by over extending one virtue. Even the combination of any four virtues without the fifth still cannot be considered healthy. If faithfulness, wisdom, courage and civility were present, but kindness was lacking, what type of a cruel force would be created? Or if kindness, faithfulness, courage and civility were present without wisdom, what kind of instrument would people become at the hands of a cunning individual? Or if wisdom, courage, kindness and civility were present without faithfulness, what type of monster would be born? Or if there were kindness, civility, wisdom and faithfulness without courage, what worthwhile or meaningful task could be fulfilled? Lastly, if courage, wisdom, faithfulness and kindness lacked civility, what kind of isolation would people suffer?

It is all right to appear lacking in all virtues, without making any one virtue stand out. This is why the ageless Lao Tzu said, "The highest virtue is to have no virtue. Inferior virtue appears to be the most virtuous." The Taoists admired the non-noticeable whole Being who is blessed by life and does not make any trouble for the world. Troublemakers are people with one or more outstanding virtues that exaggerate a particular function of life. People are only noticed when they are overly kind or not kind, overly civil or uncivil, overly intelligent or ignorant and overly appropriate or inappropriate.

Partial virtue always creates worldly confusion. Religious leaders teach faith, but they neglect to teach people to respect the wisdom that is above churches and individuality. Political freedom, equality and independence are good virtues of natural life, but national leaders neglect to inform people of the need for ethics alongside these virtues, as practiced in everyday life.

Partial virtues are the chosen weapons of one individual or a group, to seize power and take support from the undeveloped majority of society. Revolutions create chaos and destruction for momentary gain. They are only external and do not respect the long-term health of society. Whoever is concerned about saving the world must first save individuals. As an individual, you must frequently check to see if you have a strong tendency towards fulfilling only one part of life, rather than the whole. True virtuous fulfillment comes from leading a balanced life.

Conventional society encourages the pursuit of extremes. People strive to be number one. This kind of selfish pursuit forces society to create extreme measures to manage individuals with extreme needs. Therefore complicated social and law enforcement systems are created to maintain order. Such an overly externalized life does not respect the value of peacefulness, or the great blessing of a normal life. These bulky and complicated social systems are proof enough that human nature has become corrupt, and that the result of its corruption is a sick society and culture.

You would expect modern people to be very developed, but the convergence of intellectual energy with social confusion has created a condition of interactive slavery. This is a great mischief that most do not understand. Modern society is an unconscious mistake! People who work very hard at their jobs only contribute their strength to support a complex system of interactive slavery, but how many of them are aware of this trend?

The PCL can teach you to subdue your overactive monkeys. It can help you break through the artificial and false, social network or bondage that keeps you from living a natural life.

The complete virtue of a natural life goes beyond the dualistic pattern of an unspiritual mind. Instead of thinking of your mistakes as good or bad, see yourself as one still in the process of learning. If you haven't found the right response to a particular situation, the best thing to do is to keep your balance and manage your energy. Do not think you have achieved a great merit or committed a sin rather accept each result as part of your growth.

The Way of which we speak is so much broader than the preferences people hold as good or bad, based on what they like or dislike. Modern people do not see the danger of neglecting the naturalness of life. The naturalness of life is achieved by doing nothing extra. By pursuing peace rather than extra activity, nature rather than unnatural creations, and by living an unemotional, calm life, you then receive the naturalness of life.

Do not miss the boat by listening to someone else's comments or by taking sides in irrelevant matters. Do not waste your life judging every action of other people. Save your time and attention for your goodness and the goodness of others. If you stop worrying about other people being good or bad, you will be safe from their sharp judgments of you. If you don't need the extra attention, then you won't have a nervous breakdown.

Most undeveloped lives are filled with tremendous desires. They spend a lifetime trying to become the best, the most important, or the richest. All of these pursuits are part of the sickness of "extraneousness." Extraneousness is disrespect for your own life. A wise person's life needs no throne to honor it. Life is simple and natural. It has its own dignity and respect. To ask more of life than to just respect its simple essence is disrespectful of the naturalness of life. You might say that doing nothing extra promotes laziness and mediocrity. What we are saying is to allow things you value to come to you naturally without turning them into goals and striving for them. We see many young people ignore the limitations of their physical health and meet an early death, for the sake of a gold medal, or first place in a marathon, car race, or mountain climb. We do not mean that people cannot enjoy doing these things, but such activities should serve life, not the other way around.

We are not saying that you cannot accomplish great things. We are only suggesting that things of great meaning are not necessarily big. In fact, they usually seem small and insignificant. Most things that you want to do, or are interested in, are motivated by the desire to satisfy your ego. Before reaching maturity, you may feel ready to give your life to your ambitions. Any damage you do to yourself depends on how hard you push yourself. You may not intend to damage your life or the lives of others around you, but you are mesmerized by external pressures, or by the influence of the media. Sometimes you do strange things as a reaction to pressure from your parents or from your job. Actually, there is no real pressure, only your own weakness leading you to chase after something extra, something that goes beyond the simple dignity of life. Even if you succeed, your success does not justify deception of yourself.

A student once asked, "What is the first step I can take to bring the five virtues into balance?" The first step is to thoroughly understand each virtue, so that you may achieve a balanced personality by observing the five basic virtues of nature.

Remember: don't practice a single virtue by itself. Always follow the gentle way that is the middle range of human activity. Never try to be special. By living a simple life, you are on the Way. You don't need to search for something extra in your life. Most people live partial lives, but we hope you will become a complete person, a complete soul and a being of wholeness.

The Way to which we point is above all comparisons, concepts and worldly confusion. The indescribable greatness is natural, normal and ordinary. All of you will find greatness in your commonness. Our job is to help you discover the greatness in living a simple, balanced life through balanced behavior. By so doing, you will be above judgment. When you live simply, and when your country lives simply, there is no need for bulky and burdensome social systems.

The social system of which you have been educated to be a part, is going in the wrong direction. It doesn't spend a cent on supporting the dignity of life. Your hard work is mostly spent on your emotions and desires, and what's left goes to support the overgrown and complicated social establishments in which you live.

All the education, advertising and social illusions you live among make you think you will benefit by trying to do something extra to become "number one." You will not benefit one bit by chasing these illusions. We are pointing you towards the simple Way. We offer you a chance to discover your own beauty. The natural reward for living a simple life is "Heaven on Earth." Learn about the five virtues and make them one within you, within the core of your being. Discover the virtues that are already there, water them deeply, and watch the natural garden blossom within you and all around you.

Question: Does your main teaching apply to spiritual cultivation as well as behavior? In other words, are we trying to harmonize the five virtues in our meditation and in our t'ai chi and chi kung practices, as well as fulfill them in our behavior?

Human nature is indistinguishable from wholesomeness. All practices are done for the purpose of reconnecting with this reality. The benefit of any style of *chi kung* or *t'ai chi* comes from truthfully following the principle of naturalness. Even the principle of balance, which I emphasize on many occasions, is contained in the wholeness of a healthy, normal life.

Question: How can a beginner make sure that all virtues are present in his or her life? If faced with a decision, should we ask ourselves: "Is this appropriate? Is this kind? Is this wise? Is this being faithful? Is this orderly?"

That is too fragmented. It is the same misapplication of the natural mind that religions promote. In the natural training that we received, conscience appears in the first thought or idea towards a positive matter, and it appears in the second thought or idea towards a negative matter or harmful idea. You do not need to search far for the natural healthy mind. It is simply your conscience, and it is the best prevention for cancer or any disease.

The Five-Star Practice: A Two-Fold Enhancement of Your Life Being

There are three important partners that comprise a complete life: health, which is necessary for the body; understanding, which is necessary for the mind; and wisdom, which is necessary for the soul. Together, these partners support life. If the mind loses its understanding or the soul loses it wisdom, the body loses its health.

Invocation for a Constructive Life

No difficulty is insurmountable, when I set my heart to it.
I shall live a constructive life.
Wherever whole-hearted dedication is directed,
the world will step aside to let me by.
When I live a constructive life, it cannot be otherwise.
Absolute sincerity melts the hardness of stones.
This describes my commitment to a constructive life.
Faith in a constructive life enables me to move mountains.
Because I live constructively, my life is everlasting.
Nothing is impossible for a willing heart.
This is the power of my constructive life.

Invocation for Integrating the Mind and Body

The Tao has equipped my life completely and wholly.
I renounce my ignorance.
Spiritually, I am supported by five groups of spirits.
On my left, I have the spiritual support of *Hun*, the pure life spirits.

On my right, I am supported by the vital essence of *Po*, my semi-spiritual life force.
On my upper body, there is the Power of the Great Unison.
On my lower body, there is the Power of the Reproductive Force of natural health.
In the center of my body, the Coordinator of my life provides balance and harmony,
this is the all-embracing heart of my developed spiritual life.

(You may draw the Southern Cross on your body with your right hand in the sword position. The sword position is formed by bringing your thumb, ring and small fingers together, and extending your index and middle finger.)

My head is the high mountain
where the high gods and spirits dwell and visit.
Behind my eyes is the throne of *Kwan Yin*,
my spiritual visual power;
I am endowed with the transpiercing vision of the Goddess of Mercy.
The smile on my face reflects the truth of life and happiness.
I live my happy, divine life.
As the awakened one, I am able to dispel ignorance from my life.
I no longer live in confusion.
I am empowered with a tolerance
that enables me to disarm the hostility of troops of darkness.
With a broad and open chest,
I am able to take all events in my stride.
The depth of my belly
can accept and digest the variety of all people.
The four capable limbs of my body
are the four Heavenly Generals who fulfill the greatness of my life.
The rhythm of my breath
consists of two Heavenly kings
that attune the ebb and flow of *yin* and *yang* in my life
with the deep pulse of nature,
with each inhalation and exhalation that I take.

On both of my palms
there are the Five Pillars of my enduring life:
my small finger indicates that there should be no withdrawal from
expressing the positive nature of life;
my ring finger reminds me to not be overly aggressive or greedy;
my middle finger expresses firmness and resolve;
my index finger guards against excessive emotion and sentimentality;
my thumb displays the truth that psychological shadows
cannot cloud my clarity and stability.
Therefore my life is accomplished with all five virtues
to become the Star of Five Beams.

(With your right hand in the sword position, start from the left upper side of your body and say, "Kindness." Then with your right index and middle fingers draw all the way to the right upper side and say, "Righteousness." Then, turn the sword to draw all the way to the lower left side and say, "Civility." Now raise the sword from the lower left to the middle upper part and say, "Wisdom." Then turn the sword all the way to the lower right side and say, "Faithfulness." From the lower right, the sword turns to draw all the way to the left upper side to connect with the starting point and say, "The completion of the greatness of my life being.")

Chapter 21

Vampirism and Dual Cultivation

In the West people believe in vampires, which can either be male or female. Do they really exist? Yes, they do. A man or woman can be attacked in certain circumstances. The experience can be similar to a nightmare where you feel pressed down by an assailant. The vampire does not suck your blood, but your vital energy (which produces blood, secretions, etc.) so that its ethereal body can survive. These "vampires" are merely undelivered souls who still have an earthly connection. They live in society with you.

If you are spiritually weak, you can protect yourself by using the invocations in the *Spiritual Workbook*. But if you are spiritually cultivating and achieving yourself, it would be kinder to deliver them instead of destroying them or scaring them away. Traditionally, you can effectively send them away without creating or expressing hostility by mentally reciting the following prayer at least ten times, "Venerable One of *T'ai Yi,* please deliver the soul and spirits of the lost."

T'ai Yi is the constellation of stars around the North Star. She has spiritual sovereignty over all beings and lives beneath her including souls, as souls are slimmer beams of light with a different range of color and radiation.

It is important to protect and nurture your vital energy. It is the foundation of your health and spiritual growth. You need to strengthen yourself against invisible forces as well as visible ones in the form of teachers and practices that you may be attracted to, since some of them can be harmful to your vitality. Some practices can have the effect of vampirism in human form. Do not be carried away by short-lived gains, but search for and practice the true internal practice. The following discussion can help you in this pursuit.

The Serious Internal Spiritual Pursuit

The power of nature affects your physical appearance and health, as well as your behavior, mentality and destiny. Without spiritual cultivation your life is subject to nature's mechanical and physical operation. Truthfully, you cannot expect to enjoy a free ride from universal nature; you need to make real efforts to grow. To understand nature's influence, recognize that the subtler the influence, the stronger and more important it becomes. Knowing this can reduce trouble and lead to valuable growth.

Is there any human effort that can change the natural destiny of life? This question represents the constant pursuit of the pioneers of the Integral Way.

Generally, people's spiritual essence is weaker than their reproductive or sexual force. People tend to waste or overly expand their sexual force, which means that in most practical situations the power of the brain is weaker than sexual desire. This situation inspired the efforts of wise pioneers such as Master Lu, Tung-Ping, who lived around the end of the Tang Dynasty (618–906 CE), and Chen Tuan (871–989 CE). They offered ways to change personal destiny, because by changing personal destiny an individual can change the pre-existing imbalances in his or her life.

In this pursuit the pioneers used the eight *gua*, which are the eight trigrams or the eight manifestations of natural energy as depicted in the *I Ching*. These metaphoric illustrations describe how "to take the overflow of *Kan*," (see the trigram) "the water, which symbolizes the sexual fluid, to fill up or to support the empty middle of *Li*," (see the trigram) "the fire or the mind." *Kan* symbolizes the overly full sexual energy of young people, and *Li* symbolizes the weak condition of intelligence in most people. The aim of the practice is to sublimate the sexual or reproductive energy of life and transform it into high spiritual energy. General sitting meditation cannot achieve this purpose.

As a result of their efforts, the pioneers established the essential practice of Internal Refinement, or the Transformation of the Internal Life Force. Generally it is known as the refinement of the internal immortal medicine. Real achievement is known by seeing the Light, and then internally forming the red baby, *Kwan Yin,* or the Jade Maiden, which are all titles for the newly formed and integrated being of your life. Both my book of *Nurture Your Spirits* and Dr. Carl Jung's translation of *The Golden Flower* clearly point out the principle of this practice. You can use the practices in those works to help you attain real and beneficial proof.

You should be aware that there are some individuals who, while still in the exploration stage, proclaim to be true teachers of the internal practice—yet they do not honestly present it. They do not respect the experience and traditional values of the achieved masters who reveal its true purpose and the way of its achievement. Instead, those self-proclaimed individuals use stolen theories and untested practices to teach the public.

Both Master Lu and Chen Tuan made real examples of this practice in their own lives, but none of the self-proclaimed teachers of our time have done so. We suggest that teachers do not fool the public by introducing personally invented and ungrounded practices, out of a need for self-establishment. We also encourage the public to use their discernment to avoid following teachers who do not have a deep or real practical understanding of the profound and original concepts.

Dual Cultivation and the
Standard of the Universal Way

In the vast culture of ancient China, with its generations of deep life experience, sexual education was passed down to true seekers as part of the tradition of everlasting life. Sexual education, as part of immortal pursuit, confirms the value of a paired life with the mutual ability to help one another live a spiritually

purposed life. Naturally, such a life includes a special design of sexual cooperation between partners.

Dual or Twin Cultivation means the integration of the mind and the body, with
the spirit behind them. It is an important spiritual practice that seeks internal
balance. It is important both for internal integration and for suitable external
fulfillment. However, there are very few people who pursue its more valuable
aspect of internal cultivation. There are even fewer teachers who like to share
the information of such a meaningful practice. In contrast, it is easy in any time
or generation to find a big market that teaches sex under the name of dual cultivation. It is a great loss that some so-called teachers and cunning individuals have
to narrow down the sacred practice of dual cultivation to merely sex.

When I came to the West in the 1970s, I presented the teachings of essential
Taoism alongside my traditional Chinese medical practice. The foundation of
my teaching was to continue the pursuit of all developed individuals, who are the
immortal teachers before me. All of my books are written as a service to the
public, to assist its current stage of spiritual understanding. They are not for
serving myself.

As the most important principle and practice, I encouraged people to attain
health and balance in the three spheres of the spirit, body and mind. This practice
is known as spiritual self-cultivation, or the cultivation of the tri-partnership,
which also means the integration of Heaven, Earth and People. The harmony and
cooperation among all three partners of life ensures your happiness, health and
long life. The term "dual cultivation" first appeared in my edition of the *Hua Hu
Ching* around that same time.

Then, in the 1980s, some other individuals started to be active, and introduced
the sexual styles of Chinese folk or religious Taoism to the West. Those new
teachers unfairly and untruthfully placed these overly extended sexual practices
under the name of Taoism. This has caused confusion for people who mistake

244 PART III: CHAPTER 21

those sexual practices and teachings to be the same as the spiritual pursuit of original Taoism, and particularly of the Immortal Life tradition. Those new teachers were purely self-serving. They do not teach with a social conscience.

One teacher took the term "dual cultivation" and made it the equivalent of sex. He wrote about it and started to teach the sexual practices of folk Taoism. These practices are intended to exercise and prepare the sexual organs for more frequent and stronger sex. They are not about looking for harmony and mutual benefit between sexual partners. What this teacher is ridiculously suggesting is to take the partner's energy. This is just one of the superstitious notions among the underdeveloped and uneducated people of China. It is not a real fact.

Folk Taoists teach male students to hang heavy objects from their sexual organs to strengthen their male energy. Once their sexual strength is high, they look for female partners to serve their purpose of taking the female energy. The practice is taught to young males. This is how folk teachers promote their untruthful theory. It can do more harm than good by leading to testicular problems and the possibility of becoming a vampire in human form.

The same type of teacher teaches females a practice called "internal massage," whereby a wooden egg is placed in a woman's vagina to strengthen it and prepare her to be a female vampire. Women are even certified to teach this practice. These practices have no connection with the teaching and learning of the Way, or the spiritual pursuit of Taoism. The Way looks for health, balance and normality as the safe way to enjoy and live life. Taoism is the search for the spiritual support from nature. Those self-proclaimed teachers have misrepresented the practices they teach to be Taoism.

The *Hua Hu Ching* was written to accompany the *Tao Teh Ching* in my book *The Complete Works of Lao Tzu*. The *Tao Teh Ching* means "universal spiritual morality." The reference to dual cultivation in the *Hua Hu Ching* is different to the pro-vampire group of people who used the term as equivalent to sex. Using it as equal to sex has no spiritual benefit. It actually takes one in the opposite direction of the Way. To correct the misinterpretation, I published *The Story of Two Kingdoms*. That book explains that the overly expanded sexual desire is a dark force in life, and can harm the balance of your life being. Healthy people find this fact difficult to accept.

Later, I produced *Harmony, the Art of Life* with the aim of teaching the art of balance and harmony between men and women, over mere sexual skill. I hope the editors and readers of that work have not deviated from my original intention. In any case, I suggest you read the *I Ching* for your deeper understanding and support.

Truthfully and deeply, dual cultivation is an internal marriage. It is practiced for spiritual benefit with the purpose of pursuing everlasting life. The early Christians, such as the early Gnostics, followed the practice, as did the teachers and followers of the system of Manichaeism, although they took it to an extreme. Tibetan Buddhism continued the practice from Manichaeism, but its followers greatly modified and developed it. They simplified the teachings by making the sun Buddha and Buddha the sun, but they relied too much on rituals.

In *The Story of Two Kingdoms*, I offer the principle of balance to conserve the essence of life. This principle is derived from the *I Ching*. The rotating nature of the universe, as expressed by the *I Ching*, is the real source of all teaching, inspiring Christ, Mani and the system of Tibetan Buddhism.

The developers of the system of Universal Rotation taught the Way. The Way is the course of universal nature. It has been extended to include the natural and regular process of human life and society. Those developers were the early leaders: Fu Shi (whose epoch was prior to Shen Nung, but the exact date is not known), Shen Nung (3218–3078 BCE, 140 years of reign), the Yellow Emperor, as well as a few writers in the time of the Epoch of Spring (beginning in 722 BCE) and the Warring Period (beginning 403 BCE). As a result of the progress in writing, these writers recorded and developed the thoughts and intuitions of the early leaders. It was during this period that the classic books and teachings of the Way appeared. Those classics establish the standard and philosophy of the Way. They give directions on the health of life. Among them is the *Yellow Emperor's Internal Classic* or the *Neijing*. It is the essential work of the ancients and covers all-important subjects, offering guidance for the complete health of life.

Both the *I Ching* and the *Neijing* teach the need for a balanced life. All of life's aspects, including sexual activity, should be governed by the principle of balance. Nothing should be overly extended.

Chinese Taoism is the spiritual effort of the Chinese people throughout many generations. Its teachers were very serious, and they did their best to formalize the spiritual practices with their early respect for nature. It has been mixed with different influences however. The later folk or religious Taoism contributes some new life experiences, but it gets carried away with the new fashions of spiritual life. Conversely, in Buddhism the new leaders tried to preserve the essence of the early Taoist classics, such as in Zhan (Zen) Buddhism. Although Taoists aimed to preserve their traditional style, and their teachings can be just as serious as any world religion, their teachings may not directly present the depth and the maturity of the early classics. I personally prefer to continue the efforts of those individuals who came from the beginning of the teaching of the Way.

In our spiritually troubled times, many individuals have been teaching and writing about so-called "Taoism," but whatever their background and motivation, it is only their personal presentation. Rather than improve it, they degrade it. The so-called Taoist writings on sexual subjects that can be found in stores today are merely the promotion of different styles of human sex. To call it Taoist sex is not correct.

You should not expect all cultural activities and writings to be dutifully motivated to serve people's health. Many presentations and publications attract curiosity, but not all of them are seriously grounded. You need to make a discerning choice about what to read and learn. The top priority in any stage of your life should be improving your spiritual condition.

The troubling situations that I have mentioned do not affect Maoshing's and my personal devotion to present the constructive nature and integral truth of humanity to the universal society. Our teaching has different levels to respond to the different stages of people, and its purpose is the pursuit of universal spiritual benefit for all people. In order to directly continue the humanistic, spiritual effort of the early sages, and be spiritually responsible to the public, we need to ensure that our teachings are not connected to or confused with any shallow, cultural or new age teaching. Therefore, we have repackaged our work into the vehicle of the PCL. To avoid confusing our work with other teachings, people of the Integral Way should stop using the term "dual cultivation" and in its place, and for their promotion, they may use the title Path of Constructive Life.

The spiritual effort of the PCL values the positive essence of conventional cultures, and the positive spiritual achievement of all people. Above all, it values the spiritual inspiration of nature in presenting the Spiritual Unity on which to base the Spiritual Integral Truth of the universe. It certainly does not support the old or new vampirism, whose harm to life can easily be seen.

The simplest way to present the universal spiritual truth, which is the spiritual essence in life and in nature, is nonverbally. That is, beyond any conceptual presentation and exploration. The essential practice is to live and embrace the simple essence of life above any cultural complication or flowery presentation. However, it requires a lot of learning and a lot of achievement to be simple, and it may appear rude if you present it in such a manner.

The exploration in the *I Ching* and the *Tao Teh Ching* is simple, but you may ask how to fulfill it in life? This is why we need a vehicle to convey the deep spiritual life. The recently founded PCL is intended to be this vehicle for the service of the

Universal Integral Way. The presentation to society of a new religious path is based on the reality that spirituality cannot be without religiosity, and vice versa. Further, it takes the willingness of people to stand above the confusion of internal and external sources.

Sexual practice is one important aspect of life. The pursuit of an immortal life has its root on Earth. The longest tradition is the Way. It is the spiritual source of Jesus's pursuit of everlasting life.

Sexual   Practices

There are many levels of healthy sexual practice, based on the different ages and personal conditions of people's lives. These practices are hidden in the vast volumes of the *Taoist Canon*. Tremendous research is required before you can completely understand them.

On a general level, there is the sexual style of Tantra or Tantric Practice, which differs from the normal, vigorous sexual performance of people. It is still popular in Tibet, India and Nepal. Tantra can be used as sexual education, provided you are not motivated to extend your life just for Tantric sex, as the so-called experts are.

The sexual style of Tantra can have a good affect on your health and keep you looking young. Unfortunately, it has been over promoted as the way to become Buddha. However, any person of spiritual self-awareness, who has a strong consideration for others, is a Buddha in life. Buddhas and living Immortals are not necessarily those individuals who live in monasteries and nunneries. Rather many such individuals have led simple lives within society, and their lives included sexual relations. Some examples are described below.

Legend has it that the Yellow Emperor, who was the direct ancestor of my family, had 1200 wives. Truthfully, his wives were the gestures of friendship and alliance

from the different tribes and communities throughout ancient China. They symbolized the communities' early mutual political alliances. His first and formal
wife, Rei Tzu, was a leader among women. She mobilized all the women to join
her in initiating the silk and weaving industry in China.

However later Taoists, who used sex for the sake of sex alone, believed that those
1200 women were virgins given to the Yellow Emperor to help his ascension at
the age of 120. I trust that the Yellow Emperor was an individual who truly knew
how to live his life well, and not abuse it with unlimited sex. The later Chinese
emperors enjoyed expanded privileges, including sexual ones, as they were the
alpha male among all males in the vast nation. Due to such excess they died
young—their average age was only around fifty.

Among the Yellow Emperor's descendants, one man known as Pang Tzu lived for
800 years and married 49 times. He was active around Emperor Yeo's reign,
(2367–2257 BCE). People marveled at his longevity and many marriages, but
they did not pay enough attention to the fact that he developed cooking and
nutrition, Dao-In exercise and self-massage. All of which contributed to his health
and longevity. King Jou (reign 1154–1122 BCE), the last emperor of the Shang
Dynasty, pressured him for his secrets on sexual performance, but Pang Tzu
avoided the king by relocating his clan to the wilderness of the west. It is believed this was how Hatha Yoga was initiated outside of China.

Emperor Wu of the Han Dynasty (reign 140–86 BCE) collected all the earlier
longevity skills, and engaged a large number of virgins. His last comments were
that such things can help your health and help you live a relatively longer life, but
they make it impossible to achieve immortality. I value his wise comment as the
genuine result of his objective experiment.

The Szechwan province is famous for the long lives of its people. One individual,
Mr. Lee, Ching-Yung, lived for 250 years. He lived the same general lifestyle as the
other villagers. He married many times and collected herbs as his profession.

People only knew him for his secret knowledge about sex, but they did not see that he also took care of his physical health with herbs and by living a simple country life.

Another individual, Mr. Lee, Cheng-Yun, lived for 250 years. He diligently exercised and frequently visited mountains. Most people think that his long life was supported by special sexual skills. His real secret was a regular and healthy sexual life with spiritual discipline.

Chen Tuan, who lived for 120 years, practiced internal breathing and fasting, and most of the time he hibernated the active mind. Master Lu was spiritually active for some 400 years. His view was that spiritual life can include sex, and he agreed that senior men can have a sexual life. Master Chang, San-Fung continued the principle that spiritual pursuits can include a sexual life. He became famous as one of the developers of *t'ai chi*. He may have been physically active for up to 400 years.

Sexual practices were not necessarily male-centered. In ancient Chinese society, communities were female-centered. Such old tribes still exist today in China's west.

The Path of Constructive Life and Faith in the Subtle Light

The PCL is the harvest from the Han Dynasty and from the early societies of Fu Shi, Shen Nung and the Yellow Emperor. This harvest covers the humanistic achievement of prehistoric times. The Yellow Emperor's *Internal Classic* is a collection of the early views of life and health by the ancient developed sages. It is not about sexism, which is how the folk stories treat those classic works and describe their ancestors.

You should know that the value of life is not measured by the quantity of wealth you have, or the number of years you live, but by the spiritual quality of your life. This quality is refined and cultivated by all types of life experiences, including sexual behavior. Wealth, power and longevity are simply the by-products of your spiritual quality.

The correct direction to move is towards human health in all aspects of life and without deviation.

Dual cultivation is part of the immortal teaching. It is related to Master Lu's principle of sex for health and mutual benefit. Master Lu emphasized these principles in order to correct the negative effect of celibacy in Buddhism, and other similar practices in people's personal lives.

The spiritual teaching that comes from our deep heart continues and develops Master Lu's and Chen Tuan's work to assist people in living a universal, spiritual life. In the troubled state of today's world, you should not be any less spiritually romantic or poetic than these teachers were in their time, when the world was also in chaos.

Please look up at the sky frequently. The Big Dipper in the northern hemisphere of the sky is a group of seven stars. My mother described them to me as the seven daughters of Mother Universe. Each bright star can remind you of one of the following lines that we offer to you.

To live correctly and normally is more truthful to life than being conventionally religious.

To live frugally within reason is more effective than struggling for great wealth.

To live healthily is more supportive than wanting to be extremely macho or overly sports oriented.

To have a natural and healthy sexual life is more important than experiencing all your sexual fantasies.

To ignore the conditions that lead to temptation and fantasy is more strengthening than gaining tremendous power, wealth or romantic love to support your emotional ego.

To be positive towards what you are able to spiritually achieve can be more practical than trying to become a Buddha and live in Blissful Spiritual Paradise. Truly recognize that the essence of your life is eternal and everlasting, and it involves all kinds of external experiences. Therefore, know the value of being less picky. This last line is the reality of spiritual immortality.

To continue to unite your life and emotions to the natural movements of the sky can be more enduring than struggling against the natural cycles, and it can help you to avoid frown lines.

Chapter 22

顓頊和合道
The Way of Harmonizing Yin *and* Yang
from Emperor Chuan Hsu

時在人類進入家庭與社會不久,
亦堪為新時代,新理想之婚姻觀念.

(Note: Below is the spiritual guidance for sexual union. It comes from the ancient achieved ones. Although it came from a time when humans first entered family-centered society, the instruction still provides useful guidance for today's relationships, offering a new vision for the union of yin and yang. OmNi has translated the following piece from his original in Chinese. Both texts are kept for cross-reference and as guidance for our Chinese-speaking friends.)

黃帝有孫名顓頊,
遠在史前約三千.
不事征伐起戰端,
但願人間無疾苦.
殷勤求索醫與藥,
健康治世便是他.
世人有病可求藥,
只有一病藥難求.
孤陰孤陽心鬱鬱,
男女不諧多懸想.
故此常有情志病,

人間痛苦多因它.
上古神農嘗百草,
只有此病無藥用.
從此闡明和合道,
立定寶則傳後世,
不是上品不可言.
易經重漸家宜恆,
千秋萬世難可變.

Chuan Hsu was born around 3000 years ago, before the Common Era. He was the grandson of the Yellow Emperor. When Chuan Hsu became emperor, he did not delight in wars for conquering. Instead, he devoted himself to the physical suffering of his people. He diligently studied and searched for effective healing arts and medicine. The health of humanity was his pursuit.

Emperor Chuan Hsu realized that when people became ill, medicinal herbs could cure them. Yet one sickness had no easy remedy: the unhappy hearts among unpaired women and men. Their single lives caused them much longing and anxiety. This was the common emotional turmoil among people. They suffered from the many pains that result from the unachieved union of the *yin* and *yang* energies.

Even the sagely King, Shen Nung, who had tested many kinds of plants and herbs, found no medicine for this disease. So Emperor Chuan Hsu expounded on the Way of Harmony, an invaluable instruction on sexual practice, both for his own generation and the generations to come. Do not speak of these things to people of inferior spiritual virtue though, as they would not respect them.

It seems that even though the *I Ching* teaches the principle of gradualness in getting married, and the principles of constancy and persistence in establishing a family, the following precepts on the union of *yin* and *yang* are still needed. And, they will remain suitable for generations to come.

言語不順非眷屬,

The first important requirement is good communication, with mutual respect and understanding between partners.

情意先通水和乳.

When they come together, the spiritual concordance between them must cohere like water and milk.

男敬女,如尊貴;

The man must respect the woman as if she were the wise noble one.

女敬男,如事君.

The woman must care for the man as if he were the king.

心用敬,志宜專.

Their hearts should be filled with respect, and their will should be pure in concentration.

然後入室修上法,

Then, they are ready to enter the inner chamber to cultivate the high practice.

濁質凡夫不堪言.

This practice should not be shared with people of low spiritual virtue.

心存不敬反失笑,

They would only scorn it and laugh about it.

反將至眞視等閒.

They would think the teaching has no high value.

行此道,須至誠,

To perform this practice, you need to be of utmost sincerity.

男不寬衣女亦然.

The man does not take off his clothes, and neither does the woman.

相擁而坐面對面.

Together, you hold each other face-to-face,

聽呼吸,息綿綿,

and listen to the breath in its smooth, unceasing rhythms.

太上忘情在此時.

At this moment, you begin by letting go of the impulse to maximize the excitement and simply be with the joy of pure pleasure.

意在有慾無慾間.

This can be achieved by placing the mind in between the states of desire and no desire.

二氣相和漸忘己.

Gradually, as you both unite your *chi*, you forget the existence of your individual selves and no longer feel your separate bodies.

陰陽交凝復歸一.

With the interweaving of *yin* and *yang*, the two types of chi return to the oneness of the origin of life.

求長生, 須歸一,

In the search for everlasting life, you need to return to the oneness of life.

不歸一, 氣不全.

If you cannot achieve that, the *chi* of your life will remain separate and incomplete.

和合道，存至眞，

The Way of harmonious union takes you to the depth of True Life.

至眞要妙在氣交，

The true practice is the intercourse of the two *chi*—the vitality of two people becoming one.

心若不交氣不交，

If you project your mind separately, there will be no interweaving of the *chi*.

氣若不交有何益，

If there is no interweaving of the *chi*, there will be no benefit from this practice.

僅有體交是馬牛.

If the two bodies are linked together, but there is no union on the other two levels of the mind and spirit, it would be like the horse and ox merely joining their sexual organs together.

此際全心與全意，

Thus, you must be whole-hearted and fully aware.

不雜他念與妄想.

There should not be any other thoughts.

男子頭爲陽來腹爲陰，

To the man, the head is *yang*, and the lower abdomen is *yin*.

女子頭爲陰來腹是陽.

To the woman, the head is *yin*, and the lower abdomen is *yang*.

陰交陽,陽交陰，

Yin intercourses with *yang*, and *yang* intercourses with *yin*.

二陽二陰相交叉.

The two sets of *yin* and *yang* intersect.

若全無慾氣不交,

If you remain completely desireless,

氣不交時形無益,

the energies will not intersect, and there will be no benefit for your life.

若然慾熾火焚時,

And if your desire is overly strong, it will burn up the newly growing tender energies inside more quickly, causing you to age faster and die sooner.

雙雙墜落無岸海.

Engaging in that style of intercourse, will lead both of you to drown in the shoreless sea of Desire.

此等事, 俗難行,

Ordinary people cannot practice these requirements.

不如閉口藏寶秘.

It is better to be quiet and keep the most precious treasure hidden.

從此傳女不傳男,

In early times, for sexual management, this practice was taught only to women, not men.

入選男子須女教,

Only the men chosen for mating could receive the training from the women.

調教不善反遭辱.

If a woman did not train a man well, she could be disgraced by that man.

男壓女，肆暴虐，

The man, out of impatience, would press the woman down with violence and cruelty.

無敬意，無顧惜，

And with no respect or tenderness the two would part.

一時得逞便棄去，

For once the desire was fulfilled, the woman was discarded.

從此人間多悲事．

Since then, there have been too many sad stories.

和合道，戒多言，

You should not talk of these things in practicing the Way of Harmonious Union.

雙方須得伸盟約，

The man and woman should extend their vows.

月下神前表志堅．

This is best done under the bright full moon, or in front of one's spiritual altar.

男顧女，女顧男，

The man should care for the woman.
The woman should care for the man.

永不相負無敵對．

Between them, they should harbor no hatred or conflict in any circumstance.

若有此德存誠敬，

If they have sincere respect and virtuous appreciation for each other, they can then accept each other as partners.

男可寬衣女解帶.

The man can take off his clothes and the woman can do the same.

從此誠心修和合,

From now on, they are partners on the Way of Harmonious Union.

不雜不亂不生災.

If there is no confusion in their behavior, no disaster will happen to them.

雜病不生人長壽,

They will suffer no sickness and enjoy longevity.

從此人間少爭鬥.

By practicing the correct sexually harmonious way, the world will have less struggles.

女貴從一男宜端,

The woman should value having only one man in her life. The man should also value having only one woman in his life. This will prevent the scattering of their energies.

一女一男最和順.

One man to one woman is best for harmony.

神仙家庭神仙侶,

An angelic family with angelic individuals forming the complete union

樂樂融融眞天界.

realizes the happiness of Heaven on Earth.

和合仙人是男子,

The man prepares to be an immortal.

和合仙子是女人.

The woman prepares to be an angel.

慾念形式若改變,

If the pattern of human desire can be improved and changed,

人間太平始可望.

there is hope for peace and harmony in the world.

Chapter 23

The Power of Love

Open your heart.
Love those who accept you,
without calculation and
without bargain.
Love others with kindness.
Love others with consideration.
Do not use the concept of gain in love.
Love is produced by fondness, respect and care.

Love your partner without pushing towards any end.
Purely enjoy the emotional union that satisfies your
longing, your needs and your wants,
without demanding immediate physical union.
It is important not to cause any tension to your beloved.

To achieve spiritual union,
enjoy the love without pushing for physical contact.
There is no lack of subtle union between true lovers.
Achieving that, both sides can enjoy mental and spiritual contact
without harming each other.

Be a human of loving.
Be an angel by living always in the air of love.
Be an angel who loves their companions
without pulling then into a sentimental whirlpool.
Be an angel by conducting your life without hard physical struggle,
and emotional stress.

Love is a style.
Love is a personality.
Love is a harmless medicine.

Merely living in the world
may not lead to any real significant achievement.
Real achievement comes from loving the world
without being harmed by the world.

Who taught this?
The great Emperor Chuan Hsu.
And who else taught and exemplified this?
The Immortal, Master Lu, and his friends.

Unless men and women achieve themselves through spiritual cultivation,
and come to know that change in their sexual styles is necessary
from one of force and friction to one of gentleness and appreciation,
there is no hope for a painless and joyful life.

Why has the world changed to be so bloody?
And why have people become so beastly?
It is because people are too physical,
and they live sloppily and love narrowly.

Be open to see the Light.
Paradise is right here: in the world, in life and in love.

Chapter 24

Emotional Love and Moral Love

General love is an emotion. It is an expression of strong fondness between two individuals. How long can such narrow love last? That depends on the different factors and the motivation that support it.

When we examine the emotional bond between two individuals, which is often considered to be "love," we see that this love only exists in a particular psychological condition, and it changes or disappears when that psychological condition changes. Therefore being attached and in love, or detached and not in love is just a matter of one's psychological condition or emotion. This kind of emotional exercise is limited to the physical level of life, and is not a worthy offering to the world. The love you offer to the world should be stable and secure. It should come from your own deep moral development. An individual of moral depth and moral love has risen above mere emotion and wit.

Some teachers live off the public's support. Both Maoshing and I support the public. We live off our own strength, while working for the spiritual health of humankind. The teachings of those former teachers' have produced loafers, whereas our teaching produces healers. The background of the former teachings is from a religious mix. Our background is from the ancient humanistic, moral culture of China.

Many individuals have caused spiritual confusion by playing ideas and thoughts to the unlearned world. As seriously trained individuals our path is a dutiful one. We guide people to the bright future. The Way is not sloppy. We do not use spiritual excuses to avoid life's responsibilities. We use our own decent strength, and encourage the decent strength of others to enhance and assist our moral work in the world.

Moral love is the strength to live in the world and care for the world at the same time. Emotional love is just a temporary escape.

Love without responsibility is not love, but an abuse of oneself and others.

Love is not a lullaby to put you to sleep. Love, which includes respect and appreciation, brings the lover to a deeper understanding of the love of Mother Universe.

PART IV

Realize Your Life Through Virtuous Service

Chapter 25

Universal Nature Is the Root of Your Virtuous Life (Cultivation of Cosmic Chi)

In Chapter 20, we talked about how you can realize the deep, innate virtues of life, and integrate them into your daily life through spiritual cultivation and self-discipline. You can then naturally extend these virtues into your social relationships and wider communities. The achieved ones, who were the early students of life, called this virtuous fulfillment. In this chapter, we wish to describe how cultivating healthy energy, or *chi*, and performing healing can be constructive forms of virtuous service.

The Virtuous Power of Cosmic *Chi*

The virtue of life comes from the deep root of nature, which is also the power of cosmic life energy or *chi*. One of the highest recognitions of the virtue of life comes from Lao Tzu's transmission of the *Tao Teh Ching*, where *Teh* means "virtue," or the spiritual gain of life, *Tao* means "the Way," and *Ching* means "the book." The complete vision of that teaching is the Way to an Everlasting Life.

Tao and *Teh* are the substance and function, respectively, of the same deep reality. They are the normal and healthy expression of the existence and function of nature. And nature, by expressing itself normally and constantly most of the time, is supportive and productive of all life. Therefore *Teh,* or virtue, in the teaching of the PCL, means the healthy and supportive functions of life. It does not mean the external demands or commandments from any outside authority. It is the very nature of your healthy life. Hence, a lack of healthy function in life means a loss of virtue. Virtue can also mean the spiritual merit of your personality. For further understanding you may refer to my book *Enrich Your Life With Virtue.*

The natural power of health and healing belongs to those who are spiritually aligned with the natural virtues of life. The central virtue of all the virtues is the love of life, which includes respect for life. With love, you can eliminate all prejudices and hatred, and you can receive healing from the cosmic *chi*, or you can conduct *chi* to promote healing in someone else.

Cosmic *Chi* Healing Practice Produces the Power of Natural Health

Cosmic *chi*, or cosmic energy, is the source of the universe and all life. It is also the root of your healthy life. You can cultivate this energy by living peacefully, and by doing away with unnecessary thoughts, emotions, activities and struggles, in order to remain receptive to the healing effects and healthy support of the energy.

Peacefulness can be achieved through quiet and serene sitting, standing, walking and movement. All these practices can help you achieve the health benefits and high goals of *chi* cultivation. Serene sitting can also help you reach the inner depth of your life. The practice of serenity means that when the pure and silent mind is engaged, there should be no negative thoughts or disturbing emotions creating any internal pressure.

Some of the powerful effects of cosmic *chi* cultivation and healing include mental and spiritual cleansing, mental and spiritual protection, and the remaking of your destiny through accessing your inner potential. By purifying your soul, you can reach Tao, the Way of Everlasting Life, in this lifetime. The *chi* practices heal you by directly connecting you to cosmic *chi* without using any distorted presentations or involving you in any kind of organized social manipulation.

Below is a list of benefits that can result from cosmic *chi* cultivation. By regularly practicing serenity and quietness, you may:

Clear away unnoticed tensions and obstacles in your body.

Generally temper emotions and specifically weaken negative emotions.

Increase metabolism.

Promote endocrine balance.

Restore your body's natural regenerative function.

Increase vitality and stamina.

Reduce tension and instability.

Protect your health.

Regain the power of learning and memory.

Gradually eliminate suffering from your body and mind, which can manifest as aches, pains, insomnia, chronic fatigue, and so on.

Enhance circulation and regain your life's healthy functioning.

Nurture and refresh your life essence.

Develop your bodily energy to become *chi* energy, which can be experienced as warmth, vibration and tingling, etc.

Refine your *chi* energy to enhance your life's spiritual energy, which is the subtlest of all energies at the general level.

Enhance your spiritual consciousness. Spiritual energy has consciousness. The energy of your soul produces inspiration, intuition and conscience. The spiritual function of your conscience can be called Instant Judgment. It enables you to eliminate the so-called "Last Judgment."

Strengthen your conscience through the development of your soul energy. This nurtures the power of righteousness in your life and with your worldly connections. With a spiritually developed conscience, you can achieve union with the Divine and enter the sacred realms. In this way, you can unite your whole being with the Tao in this very lifetime. This is the traditional goal of the Integral Way.

The Preparation for the Healer and the Recipient of Cosmic *Chi* Healing

Natural health seekers and healers of cosmic *chi* are those who can heal themselves and others with cosmic *chi*.

More than 2000 years ago, when life was mostly natural, people in the early Han Dynasty (206 BCE–219CE) lived a natural faith and enjoyed the healing powers of cosmic *chi* as described in the Invocation of Cosmic *Chi* Healing (see the end of this chapter). The people appreciated the vastness of nature with its hidden potential, and their accomplished healers held strong convictions about humanity's deep-rooted connection to nature. Based on this faith, the early people were able to maintain their health and develop themselves. You too can use the Invocation to support your general health, your complete development and/or prepare yourself to become a cosmic *chi* healer.

In addition, if you wish to attain the natural power of health, self-heal a serious disease, or facilitate healing for someone else, you should prepare for at least seven and up to 49 days. During this period, you can recite the Invocation and maintain a quiet and focused concentration. It is best to eat clean, healthy food, and mentally fast so that your thoughts do not scatter or entertain strong desires. This will help you nurture the purity of the cosmic *chi* and become a good healer of yourself and others. Healing can also be done in groups.

The Important Understandings of the
Power of Self-Healing From Cosmic *Chi*

Cultivating and receiving cosmic *chi*, or energy healing, can help heal many diseases including: psychosomatic illnesses, which generally avoid detection by external systems or methods, such as undiagnosed malaise; illnesses with latent spiritual causes, such as the disharmony between one's internal spiritual elements due to past and forgotten reasons; and illnesses that have been unsuccessfully treated by other methods. The healing power can therefore be channeled to heal psychological and spiritual contamination, as well as physiological conditions.

The healing comes from the spiritual energy of nature rather than from any physical or external form of medication or application. Physical healing systems usually serve as supplements to the deep life energy of nature.

In *chi* or energy healing, the source of energy moves from a purer person to a sick person, but the energy is not entirely the healer's. Rather, it is the pure piety of the healer and the recipient together, which brings forth the appropriate result.

In *chi* healing, a patient does not need to see different specialists for his or her symptoms, because the *chi* healer reaches for the root of the problem. In contrast, a specialist who limits their focus to a small portion of the whole, is like someone looking at a leaf or twig on the branch of a big tree, therefore, they may not be able to provide the essential help for a sick person. Specific knowledge and laboratory tests can supply some information, but these are usually superficial and limited. Both the doctor and patient can get lost in the details and miss the subtle and essential foundation of life. On the other hand, a cosmic *chi* healer reaches for the root of the problem, performing all-round therapy for problems on all different levels of life.

A sincere and well-trained *chi* practitioner can apply energy healing in a variety of situations. For example, it can be used as a remedy for someone who obsesses over material riches or social power. That person's excessiveness is a disease, rather than a healthy expression of natural life. Energy healing is most effectively applied to those who still maintain some level of naturalness.

The healing powers of cosmic *chi* have, unfortunately, been misused by confused individuals and corrupt groups who established themselves with spiritually misleading beliefs. In particular, some leaders have used historical evidence of particular individuals (such as Jesus) who were achieved in cosmic *chi* healing, to support their leadership ambitions. As a result of those leaders' unhealthy motivations, no one could directly experience cosmic *chi* for their life's support. Cultural confusion has arisen due to the over abundance of names and forms created to invoke the same unnamable reality.

The traditional and primary aim of cosmic *chi* healing is to help you attune yourself to life's natural virtue. Life's virtue is what you selflessly express or fulfill in your daily life and relationships. For instance, the virtue of Maoshing and I is not expressed as a desire to amass followers, but as the true, unbiased service we give to guide you in nurturing your life's perfect energy. In addition, the performance of cosmic *chi* healing is part of your personal virtuous fulfillment of life. It is usually done formlessly according to the healer's achievement. All healers accept universal discipline as the way of maintaining their health, while facing all of life's temptations.

While the tradition of the Integral Way respects the development of personal power, it also warns that the sole pursuit of power without personal discipline invites downfall, and can lead to insanity. The religious term "evil spirit" merely refers to the undisciplined and ill use of natural power, while the term "Godhood" refers to the disciplined use of natural power. Both come from nature. Spiritual development and self-discipline are both important as they enable you to learn how to ride safely on nature's power.

Those of you interested in nurturing the pure power of nature are given clear instructions how to attune to and live with its natural health. My books such as

The Foundation of a Happy Life, Enrich Your Life with Virtue, The Centermost Way, and *The Majestic Domain of the Universal Heart,* among others, are written to help you grow and develop spiritually. By using these books you may find one that personally and spiritually corresponds to you. When that happens, you'll have regained your connection to life. It can happen in a moment when the descriptions turn out to be your own truthful spiritual being that has been unfolding in front of your eyes. This is the response from your own inner, spiritual reality.

Modern minds have a hard time seeing the natural healing power of cosmic *chi.* Last century, the communist government of China banned it as superstition. They preferred to trust the discovered, mechanical patterns of nature as the complete knowledge of life. Yet numerous *chi* healing styles have been practiced in China throughout many generations. In fact, China's old communities mostly rely on the natural support of *chi* to maintain their health. Now, after a wasteful half-century, *chi* healing has been re-accepted in modern China, serving as the most powerful medicine for its vast population.

Interestingly, the Chinese communist government sees the positive result of *chi* healing, but cannot tolerate the theism. The totalitarian regime has taken advantage of the undeveloped masses by teaching them that communism is the solution for human society. In part, the government fears that *chi* healing groups may become their political rivals.

The Curative Effects of Cosmic *Chi*

Chi healing is one way of applying cosmic energy. *Chi* is the essence of life. It is the truth of universal life and the Way to everlasting life. However, people who perceive partially and narrowly have interpreted and described cosmic *chi* with limiting images. Therefore, humanity has many religions portraying cosmic *chi* in confusingly different ways. It is important to remember that religious teachings are just different metaphors for the one spiritual reality, which is, in truth, internal and indescribable.

God is the very essence of life. If Allah means God, then it describes that very same essence in life. In truth, God simply describes the natural power that exists within the vast natural background of life. Buddha in Hinayana Buddhism means an awakened one, or the specific sage who achieved enlightenment. While in Mahayana Buddhism, Buddha means the Perfect Being. Hinayana was developed so one could learn the wisdom of the awakened sage, while Mahayana was the spiritual pursuit of perfection. If you could see through to the unadorned subtle reality, and recognize that all religious systems were people's pursuit and worship that developed in different times, which one of these names could you reject?

All lives and things derive their being from the Cosmic *Chi* Being. The Cosmic *Chi* Being belongs to all lives on all levels. The universal consciousness of the Cosmic *Chi* Being does not discriminate against or create boundaries towards anything on any level. However, lives with a naturally developed conscious energy are above those lives that have not yet developed conscious energy.

The universal conscious energy encompasses all beings and things, including nonbeings and nonexistence. That is, it is above all lives of form and no form. Universal consciousness and universal conscience are achievable by beings with developed consciousness.

Cosmic energy is in a perfect and healthy condition. It is the pure original energy before any contamination. This perfect and righteous power, or *chi*, is the respectful subtle source of the universe. Its curative properties can apply to your body, mind and spiritual consciousness, producing tranquility and well-being.

Physiologically, cosmic *chi* can activate and strengthen the functioning of various tissues and organs. It can cast out negative *yin* and turbid *chi*, while nurturing *yang chi* for a quick and healthy recovery.

If sufferers can reopen their hearts to appreciate the natural virtue of life, which is the spontaneous functioning of natural life, and accept its healthy discipline, the curative effect of cosmic *chi* will be greater.

During serene sitting, a practitioner can use invocations selected from the *Spiritual Workbook*. Within that book there are five invocations of purification that are essential for the sick and troubled. Their use can invoke a cosmic response to purify the sufferer's body, mind and soul. A nexus of perfect *chi* is formed that responds and resonates to the universal cosmic energy in order to thoroughly cleanse and improve the sufferer's bodily composition.

In relation to your human body, cosmic *chi* healing is a means to completely realign and reorder your life away from the contorted conditioning of worldly experience.

Conditions Where the Healing Is Not Effective

Although there is no power higher than cosmic energy, that energy may be of little to no use to people when they:

Lack motivation to nurture perfect *chi* in their lives.

Request treatment, but lack seriousness or sincerity.

Overly damage their lives through medication, surgery, radiation, or other potentially harmful techniques.

Shorten their naturally allotted lifespan due to an unhealthy lifestyle, and/or contact with detrimental influences.

Reach the end of their lives due to self-abuse or social abuse.

Conditions Where the
Healing Is Most Effective

Cosmic *chi* healing easily lends itself to people whose minds and lives remain natural, and whose broad life attitudes enable them to recognize the following connections.

The sky is the source of life. The Earth gives form to life. All people are brothers and sisters.

In the vastness of space, the life of humankind is among the most beautiful of beings.

Many personal problems result from a lack of development.

Social trouble results from the strong abusing the weak; however, the strong usually end up abusing themselves. People, who overextend their desires for more desire, create uneasiness in the world.

The early people who lived around 2000 to 3000 years ago (particularly around the early Han Dynasty) lived a natural faith. They did not suffer from the complicated physical and mental conditions that people do today, nor did they have the complicated medical system of today. Instead, they relied on the power of natural health, occasionally receiving help from accomplished healers who upheld humanity's connection to nature.

Those people appreciated the vastness of nature with its hidden potential, and they lived according to it. However, once people started to develop literary abilities, that natural faith was presented in a new literary style, and the human mind began to deviate from the natural reality. This was the time when religions began developing. And when the literary reproductions were used to establish control of people's undeveloped minds, socialized religion emerged. Although the religious presentations appealed to people's sentimentality and emotional suffering, it only contorted their minds; just as conventional religious teaching does today.

In modern times, therefore, you have a situation where people generally do not recognize the existence of *chi* until they become sick, and receive help from a *chi* practitioner. By seeing through your mental distortion, you can come to understand that the salvation for all people comes from recognizing the value of nature, and the position of human life within it, just as the early, natural healers did.

The Principles of Cosmic *Chi* Cultivation

The body, mind and spiritual consciousness of a human being are intimately connected and interdependent.

Apart from external conditions of polluted air and water, viruses and virulent bacteria, pathogenesis can also be traced to prolonged stress and anxiety, leading to imbalances in the internal secretions of an individual. These imbalances, in turn, give rise to physical diseases, or what psychiatrists call psychosomatic illnesses.

Illness can also arise from the invisible influence of a contaminated consciousness acquired through lifetimes of experience. When the essence of a life moves through different lives it is called reincarnation. Through this long process of unfolding, the individual essence can become caught in the cyclic and recycling pattern of suffering. This can lead to various psychosomatic imbalances in that life.

Cosmic *chi* healing works when the healer, moved by the mental energy (known as the bonding force) of an individual who earnestly seeks treatment, resolves to respond with compassionate mental energy (known as the harmonizing force).

This is the way to establish spiritual communication between people, and allow for healing between two different lives.

The healer first uses The Invocation of Cosmic *Chi* Healing to connect to the spirits of the sufferer, and the healing energy of the pure beings from the healthy side of the spiritual connection. The healer's energy and the silent practice invoke the sufferer's higher level of energy. The sick energy is infused with pure healing energy when a new energy field of health is formed by reconnecting to the Cosmic Chi Being. In this subtle change, the healer repels the suffering person's pathological elements, thereby producing a therapeutic effect. This occurs through the strengthening action of the harmonizing force between the individuals and their spirits. The healer uses the harmonizing force, while the recipient uses the bonding force. These opposite forces attract each other. The healer emanates compassionate *yang* energy and the recipient emanates pleading *yin* energy. Effectiveness lies in the utter sincerity of both the healer and the recipient. Illustrations and demonstrations may be given directly for personal experience and understanding.

Life comes from the bosom of the Cosmic *Chi* Being. Healing power comes from the pure source of nature, and from where it comes, there it should return. A highly achieved life is deathless. To a being of pure energy and life, there is absolute freedom: there are no obstructions of form or no form, color or no color, sign or no sign, or whatever.

The Invocation of Cosmic *Chi* Healing

The sky is my father.
The Earth is my mother.
As the energies of the sky and Earth harmonize,
the high life of humankind is born.

All people are my brothers and sisters.
All of us are connected by bonds of mutual respect.
The whole supports the single being,
and all single beings support the whole.
In this way, we assure the health of human society.

As the energies of the sky and Earth harmonize,
the Cosmic *Chi* Being gave birth to my life.
I endeavor to fulfill my natural human potential,
to remain worthy as nature's dignified life.

Natural virtue brings forth human life.
I therefore live with the natural virtue of life,
And, above all, I will not deceive or mislead others.

Nurtured by the Cosmic *Chi* Being,
my life gains growth.
Uniting with the Cosmic *Chi* Being,
my life attains eternity.
My everlasting life can be discovered through the Cosmic *Chi* Being.
I live on the products of the Cosmic *Chi* Being
that come to me or through me.

These are my high practices in life—
I open up to the High Truth of the Cosmic *Chi* Being.
I waste nothing in order to enrich my life.
I tolerate all offenses to set myself free.
I am loyal to life's purity and decency,
and forgive others in order to support my conscious health.
I am righteous and I am dutiful towards the health of life
in order to attract bountiful, good fruit in my life.

Being upright presents my health.

Being healthy is my personal responsibility.

I am the Divine Light,

I am the Divine Truth, and

I am the Way of Everlasting Life.

When I have removed my own selfishness and egotism,

I am also capable of removing the illness and darkness of the world.

With utmost sincerity,

I help my own life and the lives of others.

Ten Prayers to Support the Subconscious Sphere of Your Life

The following ten short prayers can support the health of your subconscious as you move towards attaining a healthy and pure conscious being. Any one of the prayers may be chosen and chanted repeatedly in quiet and with a relaxed concentration. This is one way to spiritually train and calm your subconscious strength. These prayers can also keep you away from unnecessary medications and painkillers with their negative side effects. It is best to use the prayers before you have spiritually surrendered yourself to the shallow culture and dominant, external forces of society.

Some practitioners of a quiet mind may notice that modern political and commercial organizations employ a similar technique of subliminal suggestion, although their conditioning is often irresponsible and unsupportive of your health. You, therefore, need to protect yourself by replacing the unhealthy conditioning with natural, healthy and universally constructive suggestions.

Nature endows everyone with spiritual power; it just needs to be correctly invoked. Sincere and regular use of the prayers can do just that. The prayers are effective. My mother used them to help her students' consciously expand their lives. You can do the same. You may refer to my book *Mystical Universal Mother* for further details.

The invaluable prayers are:

"The Universal Divine One of All Healing"

"The Universal Divine One of All Enrichment"

"The Universal Divine One of All Empowering"

"The Universal Divine One of All Enlightenment"

"The Universal Divine One of All Harmonizing and Pacifying"

"The Universal Divine One of Helping Make the Appropriate Choice"

"The Universal Divine One of Clearing the Way to Goodness"

"The Universal Divine One of All Forgiving"

"The Universal Divine One of All Blessings"

"The Universal Divine One of All Prospering"

Each and all the prayers contribute to positive individual and group life energy.

The subconscious condition of people who do not have a specific practice is usually unruly. Those people can incur unexpected trouble in the absence of good spiritual discipline and cultivation. Therefore for them, I recommend the following prayer: "The Universal Divine One of All Blessings."

Chapter 26

How to Support the Path of Constructive Life in Modern Times? (The Foundation for Realizing Universal Morality in the World)

What is the best way to support the teachings and healing practices of the PCL, and make them available to the world?

Different religious teachings are supported in various ways. For example, Christianity relies on tithing, and Tibetan Buddhism relies on large donations of up to 30 to 50 percent of its followers' incomes. In early Chinese societies, politics and spiritual teaching were combined; there was no religion, although the Way did exist. The Yellow Emperor and six generations of his descendants were the early social leaders. Their work was a pure donation for their society's development. The so-called "emperor" donated all of his creations to society. The "throne" was not a position of personal enjoyment or self-support. The emperor's advisors, ministers, and all of his supporters performed their duties without asking for any payment over and above what was necessary to survive.

The natural social order in China that was initiated by the Yellow Emperor and the early leaders before him was destroyed by both natural and social disasters. By the end of the Chou Dynasty, some 2300 years ago, people's minds and health had begun to deteriorate due to physical and emotional competitions. Such decline continues today.

When the trouble was just beginning, Lao Tzu had the foresight to reproduce the teaching of the ancient Way, calling people to return to its natural order and balance. He guided people to give up relying on external establishments with their artificial order, suggesting, instead, that people donate to society once they have achieved what is necessary to maintain their own healthy lives. This was also the approach of later proponents of the Heavenly Way. The approach of both Lao Tzu and those later proponents came from a personal moral sense to extend their individual spiritual development in order to improve human society.

Today's social and spiritual confusion reflects that Lao Tzu's work has not yet been realized. This has inspired Maoshing and I to perceive of the possibility of achieving a more natural harmony in the world by using its positive spiritual customs, alongside the teachings of the Way of universal life in the form of the PCL. In support of these teachings, we recommend that spiritual leaders donate at least 90 percent of their life's creations to the spiritual work of the world. General people can donate at least ten percent of their life's creations for the support and realization of a morally ordered society. We do not insist that you follow these personal standards. Each individual is responsible for deciding the extent of his or her moral contribution to others, and gives what they can afford. Actually, the most fundamental help you can give the world is to lead a responsible and healthy life, and avoid creating any burden on society.

PART V

Prayers and Inspirational Readings for Spiritual Cultivation

Chapter 27

The Shrine of the Eternal Breath of Tao

The Shrine is used to remind you to value and respect your life and the greater Life with the Eternal Breath of Tao.

The Tao is the Way. The Way is the universal nature. It is the health of the universal nature. Although it cannot be contained in a small shrine, it is contained in the life of each individual. In your small life you thus have two basic responsibilities to fulfill: one is that your life should present the health of nature, and the other is that you should keep away from the contamination that damages the healthy nature of life. By respecting your life, you naturally respect the shrine and the Way of life.

The sages and wise leaders who are displayed in the Shrine of the Eternal Breath of Tao[1] represent humanistic love with their constructive life spirit. They are examples of life. In particular, Fu Shi, Shen Nung and the Yellow Emperor represent the initiating spirit of humanity, before too much bad experience had contorted its benign nature. Once human nature became contorted, people began searching for remedies to cure the trouble. By so doing, however, many helpless and wasteful creations were made, further contorting the healthy nature of life.

The healthy nature of life is itself the shrine. Life is the biggest religion above all. May each one of us spiritually devote ourselves to the natural health of life without deviation. Let human love prevail over the conflicts of minor difference. May all of us be an example of the constructive spirit of humanity, and continue to enjoy the Eternal Breath of Tao in posterity, even though we may

---

1. The Shrine of the Eternal Breath of Tao is located at Yo San University of Traditional Chinese Medicine in Los Angeles, California. Although this chapter refers to that particular shrine, its meaning applies to any shrine that is constructed with sincere and genuine intent for true spiritual growth. Guidelines for constructing a shrine can be found in the *Workbook for Spiritual Development of All People*.

have experienced occasional sickness and the sickness of some people and some leaders in the long river of our human history.

Harmony, balance and cooperation are the life spirits we appreciate to fulfill. May these great life spirits and the health of life be fortified, here, at the Shrine of the Eternal Breath of Tao.

人身如圣殿,

Our body is the holy temple.

先贤有金言.

An early great teacher commended this.

借外以修内,

Borrow the external things of life to cultivate our internal life.

道昌德乃坚.

When the Way is clearly practiced the Virtue of life (which is the Health of life) is then strengthened.

Chapter 28

My Lord, Heavenly Heart
(A Prayer for Universal Spiritual Unity)

I do not take orders from kings, but I work with those of the Heavenly Heart.
I do not subject my life to any lords, except those of the Heavenly Heart.
I obey no authority over my life, but that of the Heavenly Heart
in any person, even that of a child.

No teaching or religion shall earn my faith,
unless it correctly expresses the Heavenly Heart.
With straightforwardness, I follow the Heavenly Heart.
By following the Heavenly Heart, I avoid all detours.

I enjoy good health and a long and peaceful life
because I cherish the Heavenly Heart within me.
I happily thrive with a simple life and earnest means
because of the constructive creations from the Heavenly Heart.

I clearly recognize that the purpose of my humble life
is to serve the Heavenly Heart within and without.
I befriend people not for their riches or intelligence,
but because I cherish the Heavenly Heart within them.

If I could mean something to others,
it would be as a reminder of the Heavenly Heart.
To awaken the Heavenly Heart in others,
I strengthen the Heavenly Heart in me.

People may be lost and the world may be confused,

but it is my responsibility to help them turn back

from the steep cliff of downfall and the bottomless abyss.

In reality, there is no such abyss, only people who lose their self-reflective vision

and Heavenly Heart by following too deeply the wrong directions of each other.

The world's people have strayed from the Heavenly Heart

by engaging in competitions of swollen emotions and physical strength,

creating endless suffering and darkness.

I follow the Heavenly Heart without need of any return.

Its purity knows no bounds.

Each day, with sincerity and devotion, I continue to grow into its endless domain.

O' Heavenly Heart you have cleansed and strengthened me.

You have sustained humanity as your own infant and child.

Now each one of us, by attending to our own spiritual growth,

can help promote a long and happy survival on Earth,

and therefore fulfill the true spiritual duty of life.

Love, OmNi

Chapter 29

The Lady-In-Blue

The Lady-in-Blue is the Goddess of Wisdom.
Her voice is soft; her approach gentle.
She is a little too shy, however, to get along with the masses.

She is the Prime Minister to the Heavenly King of Humility
and the Heavenly Queen of Modesty.
Being humble and modest are divinely valued virtues.
The Mother of the Universe assigns the Divine Ruling Couple.

The official title of the Mother Universe is Unity—the highest.
Her maiden name is *Ama*.
Scholars try to please her by addressing her as the Almighty.
But she jokes to herself like this:
The Almighty is unseen and inactive,
while the minor "mighties" are very active.

The Divine Couple of Heaven rules equally
over Heaven and the human world.
The Prime Minister hasn't much to do,
though she likes to dress up in blue.
Sometimes she appears in light blue and other times in deep blue.
This is why she is nicknamed the Lady-in-Blue.

She comes down from high to visit the human world.
She needs no tax write-off for her trip,
because she manages her budget well.
She always has more than enough.

Since you are the children of the Almighty,
you may see her in the dark after you have developed your spiritual vision.
Spiritually, she appears as a royal blue light.

She can function as the developed vision of your life too.
With the name of Crystal Clarity,
she can help you in times of confusion.

Generally, people divide things and themselves into good and bad,
right and wrong, long and short, and so on.
But because people are the children of the Divine Couple,
it is not that simple.
At the level of good and bad there are no absolutes,
though people may insist so.

The Divine Parents developed the world,
by first giving birth to twins—*yin* and *yang*.
As the direct offspring of the Divine Couple,
the twins are assigned to take care of their world.
Miss *Yin* and Mister *Yang* do things differently,
if not totally oppositely.

The Divine Couple endows the twins
with no absolute authority or special spiritual power,
and this is a constant complaint between the twins.
Their authority is established, however, when they help one another.

Neither *yin* nor *yang* is absolute.
Rather, they naturally mend each other.
Things can be good at the beginning, but bad later on.
Things can be bad at the beginning, but good in the end.

How can you define good or bad,

when they are constantly interchanging?

The over extension of either side is what leads to negativity.

But *yin* and *yang* each insist that they are right.

They argue and fight among themselves endlessly.

The Divine Couple above witnesses this trouble.

The Prime Minister intends to help,

though there is not much she can do, unless she gets the twins' support.

Objectivity is the greatest offering that can be made to the Goddess of Wisdom.

Assertion or insistence is a serious blasphemy.

When blasphemy occurs, it means the Goddess' help is refused,

and she has no alternative but to give up.

The Goddess of Wisdom has four maiden assistants,

which appear in the dark with your spiritually developed vision

as different colored lights:

Lady Spring is a tiny, green light.

She helps you in matters of health.

Her name is *Vivi*,

or some prefer to say the Spring of Ever Youth.

Lady Summer appears as a tiny, sharp, red light.

She can assist your material needs and sometimes

appear as a warning of your excesses.

Her name is *Ajini* or Joy.

Lady Autumn is a tiny, white light.

She helps in matters of blessing.

Her name is Harvest.

Lady Winter appears as a tiny, purple light.
She helps you live a long life.
Her name is Longevity, the same as her function.

Each of these lights can appear as a tiny, single spark when you are at peace and in the dark. They are the result of your realistic efforts to nurture your life, rather than draining it through external searching and unhealthy living. The soul of your life is composed of tiny, light particles which, when increased, lead your life to prosperity. If these particles are lost or reduced, you know what that means. Those particles are related to your sexual secretions or reproductive force, and you can increase their number through spiritual self-cultivation.

Among the four assistants, *Ajini* or Joy, the Summer Spirit, has made a great contribution to the human world. From Heaven, she bought the skill of fire making, which led to its use for warmth and cooking, and thus the beginning of human civilization. Civilization owes a great deal to *Ajini*, the Goddess of Fire. However, she is easily irritated, thus never offend her, but treat her with respect.

The Lady-in-Blue was the divinity worshipped by women in ancient times.
She helped the women in their decision-making
during the long period of time when women led societies.

The Goddess enjoys peace, neatness, cleanliness and quiet,
and avoids places that are noisy, disorderly, smelly or unclean.
She is the inspiration of a good life.
A good life means to be healthy, naturally joyful,
simply and materially comfortable, and long-lived.
These are the four Divine assistants of the Goddess of Wisdom.

The Goddess is too profound to be known.
You can show your respect by not using your energy to create stories about her;
she is not a mythological character.
She once appeared as a woman to assist the young Yellow Emperor
to create order in the world in exactly the same way
as the Mother Universe orders the Universe.

The Lady-in-Blue can come from the sky
and also be the blue sky.
She may also imply the Mother Universe.

Ever since my childhood,
my good thoughts and good images of her have never ceased.
I prepare my life with neatness, cleanliness, orderliness, peace and quietude,
in readiness for her teaching.

Chapter 30

最高眞理道路
The Path to the Ultimate Truth

皈 依 三 一
Paying Homage to the
Universal Spiritual Trinity

皈依明.

I pay homage to the spiritual purity that needs no decoration or explanation.

皈依達.

I pay homage to the mental clarity that is never confused by my mental creations or the mental creations of others.

皈依怡悦.

I pay homage to emotional peace, lightness and joy. This is how I treat the life I live.

人 生 四 諦
The Four Truths of a Constructive Life

從苦得樂諦:
吃得苦中苦, 方爲人上人.
不經一番寒澈骨, 那得梅花撲鼻香.

I do not mind enduring hardships in order to improve my life and transform bitterness into joy.

集善得福，集德成美諦.

I trust the spiritual truth that collecting all goodness in life, in order to invite blessings and accumulate virtue is the way to happiness.

滅除障難幻想邪行諦.

I need to extinguish all illusions and right all wrongs in order to achieve life's constant renewal.

達道光明諦.

The ultimate goal of any spiritual teaching is to eliminate obstacles in order to enlighten the soul. I follow such a teaching in order to eliminate the obstacles in my life. The reward is a brightened soul shining upon my own life and the life of the world.

内 三 綱

The Three Internal Bonds in Life

心=君,體=臣；君明臣賢→在致於明.

When the heart and mind are one, the mind is the king. The functions of the body are the ministers. When the king is clear minded, the ministers are effective. Their common effort is to achieve clarity.

氣=母，神=子；母旺子強→其致在旺.

Chi is the mother. The conscious mind is the son. When the mother is healthy, the son is strong. Their common effort is to achieve strength.

外(身)=夫,裡(心)=妻；夫貴妻榮→其致在一.

The outer body is the husband. The inner mind is the wife. When the husband is honored, the wife is respected too. Their common effort is to achieve unity.

外 三 綱
The Three External Bonds in Life

君臣合義, 君=國家,社會.

The king and the subjects unite through life's virtue.

父子同心.

The parents and the offspring unite through heart.

夫妻合德.

The husband and wife unite through mutual support.

修 道 三 綱
The Three Guidelines in Spiritual Pursuit

棄小從大, 暫往從久.
= 此心從道, 從宇宙, 及從久世;
不從世教, 但備參考.

Abandon the small and the temporal for the great and the eternal. This means to follow the Way, and what is universally and everlastingly meaningful.

貴無形而惜有形.

Value the subtle power of the formless above the formed.

尊生而賤名與物.

Respect the substance of life over fame and fortune.

298 ⁓ PART V: CHAPTER 30

尊 生 五 常

The Five Principles to Live By in Order to Respect Life

重內在而薄外表.

Value the inner substance over the outer trappings.

務實而不務虛名.

Seek a firm footing above the superficial.

重實行而不貴浮言虛言.

Respect action more than words.

寧守樸實無華, 不事花巧欺世.

Maintain honesty and sincerity rather than cunning and cleverness.

不爭一日, 祇爭千秋.

Fight not for momentary glory, but the eternal truth, so as to live with the spiritual worth that lasts forever.

修 道 三 要

The Three Pivotal Approaches for Real Achievement

見道,明道,合道, 但須破障:

In order to see, realize and embody the subtle truth of universal life, three practices are fundamental. These are:

去文言思慮之惑.

Breaking off from the obstruction of conceptual snares, which means having no ideological confusion.

去煽誘激情之惑.

Casting off the bondage of desires, which includes having no religious confusion.

去情緒牽縈之惑.

Smashing through the entanglement of emotional controls, which means releaseing any sectarian spirit, partisan confusion or negative emotional attachments.

Fulfilling the Virtues in Order to Realize Life

説得海闊天空, 不如行得一寸.
漫演天花亂聚, 地湧金蓮, 豈毋如平實家風.

Rather than dreaming about the heavens, take a step on firm ground. Rather than losing yourself in fantasies, seek the normalcy of family life.

日 常 五 常
The Five Constancies in Daily Life

處世曰仁.

With humanistic love one treats the world.

仁者愛人, 愛仁以德.

A benevolent one loves virtuously.

處爭曰公.

With appropriateness one lives in society.

義者處世曰公.

A righteous individual is not partial to anyone.

義者處事曰宜.

A righteous individual behaves with propriety.

禮者知讓.

Through yielding one fulfills orderliness or civility.

禮者,重序而尊賢篤行. 敬老, 護小. 扶弱, 恤無知,及殘者.

A chivalrous individual respects the orderliness of relationships, offering consideration to the elderly, the young, the weak and the disabled alike.

治心曰智.

With wisdom one governs the mind.

尚智不尚力.

A wise one does not apply force to others.

待人曰信

With faithfulness one treats all people with universal principles.

信者誠信待人, 裡外如一.

A faithful individual treats all people equally.

外 五 常
The Five Spiritual Duties
of External Relationships

君臣曰義.

Having a rightful common goal fulfills the normal bond between superiors and subordinates.

父子曰德.

Loving virtuously fulfills the normal bond between parents and offspring.

夫婦曰和.

Living harmoniously fulfills the normal bond between husband and wife.

兄弟曰讓.

Being humble fulfills the normal bond among brothers and sisters.

朋友曰信.

Being trustworthy fulfills the normal bond among friends.

聖 者 五 常
The Constant Virtue of the Achieved Ones

知我無我,故同之以仁.

The Achieved Ones know that there is no position for the sense of self when treating others. Therefore, they are kind to all people and take people as they are without judging them or forming opinions about them.

知事無我,故權之以義.

The Achieved Ones know that there is no position for the sense of self when performing their activities. Therefore, they respect appropriate behavior and performance, and are not self-opinionated.

知心無我,故戒之以禮.

The Achieved Ones know that there is no position for the sense of self while being civil. Therefore, they respect the way people like to be treated, and are not self-opinionated.

知識無我,故照之以智.

The Achieved Ones know that there is no position for the sense of self in common knowledge. Therefore, they respect wisdom in governing all branches of knowledge, and are not self-opinionated.

知言無我,故守之以信.

The Achieved Ones know that that there is no position for the sense of self when communicating with others. Therefore, they are not self-opinionated.

以 一 通 五
Realizing Any One of the Five Virtues is to Accomplish Them All

以仁行義,禮,智,信, 則皆仁.

When you fulfill righteousness, appropriateness, orderliness or civility, wisdom and faithfulness with kindness, all the virtues express kindness.

以義行仁,禮,智,信, 則皆義.

When you fulfill kindness, orderliness, wisdom, faithfulness with appropriateness, all the virtues express appropriateness.

以禮行仁,義,智,信, 則皆禮.

When you fulfill kindness, appropriateness, wisdom and faithfulness with orderliness, all the virtues express orderliness.

以智行仁,義,禮,信, 則皆智.

When you fulfill kindness, appropriateness, orderliness and faithfulness with wisdom, all the virtues express wisdom.

以信行仁,義,禮,智; 則皆信.

When you fulfill kindness, appropriateness, orderliness and wisdom with faithfulness, all the virtues express faithfulness.

一之不膠.

Perfection is never partial.

天下名之不得.

However perfection is hard to distinguish, unlike the partial expression of any virtue or feature.

(Note: The five virtues are the natural spiritual value and natural spiritual potential of your life, provided you do not distort them through your life's experiences. In normal circumstances they are the constructive function of your spiritual nature. They are not external beliefs invented by someone.

Although worldly spiritual teachings emphasize certain parts of spirituality, at its depth, the natural spirituality is always integrated. The true spiritual reality cannot be segmented. Specific expressions can, however, be observed in certain circumstances.

If you respect the natural spiritual health and benignity of humanity, then you cannot value any partial promotion, as partiality only divides people. Understand that the numerous spiritual customs of the world are simply reactions to the stressors of a particular time and circumstance. Such customs are circumstantial expressions, and no circumstantial teaching can be insisted upon to be the common spiritual standard of all. True spirituality is the power of integrity. This is what helps you and all people overcome spiritual difficulties without physical struggle. The power of integrity carries all people to safety and unity.)

正 直 八 則

The Eight Points
for Achieving Uprightness

精神健康在無偏,
持正無邪是神力.
日常撿點, 時時撿點.

An upright spiritual teaching includes the health and dignity of life. Once a spiritual culture insists on or supports a specific promotion, spiritual harm and confusion begins. Radical approaches should not be continued.

一正破千邪:
除障而去惑.
黑夜見皓月,
陰靈悉消除.

Exorcism is performed to cast out devils. Yet devils and evils simply mean the harms to human health. All evils and devils can be overcome by maintaining an upright spirit. Uprightness can be achieved in the following ways.

正見無偏見.

By having an upright view of the world and therefore holding no partiality towards anyone.

正思非邪思.

By thinking uprightly in order to offer understanding rather than confusion.

正語無妄語.

By using upright language in all circumstances.

正業則從容.

By behaving uprightly in order to treat people equally, as you would treat yourself.

正命自安康.

By living an upright life in order to not take advantage of anyone.

正進非盲進.

By living uprightly in order to propel your life towards the one great universal life.

正念有體恤.

By thinking with upright mental projections.

正定無旁依.

By using upright spiritual concentration so you do not need to depend on anyone or anything.

古 德 心 傳

The Passage Through Emperor Yeo to Emperor Shun

道心唯微,

The quality of heart to reach the Way is very subtle,

人心唯危.

but people's minds are fragile and always wavering.

惟精惟一.

Be focused in your efforts to unify with the deep humanity of all people.

允執厥中.

This is how to overcome all confusion and trouble, and be with the Way of everlasting life.

PART VI

Conclusion

Chapter 31

The Beauty and Bounty of Your Soul

Flowery words are used to embellish and present the thin, partial truth.
The real Truth presents itself without flowery words.

Today people of the world have little to no spiritual understanding. They prefer
to land on the moon and explore other planets, rather than seek the deep understanding of their life on Earth. They become fanatical about their external beliefs,
and miss the truth that life's spirituality comes from the inside out. They fail to
see that the nature of spirituality is reflective, rather than projective like the
mind.

The natural spirituality of life is completely different to worldly spiritual conventions, which describe God as the Ruler, who holds authority over the world
and human life. Generally, people hold one of two mental extremes—they either
have a physical view of life and the world, or a sentimental one. Most people's
minds are dominated by nonsense, and their numerous different perceptions
and conceptions divide them. Who is right? None of them.

The sun or "sol" is the source of the human soul. Within the seasonal changes of
the annual solar cycle, there are 12 divisions. People born in the different divisions reflect different personality tendencies. This is an observable fact. The
"solar" or spiritual portion is the main vitality or support of your life. It is the
invisible light in your life. Generally it is hidden, except in emergencies, when it
radiates out as the last surge and vitality of your life, deciding life or death.

The human soul, like your formed life, has multiple units. Each unit may have
numerous, tiny subunits, which are all transformable. Some units come through

your earthly blood connections. The soul is a composition of nature containing various components, as well as the many sentiments of your life.

The soul lies deep beneath the mind. Even though the mind produces feelings and contains consciousness, which can transform into concepts, imaginings, images, ideas and thoughts, those mental activities are not as important as the soul. The soul provides the power and is the source of your life. The relationship between the soul and the mind is similar to that of electricity and a computer: once the power is cut off, the computer shuts down.

Although the mind has tremendous descriptive capability, it cannot fully comprehend or master the soul, because the soul is at a totally different level. The mind, through its mental apparatus, experiences the spiritual level through the soul's reflections, but it generally mistakes those inner reflections to be the outward, whole reality.

Inaccurate spiritual beliefs and confused and partial ideas arise when the mind overly trusts the signs, images and forms reflected from the soul. Those reflections are simply the soul's segmented messages to its partner, the mind. They are never the true form of the soul, which is formless. The soul reflects forms and signs in order to communicate something to its physical partner. Those bare reflections, or spiritual phenomena, provide a way to avoid trouble from mental projection and imagining.

Dreams of a divinity or Buddha are just reflections from the subconscious mind at night. Even in daytime the soul can respond to the mind's thoughts in the form of an individual. For instance, a devoted spiritual seeker named San Tze Chian, who lived in the Sung Dynasty, searched for three masters of the Thunder School from whom he desired to learn. Even though the masters had withdrawn from formed life, San Tze Chian reported meeting them while on his way to the mountains. Truthfully, his encounter with the masters was his soul's response to his search. This is just one example of millions.

Another example is Confucius' dream of Duke Chou, whom Confucius admired for his efforts in ordering the early society of China. Confucius' dream experience was caused by his strong mental appreciation for Duke Chou. This is a similar to when religious believers, who have a strong faith in their spiritual heroes, experience phenomena.

Throughout the numerous human spiritual experiences, people are often mistaking their spiritual self for someone else. The experience of seeing angels, fairies, devils and ghosts, are all associated with the reflections from the soul, which can be twisted by the suggestions of the upper conscious mind.

The mind ambitiously expects to control the soul, but this is contrary to the proper order of life whereby the soul guides the mind. Such ambition also leads to untruthful spiritual teaching, as the mind erroneously teaches its ideas to the minds of others, causing more confusion.

Entering deep tranquility and the "zero dimension" are pursuits that nurture the soul and help guide one's life constructively. Generally, it is thought that stopping conscious activities denies the soul, but, in truth, it enhances the soul by simplifying one's thoughts and emotions.

Some people pursue deep tranquility, or *samadhi*, by meditating and sitting very still. Effective progress though is very uncertain. According to Emperor Chuan Su, the secret of looking for deep tranquility of mind is through active physical movement. Various movement arts are therefore valued, and the effect of a tranquil mind is much easier to reach.

Using meditation as a painkiller weakens the soul. Whereas Chuan Shu's creative meditative approach assists the productivity of life by strengthening it to take pressure from any circumstance. Chuan Shu taught people to value their lives and all their experiences, unlike general spiritual conventions, which tend to devalue life and painful experience.

The natural purpose of the mind is to act as a simple go-between between the physical and spiritual partners of your life. But when your mind becomes intellectually over developed, it enslaves the body and soul and usurps the soul's rightful role as master. This is the unfortunate case for many people today.

The physical and spiritual partners of most people's lives tend to act independently. When their life is physically active, they are spiritually inactive, and vice versa. Therefore, when a poorly guided life is physically active, it tends to be managed by impulse and creates chaos; and when that life is mentally active, it tends to experience disorder and confusion. Obviously, the spiritual and physical partners of life need to cooperate and connect with each other.

The spiritual sphere is composed of two spheres: the high self and the low self. The low self is the undeveloped spiritual elements of your life—the raw and undisciplined sphere that is associated with your desires and emotions. While the high self, or the God within, is associated with rationality, conscience, moral sense and transcendence. It is a valuable navigator through life. The high self is effective when the mind with high understanding willingly steps aside. Once your mind is consumed by strong desires or emotions, it becomes unable to perceive the God within or without, and darkness befalls your life. That is a real tragedy.

The ancients described the spiritual sphere, which cannot be completely known, as God. This is suitable only when the high self supports and guides your life, because if the low self runs your life by ignoring or disobeying the high self, your life can become a monster.

Your human spiritual experience of seeing images is produced from a spiritual response. That spiritual response can be twisted by your emotions, such as fear and ecstasy, and by your personal imagination and ideas. When experienced frequently, such images reflect your spiritual ill health rather than health. When both the physical and spiritual partners are tightly united, spiritual signs are not seen. However, the spiritual sphere is still available to respond to your life's research through inspirations, enlightenment, and visions to help bring about new insights and breakthroughs, or in response to your life's needs.

Spirituality remains a riddle to most people. If spirituality is not available to society, people can go astray, and if it is available, people can be fooled by leaders who have unhealthy or incorrect spiritual beliefs or poor vision in life. Cunning individuals without true spiritual depth, take advantage of the majority of people's spiritual ignorance. Yet, the dilemma people face is that without the artificial establishments of something or someone as their God to help them, they are unable to control themselves. Religions are therefore created and supported, but these have come at the expense of people's real development.

This is the situation of today, unlike that of 4500 years ago, when the division of the mind and spirit was not so sever. There are still some individuals, though, who make the effort to develop spiritually and attain spiritual independence without allowing the world to debase their lives.

For those individuals who are able to nurture the soul and high self, there is the boundless internal source that responds to support their lives. That is the nature of spiritual self-cultivation.

The best model of life is to unite your individual heart with the Heavenly Heart by dissolving your personal soul and uniting with the universal soul. In that instant, the new God is born within you. How can you do this? Simply, live the Constructive Life.

Chapter 32

Embrace the Heavenly Heart
by Living the Constructive Life

The Path of Constructive Life not only equips you with intellectual notions to live in the world; it also guides you to the spiritual power of the Heavenly Heart deep within your life. Embracing the Heavenly Heart can transform your whole life, eliminating the darkness that is caused by neglecting or ignoring the existence of the innate, inner Light in your life.

Most people today know that the most truthful support of their lives comes from the three partners of a bodily life, a clear mind, and the subtle soul, when these are in a healthy condition.

The soul is behind the mind. It is one step behind the screen of the deep conscious self. It is the inexpressible center of your being. Although inexpressible, the soul can manifest in your lifetime—it all depends on how you manage your life.

Your life can be influenced and confused by the mental attitudes from your environment, such as your family and society, as well as by your emotions that arise from the internal and external pressures of your life. Many young lives have created holes in their hearts, due to the pain and regret they suffer because of insufficient life knowledge and insufficient opportunity. What is the remedy to help them in the next stage of their lives? Have faith in the Heavenly Heart.

For all people, the new spiritual conviction is in the Heavenly Heart. The Heavenly Heart is your human heart when supported by your life's healthy conditions. The Heavenly Heart is able to transform the entire life of any person, and therefore change their fortune. The wounds of your heart can be healed in order that you may restart your life instantly with the everlasting Heavenly Heart. The Heavenly Heart emits subtle Light to disperse the obstacles, and guide you towards goodwill. With the Heavenly Heart all difficulties can be overcome and all troubles forgiven.

The spiritual reality of your life is decided by what is carried in your heart. This is the clear and steadfast spiritual truth.

The authority of life is internal, not external. The authority of life is the innate Heart of life, which embraces the Heavenly Will to be constructive. There is no way to establish a real partnership with God through conventional spiritual faith if that faith is overly externalized, because the truth of God is innate. All spiritual notions of God are just abstract notions of nature projected out by the human mind.

Clearly, Mother Nature has endowed human life with physical form and intelligence to manage their lives. Yet it remains up to you, as your individual duty of life, to fulfill a good and healthy life. The development you make depends on your own individual efforts.

Faith has two sides: a semi-internal and semi-external side, just like the T'ai Chi symbol, which has a *yin* and *yang* side. Mother Nature fulfills one half of your life; the other half is open to you, and is spiritually reliant on your efforts. This means that you need to correct the mistake of being spiritually dependent on notions of God, and instead find your own real improvement in life.

A spiritual seeker friend of mine, Peter Ngiam, realized this while on a recent trip in Asia seeking counseling from Buddhist monks on various life problems. He writes, "It was my curiosity to see what the monks could do. Though the monks had an uncanny sense of seeing the problems via birth dates and palmistry, and although they alleviated some of the emotional burden, I do not think life is cast in stone. I was also exposed to various social problems while accompanying an elderly and very perceptive Buddhist lady on her counseling rounds. The only conclusion I have is that there is no perfection in life. Behind the artificial façade, every face tells a story. It seems that people's problems are caused by their own greed, competition and selfishness. And while the religions and their representatives can offer some help through emotional counseling, the Universal Integral Way, through the PCL, can help prevent troubles by the cultivation of one's own balance and wisdom in life."

The teaching of the Universal Integral Way, through the PCL, is for those people who accept that spirituality in human life is their own responsibility. The PCL suggests a good diet, appropriate exercise, a correct life attitude and useful spiritual practices for health and spiritual protection. If you fail to do these, God, Buddha, Allah, and whatever other name you use to call the great spiritual reality cannot help you.

For the new sense of your spiritual life, your worship and prayers are best addressed to the Heavenly Heart. Although God, Mother Universe, Allah and the True Lord are all suitable too, the correct understanding is that Mother Universe is the background of nature and the Heavenly Heart is the spirit of nature.

You may view the Heavenly Heart as the function of nature, in which you have a 50 percent share of the duty. You need to claim your natural right in the divine share of life by removing the blockages that have been created through many years of cultural confusion. Mother Nature enables you to stand upright, to walk and to jump, but the extent to which you achieve spiritually depends on your own constructive efforts and choices.

God supports your human will, when that will chooses good health in all aspects of life. You need healthy legs, before you can run, jump and leap. Choosing health is the divine choice in life.

May the Heavenly Heart bless all of you who walk the Path of Constructive Life.

With deepest love to you all,
OmNi.

ACKNOWLEDGEMENTS

The following students, all volunteers, were instrumental in bringing this work to fruition.

Phoenicia devoted her time to reading, selecting, editing and shaping the vision for this book. She has done a tremendous job.

Barbara and Pieter from New Zealand spent long hours editing and proofing despite busy work schedules. They were greatly supportive.

Tom, a young Yo San University student, gave his keen eye for proofing around a full-time school program.

John gave his understanding and clarity in translating OmNi's "Chinglish."

Mary A. devoted much time and lent her excellent eye to typesetting and perfecting the finishing touches.

The cooperative and heartfelt efforts of all those who worked together on this book are a living testament to its message and spirit. Thank you.

INDEX

TEACHINGS OF THE HEAVENLY HEART BY THE NI FAMILY

The Power of the Feminine: Using Feminine Energy to Heal the World's Spiritual Problems—The wise vision of the feminine approach is the true foundation of human civilization and spiritual growth. When positive feminine virtues are usurped in favor of masculine strength, violence and aggressive competition result, leading the world to destruction. In this book, Hua-Ching Ni and Maoshing Ni touch on how and why this imbalance occurs, and deeply encourage women to apply their gentle feminine virtue to balance masculine strength and reset the course of humanity.
#BFEM—270 pages, softcover. $16.95

The New Universal Morality: How to Find God in Modern Times—An in-depth look at living in accord with universal virtue; particularly relevant with the disappointing failures of conventional religious teachings and the degraded condition of modern morality. Authors Hua-Ching Ni and Maoshing Ni Ph.D. reveal a natural religion in which universal morality is the essence, the true God that supports our lives and all existence. A direct discussion of the nature of God and the process of becoming a spiritual coach to serve both our community and ourselves.
#BMOR—280 pages, softcover. $16.95

The Majestic Domain of the Universal Heart—By Hua-Ching Ni and Maoshing Ni Ph.D. This book examines the power of universal love and wisdom and shows you how to integrate these life forces into your life through deepened spiritual awareness. In addition to drawing from the teachings of Lao Tzu and Chen Tuan, Hua-Ching Ni offers his own inspiring guidance for all who are seeking spiritual growth through an integral way of life.
#BMAJ—115 pages, softcover. $17.95

The Centermost Way—Hua-Ching Ni has written an inspiring account of human spiritual development, from its earliest stages, through the course of the last two millennia, up to today. It is a guidebook for those seeking a way of life that includes family, work, social activities and interests, scientific and religious pursuits, art, politics, and every other aspect of existence that we know and experience in the course of a lifetime on earth.
#BCENT—181 pages. $17.95

Enrich Your Life With Virtue—By Hua-Ching Ni. By embracing a life of natural virtue, one reduces conflict in the world. However humble this may seem, its personal spiritual and social implications are far-reaching. By examining the history of human relationships from this perspective, Hua-Ching Ni offers a broad study of human nature and draws on a centuries old tradition of natural life that transcends cultural and religious difference.
#BENR—173 pages. $15.95

Foundation of a Happy Life—By Hua-Ching Ni. A wonderful tool for making spiritual life a part of everyday life through instructive readings that families can share together. The future of the human world lies in its children. If parents raise their children well, the world will have a brighter future. A simple family shrine or alter, and regular gatherings to read the wisdom and advice of spiritually achieved people, can contribute profoundly to the development of strong characters and happiness.

#BFOUN—190 pages. $15.95

Secrets of Longevity: Hundreds of Ways to Live to be 100—By Dr. Maoshing Ni, Ph.D. Looking to live a longer, happier, healthier life? Try eating more blueberries, telling the truth, and saying no to undue burdens. Dr. Mao brings together simple and unusual ways to live longer.

#B-SEC—320 pages, softcover. $14.95
Published by Chronicle Books

Strength From Movement: Cultivating Chi—By Hua-Ching Ni, Daoshing Ni, and Maoshing Ni. *Chi*, the vital power of life, can be developed and cultivated within yourself to help support your health and your happy life. This book gives the deep reality of different useful forms of *chi* exercise and why certain types are more beneficial for certain types of people. Included are samples of several popular exercises.

#BSTRE—256 pages, softcover with 42 photographs. $17.95

The Time Is Now for a Better Life and a Better World—The purpose of achievement is on one hand to serve individual self-preservation and also to exercise one's attainment from spiritual cultivation to help others. It is expected to save the difficulties of the time, to prepare ourselves to create a bright future for the human race, and to overcome our modern day spiritual dilemma by conjoint effort.

#BTIME—136 pages, softcover. $10.95

The Way, the Truth, and the Light—This is the story of the first sage who introduced the way to the world. The life of this young sage links the spiritual achievement of East and West, and demonstrates the great spiritual virtue of his love to all people.

#BLIGP—232 pages, softcover. $14.95
#BLIGH—Hardcover. $22.95

Life and Teaching of Two Immortals, Volume 1: Kou Hong—Master Kou Hong, who was an achieved Master, a healer in Traditional Chinese Medicine, and a specialist in the art of refining medicines, was born in 363 A.D. He laid the foundation of later cultural development in China.

#BLIF1—176 pages, softcover. $12.95

Life and Teaching of Two Immortals, Volume 2: Chen Tuan—The second emperor of the Sung Dynasty entitled Master Chen Tuan "Master of Supernatural Truth." Hua-Ching Ni describes his life and cultivation and gives in-depth commentaries that provide teaching and insight into the achievement of this highly respected Master.

#BLIF2—192 pages, softcover. $12.95

Esoteric Tao Teh Ching—*Tao Teh Ching* expresses the highest efficiency of life and can be applied in many levels of worldly and spiritual life. This previously unreleased edition discusses instruction for spiritual practices in every day life, which includes important in-depth techniques for spiritual benefit.

#BESOT—192 pages, softcover. $13.95

The Uncharted Voyage Toward the Subtle Light—Spiritual life in the world today has become a confusing mixture of dying traditions and radical novelties. People who earnestly and sincerely seek something more than just a way to fit into the complexities of a modern structure that does not support true self-development, often find themselves spiritually struggling. This book provides a profound understanding and insight into the underlying heart of all paths of spiritual growth, the subtle origin, and the eternal truth of one universal life.

#BVOY—424 pages, softcover. $14.50

Golden Message, A Guide to Spiritual Life with Self-Study Program for Learning the Integral Way—This volume begins with a traditional treatise by Daoshing and Maoshing Ni about the broad nature of spiritual learning and its application for human life. It is followed by a message from Hua-Ching Ni. An outline of the Spiritual Self-Study Program and Correspondence Course of the College of Tao is included.

#BGOLD—160 pages, softcover. $11.95

Mysticism: Empowering the Spirit Within—For more than 8000 years, mystical knowledge has been passed down by sages. Hua-Ching Ni introduces spiritual knowledge of the developed ones, which does not use the senses, or machines like scientific knowledge, yet can know both the entirety of the universe and the spirits.

#BMYSM—200 pages, softcover. $13.95

Ageless Counsel for Modern Life—These sixty-four writings, originally illustrative commentaries on the *I Ching*, are meaningful and useful spiritual guidance on various topics to enrich your life. Hua-Ching Ni's delightful poetry and some teachings of esoteric Taoism can be found here as well.

#BAGE—256 pages, softcover. $15.95

The Mystical Universal Mother—An understanding of both masculine and feminine energies are crucial to understanding oneself, in particular for people moving to higher spiritual evolution. Hua-Ching Ni focuses upon the feminine through the examples of some ancient and modern women.
#BMYST—240 pages, softcover. $14.95

Harmony, The Art of Life—Harmony occurs when two different things find the point at which they can link together. Hua-Ching Ni shares valuable spiritual understanding and insight about the ability to bring harmony within one's own self, one's relationships and the world.
#BHAR—208 pages, softcover. $16.95

Moonlight in the Dark Night—The difficulty for many people in developing their spirituality is not that they are not moral or spiritual enough, but they are captive to their emotions. This book contains wisdom on how to guide emotions. It also includes simple guidance on how to balance love relationships so your life may be smoother and happier and your spiritual growth more effective.
#BMOON—168 pages, softcover. $12.95

Attune Your Body with Dao-In—The ancients discovered that Dao-In exercises solved problems of stagnant energy, increased their health, and lengthened their years. The exercises are also used as practical support for cultivation and higher achievements of spiritual immortality.
#BDAOI—144 pages, softcover. $16.95
Also on VHS & DVD. $24.95

The Key to Good Fortune: Refining Your Spirit—"Straighten your Way" (*Tai Shan Kan Yin Pien*) and "The Silent Way of Blessing" (*Yin Chi Wen*) are the main guidance for a mature, healthy life. Spiritual improvement can be an integral part of realizing a Heavenly life on earth.
#BKEY—144 pages, softcover. $12.95

Eternal Light—Hua-Ching Ni presents the life and teachings of his father, Grandmaster Ni, Yo San, who was a spiritually achieved person, healer and teacher, and a source of inspiration to Master Ni. Deeper teachings and insights for living a spiritual life and higher achievement.
#BETER—208 pages, softcover. $14.95

Quest of Soul—Hua-Ching Ni addresses many concepts about the soul such as saving the soul, improving the soul's quality, the free soul, what happens at death, and the universal soul. He guides and inspires the reader into deeper self-knowledge and to move forward to increase personal happiness and spiritual depth.
#BQUES—152 pages, softcover. $11.95

Nurture Your Spirits—Hua-Ching Ni breaks some spiritual prohibitions and presents the spiritual truth he has studied and proven. This truth may help you develop and nurture your own spirits, which are the truthful internal foundation of your life being.

#BNURT—176 pages, softcover. $12.95

Power of Natural Healing—Hua-Ching Ni discusses the natural capability of self-healing, information, and practices which can assist any treatment method and presents methods of cultivation which promote a healthy life, longevity, and spiritual achievement.

#BHEAL—143 pages, softcover. $14.95

Essence of Universal Spirituality—In this volume, as an open-minded learner and achieved teacher of universal spirituality, Hua-Ching Ni examines and discusses all levels and topics of religious and spiritual teaching to help you understand the ultimate truth and enjoy the achievement of all religions without becoming confused by them.

#BESSE—304 pages, softcover. $19.95

Guide to Inner Light—Drawing inspiration from the experience of the ancient ones, modern people looking for the true source and meaning of life can find great teachings to direct and benefit them. The invaluable ancient development can teach us to reach the attainable spiritual truth and point the way to the inner Light.

#BGUID—192 pages, softcover. $12.95

Stepping Stones for Spiritual Success—In this volume, Hua-Ching Ni has taken the best of the traditional teachings and put them into contemporary language to make them more relevant to our time, culture, and lives.

#BSTEP—160 pages, softcover. $12.95

The Complete Works of Lao Tzu—The *Tao Teh Ching* is one of the most widely translated and cherished works of literature. Its timeless wisdom provides a bridge to the subtle spiritual truth and aids harmonious and peaceful living. Also included is the *Hua Hu Ching*, a later work of Lao Tzu, which was lost to the general public for a thousand years.

#BCOMP—212 pages, softcover. $13.95

I Ching, The Book of Changes and the Unchanging Truth—The legendary classic *I Ching* is recognized as the first written book of wisdom. Leaders and sages throughout history have consulted it as a trusted advisor, which reveals the appropriate action in any circumstance. Includes over 200 pages of background material on natural energy cycles, instruction, and commentaries.

#BBOOK—669 pages, hardcover. $35.00

The Story of Two Kingdoms—This volume is the metaphoric tale of the conflict between the Kingdoms of Light and Darkness. Through this unique story, Hua-Ching Ni transmits esoteric teachings of Taoism that have been carefully guarded secrets for over 5,000 years. This book is for those who are serious in achieving high spiritual goals.
#BSTOR—223 pages, hardcover. $14.00

The Way of Integral Life—This book includes practical and applicable suggestions for daily life, philosophical thought, esoteric insight and guidelines for those aspiring to serve the world. The ancient sages' achievement can assist the growth of your own wisdom and balanced, reasonable life.
#BWAYP—320 pages, softcover. $14.00
#BWAYH—Hardcover. $20.00

Enlightenment: Mother of Spiritual Independence—The inspiring story and teachings of Master Hui Neng, the father of Zen Buddhism and Sixth Patriarch of the Buddhist tradition, highlight this volume. Hui Neng was a person of ordinary birth, intellectually unsophisticated, who achieved himself to become a spiritual leader.
#BENLP—264 pages, softcover. $12.50
#BENLH—Hardcover. $22.00

The Gentle Path of Spiritual Progress—This book offers a glimpse into the dialogues between a master and his students. In a relaxed, open manner, Hua-Ching Ni explains to his students the fundamental practices that are the keys to experiencing enlightenment in everyday life.
#BGENT—290 pages, softcover. $12.95

Spiritual Messages from a Buffalo Rider, A Man of Tao—Our buffalo nature rides on us, whereas an achieved person rides the buffalo. Hua-Ching Ni gives much helpful knowledge to those who are interested in improving their lives and deepening their cultivation so they too can develop beyond their mundane beings.
#BSPIR—242 pages, softcover. $12.95

8,000 Years of Wisdom, Volume I and II—This two-volume set contains a wealth of practical, down-to-earth advice given by Hua-Ching Ni over a five-year period. Drawing on his training in Traditional Chinese Medicine, Herbology, and Acupuncture, Hua-Ching Ni gives candid answers to questions on many topics.
#BWIS1—Vol. I: (Revised edition)
Includes dietary guidance; 236 pages, softcover. $18.50
#BWIS2—Vol. II: Includes sex and pregnancy guidance; 241 pages, softcover. $12.50

Footsteps of the Mystical Child—This book poses and answers such questions as, "What is a soul? What is wisdom? What is spiritual evolution?" to enable readers to open themselves to new realms of understanding and personal growth. Includes true examples about people's internal and external struggles on the path of self-development and spiritual evolution.

#BFOOT—166 pages, softcover. $9.50

Workbook for Spiritual Development—This material summarizes thousands of years of traditional teachings and little known practices for spiritual development. There are sections on ancient invocations, natural celibacy and postures for energy channeling. Hua-Ching Ni explains basic attitudes and knowledge that supports spiritual practice.

#BWORK—240 pages, softcover. $14.95

The Taoist Inner View of the Universe—Hua-Ching Ni has given all the opportunity to know the vast achievement of the ancient unspoiled mind and its transpiercing vision. This book offers a glimpse of the inner world and immortal realm known to achieved ones and makes it understandable for students aspiring to a more complete life.

#BTAOI—218 pages, softcover. $16.95

Tao, the Subtle Universal Law—Most people are unaware that their thoughts and behavior evoke responses from the invisible net of universal energy. To lead a good stable life is to be aware of the universal subtle law in every moment of our lives. This book presents practical methods that have been successfully used for centuries to accomplish this.

#BTAOS—208 pages, softcover. $12.95

Concourse of All Spiritual Paths—All religions, in spite of their surface differences, in their essence return to the great oneness. Hua-Ching Ni looks at what traditional religions offer us today and suggest how to go beyond differences to discover the depth of universal truth.

#BCONC—184 pages, softcover. $15.95

From Diversity to Unity: Return to the One Spiritual Source—This book encourages individuals to go beyond the theological boundary to rediscover their own spiritual nature with guidance offered by Hua-Ching Ni from his personal achievement, exploration, and self-cultivation. This work can help people unlock the spiritual treasures of the universe and light the way to a life of internal and external harmony and fulfillment.

#BDIV—200 pages, softcover. $15.95

Spring Thunder: Awaken the Hibernating Power of Life—Humans need to be periodically awakened from a spiritual hibernation in which the awareness of life's reality is deeply forgotten. To awaken your deep inner life, this book offers the practice of Natural Meditation, the enlightening teachings of Yen Shi, and Hua-Ching Ni's New Year Message.

#BTHUN—168 pages, softcover. $12.95

Internal Growth Through Tao—In this volume, Hua-Ching Ni teaches about the more subtle, much deeper aspects of life. He also points out the confusion caused by some spiritual teachings and encourages students to cultivate internal growth.

#BINTE—208 pages, softcover. $13.95

The Yellow Emperor's Classic of Medicine—By Maoshing Ni, Ph.D. The *Neijing* is one of the most important classics of Taoism, as well as the highest authority on traditional Chinese medicine. Written in the form of a discourse between Yellow Emperor and his ministers, this book contains a wealth of knowledge on holistic medicine and how human life can attune itself to receive natural support.

#BYELL—316 pages, softcover. $19.95
Published by Shambala Publications, Inc.

The Eight Treasures: Energy Enhancement Exercise—By Maoshing Ni, Ph.D. The Eight Treasures is an ancient system of energy enhancing movements based on the natural motion of the universe. It can be practiced by anyone at any fitness level, is non-impact, simple to do, and appropriate for all ages. It is recommended that this book be used with its companion videotape or DVD.

#BEIGH—208 pages, softcover. $17.95

The Gate to Infinity—People who have learned spiritually through years without real progress will be thoroughly guided by the important discourse in this book. Hua-Ching Ni also explains Natural Meditation. Editors recommend that all serious spiritual students who wish to increase their spiritual potency read this one.

#BGATE—316 pages, softcover. $13.95

Entering the Tao—Traditional stories and teachings of the ancient masters and personal experiences impart the wisdom of Taoism, the Integral Way. Spiritual self-cultivation, self-reliance, spiritual self-protection, emotional balance, do's and don'ts for a healthy lifestyle, sleeping and dreaming, diet, boredom, fun, sex and marriage.

#BENT—153 pages, softcover. $13.00
Published by Shambala Publications, Inc.

The Tao of Nutrition—By Maoshing Ni, Ph.D. with Cathy McNease, B.S., M.H. Learn how to take control of your health with good eating. Over 100 common foods are discussed with their energetic properties and therapeutic functions listed. Food remedies for numerous common ailments are also presented.

#BTAON—214 pages, softcover. $14.95

Revealing the Tao Teh Ching: In-Depth Commentaries on an Ancient Classic—By Xuezhi Hu. Unique, detailed, and practical commentaries on methods of spiritual cultivation as metaphorically described by Lao Tzu in the *Tao Teh Ching*.

#B-REV—240 pages, softcover. $19.95
Published by Ageless Classics Press

Chinese Herbology Made Easy—By Maoshing Ni, Ph.D. This text provides an overview of Oriental Medical theory, in-depth descriptions of each herb category, over 300 black and white photographs, extensive tables of individual herbs for easy reference and an index of pharmaceutical names.

#BHERB—202 pages, softcover. $18.95

101 Vegetarian Delights—By Lily Chuang and Cathy McNease. A lovely cookbook with recipes as tasty as they are healthy. Features multicultural recipes, appendices on Chinese herbs and edible flowers, and a glossary of special foods. Over 40 illustrations.

#B101—176 pages, softcover. $12.95

Chinese Vegetarian Delights—By Lily Chuang. An extraordinary collection of recipes based on principles of traditional Chinese nutrition. Meat, sugar, dairy products, and fried foods are excluded.

#BVEG—104 pages, softcover. $7.50

The Power of Positive Living—By Hua-Ching Ni. Ideas about simple improvements and changes in attitude that can be made in everyday life to increase our positive energy and health. Attain real internal peace while attaining external success and security.

#BPOWE—65 pages, softcover booklet. $8.50

Self-Reliance and Constructive Change—By Hua-Ching Ni. Being attached to cultural and religious fashions can hinder personal health. Hua-Ching Ni presents the Integral Way of spiritual discovery that is independent of cultural, political or religious concepts.

#BSELF—54 pages, softcover booklet. $7.00

The Universal Path of Natural Life—By Hua-Ching Ni. Study the ancient spiritual practices of *Yin Fu Ching*, a predecessor of the *Tao Teh Ching*. Connect with the natural unity and balance of the universe to nurture our spiritual essence and natural vitality.

#BPATH—109 pages, softcover booklet. $9.50

POCKET BOOKLETS & MISCELLANEOUS

Guide to Your Total Well-Being—Simple, useful practices for self-development, aid for your spiritual growth, and guidance for all aspects of life. Exercise, food, sex, emotional balancing, and meditation.

#PWELL—48 pages, paperback. $4.00

Progress Along the Way: Life, Service and Realization—The guiding power of human life is the association between the developed mind and the achieved soul, which contains love, rationality, conscience, and everlasting value.

#PPROG—64 pages, paperback. $4.00

The Light of All Stars Illuminates the Way—Through generations of searching, various achieved ones found the best application of the Way in their lives. This booklet contains their discovery.

#PSTAR—48 pages, paperback. $4.00

The Heavenly Way—"Straighten Your Way" (*Tai Shan Kan Yin Pien*) and "The Silent Way of Blessing" (*Yin Chi Wen*) are the main sources of inspiration for this booklet that sets the cornerstone for a mature, healthy life.

#BHEAV—42 pages, softcover. $2.50

VIDEOTAPES & DVDS

Harmony T'ai Chi Short Form (DVD)—By Maoshing Ni, Ph.D. Easy to learn 18 steps *t'ai chi*. Simplified from the regular 108-step T'ai Chi Chuan Parts I & II Harmony Style Form. Graceful movements for balance, peace and vitality.

#DSTEP—DVD, 28 minutes. $24.95

T'ai Chi Sword Form (DVD)—By Maoshing Ni, Ph.D. A short, instructional 10-minute sword form to help sweep away emotional obstacles and enhance protective energy. Excellent for developing spiritual focus.

#DSWORD—DVD, 19 minutes. $24.95

Crane Style Chi Gong (VHS, PAL & DVD)—By Daoshing Ni, Ph.D. Crane Style standing exercises integrate movement, mental imagery and breathing techniques, and are practiced for healing purposes. They were developed by ancient Taoists to increase energy and metabolism, relieve stress and tension, improve mental clarity, and restore general wellbeing. We are thrilled to also offer a reshoot on DVD of this incredibly beautiful old classic.

#VCRAN—VHS video, 120 minutes. $24.95

#VPCRAN—PAL video, 120 minutes. $24.95

#DCRAN—DVD, 120 minutes. $24.95

Attune Your Body with Dao-In (VHS, PAL & DVD)—By Hua-Ching Ni. The ancient Taoist predecessor to T'ai Chi Chuan. Performed sitting and lying down, these moves clear stagnant energy. Includes meditations and massage for a complete integral fitness program.

#VDAOI—VHS video, 60 minutes. $24.95

#VPDAOI—PAL video, 60 minutes. $24.95

#DDAOI—DVD, 60 minutes. $24.95

Taoist Eight Treasures (VHS, PAL & DVD)—By Maoshing Ni, Ph.D. Unique to the Ni family, this 32-movement *chi* form opens blocks in your energy flow and strengthens your vitality. Combines stretching, toning, and energy conducting exercises with deep breathing.

#VEIGH—VHS video, 46 minutes. $24.95

#VPEIGH—PAL video, 46 minutes. $24.95

#DEIGH—DVD, 46 minutes. $24.95

T'ai Chi Chuan, An Appreciation (VHS)—By Hua-Ching Ni "Gentle Path," "Sky Journey," and "Infinite Expansion" are three Taoist esoteric styles handed down by highly achieved masters and are shown in an uninterrupted format. Not an instructional video.

#VAPPR—VHS video, 30 minutes. $24.95

T'ai Chi Chuan, Parts I & II (VHS & PAL)—By Maoshing Ni, Ph.D. This Taoist style, called the style of Harmony, is a distillation of the Yang, Chen, and Wu styles. It integrates physical movement with energy and helps promote longevity and self-cultivation.

#VTAI1, #VTAI2—VHS videos, 60 minutes each. $24.95

#VPTAI1, #VPTAI2—PAL videos, 60 minutes each. $24.95

Self-Healing Chi Gong (VHS & PAL)—By Maoshing Ni, Ph.D. Strengthen your own self-healing powers. These effective mind-body exercises strengthen and balance each of your five major organ systems. Two hours of practical demonstrations and information lectures.

#VSHCG—VHS video, 120 minutes. $24.95

#VPSHCG—PAL video, 120 minutes. $24.95

Cosmic Tour Ba-Gua (VHS, PAL & DVD)—By Hua-Ching Ni. Cosmic Tour Ba-Gua has healing powers similar to T'ai Chi, but the energy flow is quite different. Ba-Gua consists of a special kind of walking which corrects the imbalance and disorder of "having a head heavier than the rest of the body."

#VCOSM—VHS video. $24.95
#VPCOSM—PAL video. $24.95
#DCOSM—DVD. $24.95

T'ai Chi Chuan: The Gentle Path (VHS)—By Hua-Ching Ni. The movements of *The Gentle Path T'ai Chi* guide us to follow the gentle, cyclical motion of the universe. By gathering energy in the lower *tan tien*, the root center, the movements will change our internal energy and guide us to a peaceful and balanced life.

#VGENP—VHS video. $24.95

AUDIO CASSETTES

Invocations for Health, Longevity and Healing a Broken Heart—By Maoshing Ni, Ph.D. "Thinking is louder than thunder." This cassette guides you through a series of invocations to channel and conduct your own healing energy and vital force.

#AINVO—Audio, 30 minutes. $9.95

Pain Management with Chi Gong—By Maoshing Ni, Ph.D. Using visualization and deep breathing techniques, this cassette offers methods for overcoming pain by invigorating your energy flow and unblocking obstructions that cause pain.

#ACHIP—Audio, 30 minutes. $9.95

Tao Teh Ching Cassette Tapes—This classic work of Lao Tzu has been recorded in this two-cassette set that is a companion to the book translated by Hua-Ching Ni. Professionally recorded and read by Robert Rudelson.

#ATAOT—Audio, 120 minutes. $12.95

COMPACT DISCS

The Five Clouds Meditation—With James Tuggle. Three important practices from the Shrine Ceremony of the Eternal Breath of Tao and the Integral Way of Life. Beginning with a guided relaxation to increase your receptivity, you are then guided through the five energy systems and related organs to help thoroughly cleanse and balance your internal energy. It ends by refining your energy through the deeply potent Golden Light Meditation and Invocation.
#CD5CLOUDS—60 minutes. $10.95

Meditation for Stress Release—Dr. Mao's breath/mind exercises help us counter the ill effects of our stress filled lives by awakening our protective healing mechanisms. Learn to calm your mind and restore your spirit with ten minutes of simple meditation practices.
#CDSTRESS—30 minutes. $10.95

BOOKS IN SPANISH

Tao Teh Ching—*En Espanol.*
#BTEHS—112 pages, softcover booklet. $8.95

SEVENSTAR MAIL ORDER FORM

Name: _____

Address: _____

City: _____ State: _____ Zip: _____

Phone: (daytime) _____ (evening) _____

Qty.	Stock #	Title	Price ea.	Subtotal

Sales tax (CA residents only):	
Shipping:	
TOTAL:	

Payment: Check, money order or credit card

Card number: _____ Exp. date: _____

Signature: _____

Shipping: via UPS in the continental United States. $7 for first item and 50¢ for each additional item. The *I Ching* counts as three items. Please call for international shipping rates to all other locations.

Telephone orders, questions or catalog requests: 1-(800) 578-9526

Website: www.sevenstarcom.com
E-Mail: taostar@taostar.com

Mail form with payment (U.S. funds only) to:
13315 Washington Blvd., Suite 200, Los Angeles, California 90066

SPIRITUAL STUDY THROUGH THE COLLEGE OF TAO

The College of Tao was formally established in California in the 1970s, yet the tradition from which it originated represents centuries of spiritual growth. The College values the spiritual development of each individual and offers a healthy spiritual education to all people.

The College of Tao is a school without walls. Human society is its classroom. Your own life is the class you attend; thus students grow from their own lives and from studying the guidance of the Integral Way.

Distance learning programs, based on the writings of Hua-Ching Ni and his family, are available for those who do not live near an Integral Way of Life center. For more information, visit www.sevenstarcom.com, www.taostudies.com, or www.longevity-center.com. For written information on correspondence programs, please contact the College of Tao at: P.O. Box 1222, El Prado, NM 87529.

It is recommended that all Mentors of the Integral Way use the self-study program to educate themselves. Anyone who wishes to teach the practices contained in Hua-Ching Ni's books must apply to the College for certification.

INTEGRAL WAY SOCIETY (IWS, formerly USIW)

❑ I wish to receive a list of registered Mentors teaching in my area or country.

❑ I am interested in joining/forming a study group in my area.

❑ I am interested in becoming a Mentor of the IWS.

❑ I am interested in subscribing to the IWS quarterly newsletter.

Name: _____

Address: _____

City: _____ State: _____ Zip: _____

E-Mail Address: _____

Mail this request to: IWS, P.O. Box 1530, Santa Monica, CA 90406-1530

And you can visit our website at: www.integralwaysociety.org

YO SAN UNIVERSITY OF TRADITIONAL CHINESE MEDICINE

"Not just a medical career, but a lifetime commitment to raising one's spiritual standard."

In response to the growing interest in Taoism and natural health care in the West, in January 1989 we formed Yo San University of Traditional Chinese Medicine, a nonprofit educational institution under the direction of founder Hua-Ching Ni. Yo San University is the continuation of 38 generations of Ni family practitioners who have handed down the knowledge and wisdom of ancient Chinese healing from father to son.

The foundation of Traditional Chinese Medicine is the spiritual capability to know life, to diagnose a person's problem, and to know how to cure it. We teach students how to care for themselves and others, emphasizing the integration of traditional knowledge and modern science, but the true application of Traditional Chinese Medicine is the practical application of one's own spiritual development.

The purpose of Yo San University is to train practitioners of the highest caliber in Traditional Chinese Medicine, which includes acupuncture, herbology, and spiritual development. We offer a complete Master's degree program which is approved by the California State Department of Education and which meets all requirements for state licensure.

We invite you to inquire into our program for a creative and rewarding career as a holistic physician. Classes are also open to persons interested in self-enrichment. For more information, please fill out the form below or visit our website at www.yosan.edu.

Yo San University of Traditional Chinese Medicine
13315 W. Washington Boulevard, Suite 200
Los Angeles, CA 90066
Phone: (310) 577-3000   Fax: (310) 577-3033

❑ Please send me information on the Masters degree program in Traditional Chinese Medicine.

❑ Please send me information on health workshops and seminars.

❑ Please send me information on continuing education for acupuncturists and health professionals.

Name: _____

Address: _____

City: _____ State: _____ Zip: _____

Phone: (daytime) _____ (evening) _____

MOVEMENT TRAINING & TEACHER CERTIFICATION

Chi Gong (also known as *qigong* or *chi kung*) is "energy work" and involves various methods of developing the *chi* or life energy of the body as the foundation of a healthy and happy life. The Ni Family Chi Movements Arts encompass a variety of Chi Gong forms that incorporate specific methods of breathing, meditative focus, physical movement, and energy guidance. The major benefits are general strengthening, enhanced flexibility and tone, relaxation and stress reduction, increased mental clarity, and the balancing of mind, body, and spirit leading to overall improved health, well-being, and increased longevity. These movement arts are an excellent complement to a healthy lifestyle.

The Ni family has gathered, developed, and passed down these useful Chi Gong forms through many generations, continuing their family's ancient spiritual tradition of Esoteric Taoism from the time of the Yellow Emperor and before. The Ni Family Chi Movement Arts include varieties of T'ai Chi, Eight Treasures, Dao-In, and many health and meditative practices. Please refer to *Strength from Movement: Mastering Chi* by Hua-Ching Ni for an excellent introduction.

The Ni family established the **Chi Health Institute** to promote the wider availability and more effective practice of useful forms of Chi Gong for personal and social improvement. The Institute serves as a custodian of the Ni Family Chi Movement Arts tradition, and actively works to sponsor training opportunities to develop additional training materials and to certify teachers.

We would be happy to assist you in selecting and learning a suitable form. We can provide a directory of certified teachers, information about available training workshops, ongoing classes, and self-study and distance learning options, as well as information about a variety of instructional materials. We would also be happy to assist you in becoming a certified teacher of the Ni Family Chi Movement Arts.

Please write to us at the address below for more information, and include your name, e-mail, telephone number, mailing address, and any special interests, or visit our website at www.chihealth.org. We look forward to helping you further your growth.

Chi Health Institute
P.O. Box 2035
Santa Monica, CA 90406

HERBS USED BY ANCIENT MASTERS

The pursuit of health is an innate human desire. Long ago, Chinese esoteric Taoists went to the high mountains to contemplate nature, strengthen their bodies, empower their minds, and develop their spirit. From their studies and cultivation, they developed Chinese alchemy and chemistry, herbology, acupuncture, the *I Ching*, astrology, T'ai Chi Ch'uan, Chi Gong, and many other useful tools for health and self-improvement.

The ancient Taoists also passed down methods for attaining longevity and spiritual immortality, one of which was the development of herbal formulas that could be used to increase one's energy and heighten vitality. The Ni family has preserved this treasured collection of herbal formulas for centuries.

Now, through Traditions of Tao, the Ni family makes these ancient formulas available to assist you in building a strong foundation for health and spiritual self-cultivation. For further information about Traditions of Tao herbal products, please complete the following form or visit our website at: www.taostar.com.

Traditions of Tao
13315 W. Washington Boulevard, Suite 200
Los Angeles, CA 90066
Phone: (310) 302-1206   Fax: (310) 302-1208

❏ Please send me a Traditions of Tao brochure.

Name: _____

Address: _____

City: _____ State: _____ Zip: _____

Phone: (daytime) _____ (evening) _____